Bernard Shaw and His Contemporaries

Series Editors
Nelson O'Ceallaigh Ritschel
Massachusetts Maritime Academy
Pocasset, MA, USA

Peter Gahan
Independent Scholar
Los Angeles, CA, USA

The series *Bernard Shaw and His Contemporaries* presents the best and most up-to-date research on Shaw and his contemporaries in a diverse range of cultural contexts. Volumes in the series will further the academic understanding of Bernard Shaw and those who worked with him, or in reaction against him, during his long career from the 1880s to 1950 as a leading writer in Britain and Ireland, and with a wide European and American following.

Shaw defined the modern literary theatre in the wake of Ibsen as a vehicle for social change, while authoring a dramatic canon to rival Shakespeare's. His careers as critic, essayist, playwright, journalist, lecturer, socialist, feminist, and pamphleteer, both helped to shape the modern world as well as pointed the way towards modernism. No one engaged with his contemporaries more than Shaw, whether as controversialist, or in his support of other, often younger writers. In many respects, therefore, the series as it develops will offer a survey of the rise of the modern at the beginning of the twentieth century and the subsequent varied cultural movements covered by the term modernism that arose in the wake of World War 1.

More information about this series at
http://www.palgrave.com/gp/series/14785

Stephen Watt

Bernard Shaw's Fiction, Material Psychology, and Affect

Shaw, Freud, Simmel

Stephen Watt
Indiana University
Bloomington, IN, USA

Bernard Shaw and His Contemporaries
ISBN 978-3-030-10067-4   ISBN 978-3-319-71513-1   (eBook)
https://doi.org/10.1007/978-3-319-71513-1

© The Editor(s) (if applicable) and The Author(s) 2018
Softcover re-print of the Hardcover 1st edition 2018
This work is subject to copyright. All rights are solely and exclusively licensed by the Publisher, whether the whole or part of the material is concerned, specifically the rights of translation, reprinting, reuse of illustrations, recitation, broadcasting, reproduction on microfilms or in any other physical way, and transmission or information storage and retrieval, electronic adaptation, computer software, or by similar or dissimilar methodology now known or hereafter developed.
The use of general descriptive names, registered names, trademarks, service marks, etc. in this publication does not imply, even in the absence of a specific statement, that such names are exempt from the relevant protective laws and regulations and therefore free for general use.
The publisher, the authors and the editors are safe to assume that the advice and information in this book are believed to be true and accurate at the date of publication. Neither the publisher nor the authors or the editors give a warranty, express or implied, with respect to the material contained herein or for any errors or omissions that may have been made. The publisher remains neutral with regard to jurisdictional claims in published maps and institutional affiliations.

Cover illustration: Congregation, 2003–2008 (c) Ledelle Moe North Carolina Museum of Art, Raleigh Purchased with funds from the North Carolina Museum of Art Docents, 2010.2/1 277

Printed on acid-free paper

This Palgrave Macmillan imprint is published by Springer Nature
The registered company is Springer International Publishing AG
The registered company address is: Gewerbestrasse 11, 6330 Cham, Switzerland

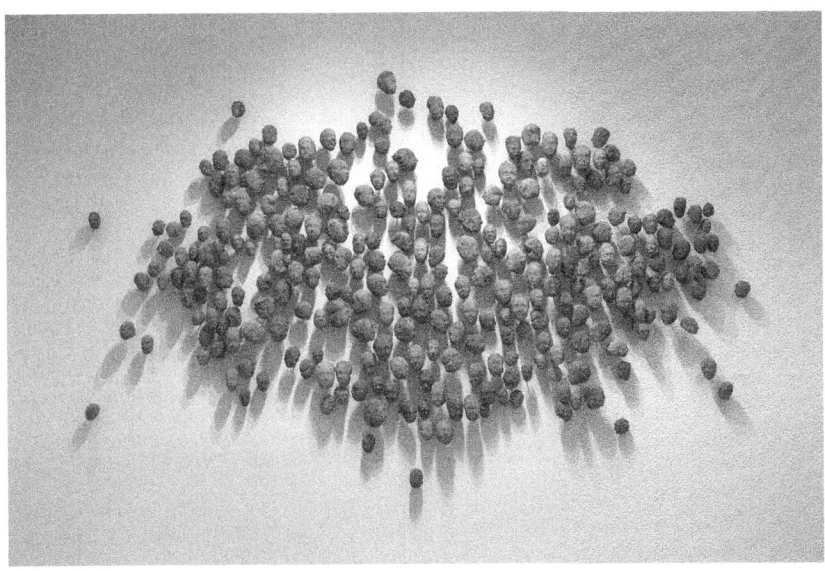

Ledelle Moe
Congregation, 2003–2008

Concrete, recycled motor oil, and steel bar

277 separate elements; dimensions variable

North Carolina Museum of Art, Raleigh, Purchased with funds from the North Carolina Museum of Art Docents, 2010.2/1 277

Acknowledgements

The genealogy of this book, like most with which I am familiar, is paradoxically straightforward and somewhat gnarled by complexities that require just a little unraveling. A summary of these latter issues might wait for another occasion, however, as the straightforward part is simply described and bears directly on the pages that follow. After agreeing some time ago to edit a special issue of *SHAW: The Journal of Bernard Shaw Studies* on the topic of "Shaw and Money," Nelson Ritschel and Audrey MacNamara approached me about contributing an article that addressed this topic through a reading of the five novels that Shaw wrote between 1879 and 1883. I was flattered to have been asked and pleased to comply with their request, the result appearing in the journal in 2016, and I am grateful that they afforded me this opportunity. For throughout the process of preparing the article—"Unashamed: Value, Affect, and Shaw's Psychology of Money," *SHAW: The Journal of Bernard Shaw Studies* 36.1 (2016): 53–72, which forms the basis of Chap. 3 of this book—I began to suspect that a good deal more might be said about both Shaw's fiction and his evolving understanding of such matters as money, the subjective quality of putatively objective notions such as value, the social performance of wealth and class, and more. However, while I was sure that these issues vitally inform, at times even dominate, both Shaw's writing and his own interior life—and, for this reason, the pages that follow include not only sustained readings of his novels, but also discussions of many of his plays, essays, and letters—I really wasn't certain that I was capable of a book that concentrated largely on the five novels he produced as a struggling young immigrant living in London.

After the article appeared, Ritschel and Peter Gahan, general editors of this series of texts on "Bernard Shaw and His Contemporaries" and both excellent scholars in their own right, wondered about much the same thing and posed a question: Did a book-length project lurk somewhere in my muddle of thoughts about Shaw's fiction and the psychical and affective implications of money, among other material entities, on both him and his characters? Uncertain of how to respond, I spent the better part of a year reading and outlining before hazarding a tepid "yes." Then, of course, more work and study followed, during which time another more precise challenge emerged: namely, how might this study contribute to the larger aims of Nelson and Peter's series? Given the fact that the pages that follow combine a morsel of economic theory of Shaw's era with more generous portions of both sociological and nascent psychoanalytic thought at the *fin de siècle* of the nineteenth century and after, several answers presented themselves. As the nonagenarian Shaw admitted in his autobiographical volume *Sixteen Self Sketches* (1949), for example, his understanding of the theories of Karl Marx in the early 1880s was subsequently revised by his conversations—and published dialogue—with Philip Wicksteed (1844–1927), who was himself greatly influenced by the marginal economist William Stanley Jevons (1835–82), a fact of which Shaw was very much aware. Both economists appear in the pages that follow, but not in the leading roles that they might. When discussing affect and performance, to take another example, prominent actors of the *fin de siècle* stage such as the Italian star Eleonora Duse (1858–1924), whose talent confirmed for Shaw that a "dramatic critic is really the servant of a high art," also appear in these pages, although again not necessarily in the spotlight their distinguished careers and international influence merit. In some ways, it seems an almost impossible task to discuss so multifoliate an intellectual as Shaw without reference to a host of composers, philosophers, actors and playwrights, politicians, economists, and more. In other words, the contemporaries who might have been featured in the limelight of this book are many, and the majority of them, regrettably, will not be.

However, some other contemporaries of Bernard Shaw *will* figure prominently in the pages that follow, ones he hardly knew or, in actuality, knew relatively little about even if on occasion he might have suggested otherwise. That is to say, while Shaw and Wicksteed may have skirmished collegially in the mid-1880s over Marx's Value Theory—a disagreement waged, as biographer Michael Holroyd terms it, in the "friendliest spirit"— they also participated convivially for some years in discussions of economics with several friends and acquaintances that Holroyd valorizes as the "closest thing" Shaw got to a university education. Shaw did not cultivate such a close relationship, however, with two European counterparts, Sigmund Freud and Georg Simmel, the former of whom Shaw was certainly aware and about whom he expressed a variety of opinions, many of them querulous or even combative, and the latter of whom Shaw apparently did not know well, if at all. Yet, these three are, quite literally, contemporaries: Freud was born less than three months before Shaw in May, 1856; and Simmel, less than two years later on March 1, 1858. And, as I have indicated, unlike, say, the close relationships Shaw enjoyed with William Archer, or with Beatrice and Sidney Webb—relationships that directly influenced his writing and thought—this trio of relative strangers had no such interactions but nevertheless shared remarkable intellectual affinities. Here I mean to reference more than Freud's admiration of Ibsen—in his "Autobiographical Study," he revealed his affinity with Dr. Stockmann in *An Enemy of the People* and his disdain for the "compact majority" that opposed him—or his quotation from the Preface of Shaw's *Doctor's Dilemma* while mourning the death of a beloved grandson in 1923. All three thinkers, for example, were compelled to engage the science of Charles Darwin, although Simmel did less of this than Freud or Shaw; all three puzzled over such issues as value and the relationships between money, capital, and people; and all three were concerned with life in the increasingly frenetic modern city and its effect on human sensibilities, as the following pages will attempt to delineate.

Such a claim may strike some as beyond counterintuitive. After all, when Shaw was not dismissive of or ambivalent about psychoanalytic thought, he was accusing Freud of lacking both "delicacy and commonsense." For over a half of a century, from the work of Brigid Brophy, Arthur Nethercot, and Sidney P. Alpert in the 1960s and 1970s, scholars have debated Shaw's knowledge of and stance toward the emergent discourse of psychoanalysis. For Brophy in *Black Ship to Hell* (1962), Freud and Shaw are "the two great mainstays" of twentieth-century thought who laid foundations for a "twentieth-century morality," and her Shaw "rarely contradicts the findings of psycho-analysis, though he is at pains to ignore them." For Albert in a seminal essay "Reflections on Shaw and Psychoanalysis" (1971), while Shaw frequently displays a "measure of familiarity with Freudian method," this is typically accompanied by "skepticism toward it." Somewhat contradictorily, he also asserts that Shaw's "approach" to the "new theory" was "decidedly open-minded and judicious." More recently, as Peter Gahan describes it in *Shaw Shadows: Rereading the Texts of Bernard Shaw* (2004), Shaw and Freud were "both rather cagey about each other's work and not because they were unacquainted with it." Yet, as I think both Albert and Gahan imply, Shaw's views of psychoanalysis were far more complicated than simple censure—or denial. The case is less complicated with Simmel who, in his *magnum opus The Philosophy of Money* (1900), which grew out of lectures he delivered in Vienna (and elsewhere) in the 1890s, makes no reference to Freud at all. Freud, however, as his distinguished biographer Peter Gay observes, certainly knew of Simmel, as Karen Horney invoked his work in criticizing the male bias inherent to much psychoanalytic thought. But neither Freud nor Shaw engaged Simmel's multidisciplinary and influential writing about money or assessed Simmel's enormous impact on modern sociology.

Happily, however, excavating relationships between these intellectual "mainstays" or "bearded masters," to borrow Brophy's terms, is not the aim of this book. Instead, the prompt to think about a project on Shaw's fiction as part of a series entitled "Shaw and His Contemporaries" led me, for reasons that I hope will become clear, to affinities between these three distinguished figures who, although working in different fields, nonetheless contributed to a discourse concerned with how modern human subjectivity—particularly as manifested in feeling and emotion—was being shaped by the velocity and increasing financialization of modern life. In some respects, this book advances an approach similar to that which Elizabeth S. Goodstein develops in those parts of *Georg Simmel and the Disciplinary Imaginary* (2017) that identify parallels between Freudian psychoanalysis and Simmelian sociology: between foreignness in Simmel's "Excurs über den Fremden" ("Excursus on the Stranger," 1908) and Freud's "The Uncanny" (1919), for example, or between the nervous exhaustion of life in the modern metropolis and Freudian assessments of the ego's functioning as a defense against the external world. However, unlike Goodstein's fine book and the work of these other extraordinary scholars, my goals here revolve, finally, around Bernard Shaw's novels and their representations of a particularly material—and at times materialist—psychology and its relation to both feeling and emotion. Throughout this book, then, and particularly in its second chapter, I attempt to delineate the ways in which Freud's and Simmel's theories of such matters as value and affect might aid in a reading of Shaw's fiction (and, occasionally, of Shaw himself).

So, many thanks to both Nelson and Peter for nudging me toward this project, and thanks as well to Richard Dietrich who forwarded very thoughtful critiques and deemed the effort worthy of a contract. Early on, two anonymous readers also made enormously helpful suggestions that have made this study much, much better than it would have otherwise been. Kudos, too, to Tom René, Vicky Bates, and the fine editorial staff of Palgrave Macmillan for making this process so professional and so easy for me in the best sense of the word "easy."

I must also express my sincere gratitude to Angela Bell-Morris and the North Carolina Museum of Art for permission to use Ledelle Moe's sculpture *Congregation* (2003–08), an installation of some 100 concrete faces positioned on a large, bright white wall. As I was finishing this book, its challenges and opportunities inscribed perhaps too indelibly in my thoughts, my daughter Caitlin and I were walking in the museum and, after rounding a corner, encountered Moe's stunning installation. Moving slowly forward to "read" its many faces, my mind ran immediately to images of faces in Darwin's *The Expression of Emotions in Man and Animals* (1872), to photographs of in Jean-Martin Charcot's study of hysteria, and to the taxonomy of affects they project. The aggregation of sculpted faces expressing a wide array of emotion also recalled for me the crowded streets of Simmel's essay "The Metropolis and Mental Life" (1902–03) and several passages in Shaw's novels, particularly a scene when the protagonist of *Immaturity* leaves the dreamy fantasy of the theatre and is jolted back to reality by the swarm of pedestrians and vendors that await him outside it. *Congregation*, in short, with its dialogue between one subject and many, its representation of a wide array of feelings etched in concrete, expresses far better than I ever could the kernel of this book. Moe has said that she intends to add faces to the sculpture from time to time, so that it is also, in a sense, an evolving community of human expression. I can't wait to see more.

My final thanks go to my support structure at Indiana University and to my family. Larry Singell, Executive Dean of the College of Arts and Sciences, generously provided a research leave, and the university awarded me a sabbatical, both of which allowed me to complete this work in a timely fashion. For over 30 years, the English department at Indiana has generously provided me with both encouragement and terrific colleagues who have helped me more than they know. These include Edward Comentale, Susan Gubar, Tom Gieryn, Shane Vogel, Jonathan Elmer, John Lucaites, Ray and Kathy Smith, Patty Ingham, and many more. Last, but certainly not least, my wife Nonie, son Brendan, and daughter Caitlin have always supported my writing. Caitlin, who has served as an editorial assistant at *Studies in Philology* for several years, is the best proofreader I have ever known (I am, perhaps, a little biased on this point). Any mistakes that remain in these pages are therefore of my own making, not hers, and most likely the product of my blindness to or just plain stubbornness about a fine point of articulation, style, or editorial consistency she endeavored in vain to explain to me. My love to all of them.

Contents

1 Introduction: On Money, Psychology, and Affect in Bernard Shaw's Writing — 1

2 The Materialist Dream Theatre: Affect and Value, Freud and Simmel — 43

3 "UNASHAMED": Negative Affect, Money, and Performance in *Immaturity* and *The Irrational Knot* — 89

4 Entr'acte at the Theatre: Marriage, Money, and Feeling in *Love Among the Artists* — 135

5 Cashel Byron's Blush—And Others — 145

6 The Antinomies of *An Unsocial Socialist* — 177

7 Postscript: Embodied Shaws — 217

Works Cited — 221

Index — 229

ABBREVIATION LIST

The abbreviations listed below refer to the editions of Bernard Shaw's works and letters cited internally throughout this book. Those abbreviations followed by a number indicate from which volume of an edition a quotation or other material is taken.

Cashel   *Cashel Byron's Profession.* 1882. *The Works of Bernard Shaw*, vol. 4. London: Constable & Company, 1930.
CL1   *Bernard Shaw: Collected Letters, 1874–1897*, vol. 1. Ed. Dan H. Laurence. London: Max Reinhardt, 1965.
CL2   *Bernard Shaw: Collected Letters, 1898–1910*, vol. 2. Ed. Dan H. Laurence. New York: Viking, 1985.
CL3   *Bernard Shaw: Collected Letters, 1911–1925*, vol. 3. Ed. Dan H. Laurence. New York: Viking, 1985.
CL4   *Bernard Shaw: Collected Letters, 1926–1950*, vol. 4. Ed Dan H. Laurence. New York: Viking, 1988.
CPP   *Complete Plays with Prefaces.* 6 vols. New York: Dodd, Mead & Company, 1963.
I   *Immaturity. The Works of Bernard Shaw*, vol. 1. London: Constable & Company, 1930.
Guide   *The Intelligent Woman's Guide to Socialism, Capitalism, Sovietism, and Fascism.* New York: Random House, 1928.

Knot *The Irrational Knot*. 1880. *The Works of Bernard Shaw*, vol. 2. London: Constable & Company, 1930.

Love *Love Among the Artists*. 1881. *The Works of Bernard Shaw*, vol. 3. London: Constable and Company, 1932.

MCE *Major Critical Essays: The Quintessence of Ibsenism, The Perfect Wagnerite, The Sanity of Art*. London: Constable and Company, 1932.

OT *Our Theatres in the Nineties*. 3 vols. London: Constable and Company, 1948.

SHAW *SHAW: The Annual of Bernard Shaw Studies*, since 2014 known as *SHAW: The Journal of Bernard Shaw Studies*. University Park: Pennsylvania State University Press, 1980-present.

Short *Short Stories, Scraps &Shavings. The Collected Works of Bernard Shaw*, vol. 6. New York: Wm. H. Wise & Company, 1932.

SSS *Sixteen Self Sketches*. London: Constable and Company, 1949.

US *An Unsocial Socialist*. 1883. *The Works of Bernard Shaw*, vol. 5. London: Constable and Company, 1932.

CHAPTER 1

Introduction: On Money, Psychology, and Affect in Bernard Shaw's Writing

> "I knew I was useless, worthless, penniless, and that until I had qualified myself to do something, and proved it by doing it, all this business of calling on people who might perhaps do something for me, and dining out without money to pay for a cab, was silly." (I, xxx)
> —Bernard Shaw, "Preface" to *Immaturity*

The project of recovering a "material psychology" from Bernard Shaw's writing—and of deploying related theoretical insights in assessing the nature of affect in his novels and thought more generally—necessitates articulations between four discourses that are often considered separately and are more than sufficiently complicated in their own right: economics, psychology, affect theory, and, perhaps surprisingly, performance studies. In addition, when juxtaposed to each other and pressed into the service of critical exegesis, these discourses might lead to even greater confusion. For these reasons, I want to take a moment, first, to outline the premises of this undertaking and then, second, to deploy Shaw's 1905 story "The Theatre of the Future" as a primer for the readings that follow. As the title *Bernard Shaw's Novels, Material Psychology, and Affect* indicates, my focus throughout, however much it might stray, is primarily on the five novels that Shaw wrote between 1879 and 1883, not long after his arrival in London in the spring of 1876. However, if Nature abhors a vacuum so, too, do Shavians.

© The Author(s) 2018
S. Watt, *Bernard Shaw's Fiction, Material Psychology, and Affect*, Bernard Shaw and His Contemporaries, https://doi.org/10.1007/978-3-319-71513-1_1

So, before engaging Shaw's novels, this chapter and the one that follows consider intellectual work at the *fin de siècle* as a context within which they were written, paying particular attention to the relationships between materialism and subjectivity in the so-called "marginal" economics to which Shaw was exposed in the 1880s and in the magnum opuses of two of Shaw's contemporaries: Georg Simmel's *The Philosophy of Money* (1900) and Sigmund Freud's *The Interpretation of Dreams* (1900).[1] Implicit in my argument is the conviction that Shaw contributed to an extant discourse on the affective dimensions of capital and exchange—which, in turn, through the process of "surrogation" inform notions of value and the myriad performances inherent to both social life and identity[2]—and that by foregrounding his insights we might better understand the relationship between subjectivity and materialism in Shaw's writing. This investigation includes, therefore, an examination of his ambivalence about perhaps the most vexed, yet semiotically resonant of all material objects—money—a topic that Shaw seemed never to tire of discussing, as several of his last plays amply demonstrate. In much of what follows, however, Shaw the accomplished playwright and public figure yields center stage to a younger, more conflicted writer, although the celebrated older man hovers backstage, emerging on occasion to seize the spotlight of our attention.

A critical genealogy of the subjectivity of this more conflicted Shaw might begin with two conjoined matters: his views of money and the psychical effects of poverty, particularly on human subjects with familial backgrounds like his.[3] Both issues inform Frank Harris's *Bernard Shaw: An Unauthorised Biography Based on Firsthand Information* (1931), which in many respects, given Shaw's participation in funneling information to Harris as he was preparing the book and correcting its proofs after Harris's death in August, 1931, might at the very least be retitled an "authorized" biography.[4] In any case, Harris establishes the relationship between poverty and intense feeling almost from the beginning, as its early chapters, much like several in Shaw's later *Sixteen Self Sketches* (1949), concern Shaw's boyhood in Dublin and the etiology of his "fierce hatred of poverty." I am less interested in origins, though, than in Harris's intimation that terms like "hatred" and "poverty" fail to capture the complexity of the matter. For although as a child Shaw did not suffer the privation of hunger, Harris observes, he could not be spared the "wounds and limitations of chronic impecuniosity and the senseless falsehood of pretending to a superior social rank with less than half the income needed to make the pretence [sic] good."[5]

Harris's phrase "chronic impecuniosity" conveys more than the term "poverty" ever could, I think, as this condition afflicted both the adolescent and older Shaw in ways that transcend material hardship. In this formulation, Harris connects materiality with a compulsory role-playing that exacerbated Shaw's pain every time he was required to participate in the mummeries that constituted genteel interaction. Shaw writes about his discomfiture in letters of the 1870s and 1880s, a period he recalls in the 1921 Preface to his first novel *Immaturity* (1879/1930) complete with memories of feeling "useless," "worthless," and "penniless." As the following pages attempt to delineate, a causal relationship emerges in Shaw's writing between these very adjectives: that is, one often *feels* worthless or useless precisely because one *is* penniless (and an opposite feeling of elation at times attends a character's financial success). Shaw's Preface to *Immaturity* is replete with similar, if less devastating, recollections of being "painfully shy" and of feeling "afraid to accept invitations" (*I*, xxx). However, the matter is more convoluted than this, as Shaw admits that underlying his reticence to accept offers of introduction or social invitations was not only the conviction that they might lead to "nothing," but also the "unspoken fear that they might lead to something I did not want" (xxx). These negative feelings rank among the most persistent consequences of his "chronic impecuniosity," inflecting both his characters' psychical lives and Shaw's as well. When invited to pay social visits on Sunday evenings in London, for example, he suffered "agonies of shyness" that led him to arrive as late as possible because he knew that interactions tantamount to "torturing" himself awaited (*I*, xlv). Such intense pains amount, in my view, to more self-defining "perennial wounds," a trope borrowed from Michel Foucault's characterization of the transformative work of Friedrich Nietzsche, Karl Marx, Sigmund Freud, and, as I hope to add, Bernard Shaw.[6] Also, if Nietzsche's claim in *On the Genealogy of Morals* (1887) is accurate that "setting prices, determining values, contriving equivalences ... preoccupied the earliest thinking of man to so great an extent that in a certain sense they constituted thinking *as such*,"[7] then one might also urge its constitutive importance to human subjectivity and feeling as well or, more modestly, to Shaw's subjectivity and that of many of his characters, particularly the protagonists of his novels.

One means of binding such wounds—including humiliation (Harris's term) and the continual "dread" of social interactions (Shaw's self-description)[8]—would seem obvious: the acquisition of money. Unfortunately, as biographers from Harris and St. John Ervine to Michael

Holroyd emphasize, Shaw's father, like his maternal grandfather, possessed little knowledge of how to earn or raise any.[9] Not so with Shaw, however, as has been described by biographers and critics alike—and by Shaw himself. While on holiday in 1895, for example, he received a request from American editor Benjamin Tucker to review Max Nordau's *Degeneration* (1892), which by that time had created an international sensation. Tucker added a further enticement for Shaw to undertake the assignment by asking him to "ascertain the highest price that has ever been paid to any man ... for a magazine article" and promising to pay him that amount, an offer Shaw puckishly described as evidence of "really great editing" on Tucker's part (*MCE*, 286). In his biography Harris, noting Shaw's reluctance to accept payment for public speaking or for appearing on radio broadcasts, similarly recalls that, some 20 years after Shaw eviscerated Nordau's screed against modernity in his "open letter" to Tucker's magazine *Liberty*, William Randolph Hearst paid him "over a thousand pounds for an article."[10] But this sum might be deemed so much small beer, as substantial as it is. For in 1919 and after considerable epistolary haggling between Shaw and Hearst's *New York American* over his fee for a series of articles, Hearst apologized for the misunderstanding and made certain that the unhappy essayist received £2800 or the equivalent of $12,500 for his labors.[11] In addition, even though Shaw privileged his writing for the theatre as essentially different from his "journalistic" work, one of his greatest American admirers, playwright Elmer Rice, was incredulous at Shaw's response to his request for permission for New York's University Settlement to stage a limited number of performances of *The Shewing-up of Blanco Posnet* (1909):

> I have never ceased to marvel at the amount of time and energy expended, by a world famous dramatist, on the licensing of a production to an obscure amateur group.[12]

More generally, Rice was amazed at how "preoccupied" writers like Shaw were with the "merchandising of their wares," a preoccupation to which Declan Kiberd alludes in *The Irish Writer and the World* (2005). Unlike European modernists, Kiberd notes, prominent writers associated with the so-called Irish Revival "did not proclaim the need for eternal antagonism between bohemian and bourgeois." He identifies Shaw in particular, who "wrote mainly for money and earned lots," as providing the most compelling evidence for his thesis, as do the entrepreneurial endeavors of James Joyce and Oscar Wilde.[13]

There exists, on the most literal level, ample justification for Kiberd's aspersion of Shaw's motives for writing. From his earliest years in London, Shaw insisted on being paid for his work, and he was quick to reiterate his stance when the situation demanded it. In September 1879, after receiving a letter from G.R. Sims, editor of *One and All*, accepting an article but not including any payment for it, Shaw responded by asking if he could expect to be remunerated for sending any "further contributions" to the periodical (*CL1*, 21). He needed the money, as he confided in a letter the same month to Arnold White, manager and secretary of the Edison Telephone Company of London: "My family are in difficulties" (*CL1*, 23). Two years later, after failing to find a publisher for *Immaturity*, he inquired of Remington and Company about the cost of printing the novel at his own expense. This plan, however, was soon beaten into "airy thinness," much like the gold in John Donne's "Valediction Forbidding Mourning." Learning that the required fee would be £95, a sum far in excess of his meager savings, a discouraged Shaw addressed his own valedictory letter to the publisher that concluded, "Let me add that if it will not pay, I had rather it remained in MS" (*CL1*: 43). Later, of course, Shaw engaged in more nuanced, even bumptious, disagreements with publishers over contracts and payments. In a 1909 letter to Constable and Company that begins bluntly with "When are you going to send me my money," Shaw observed that "with complete security" he might have invested the funds he is owed (over £1600 by his estimation) at 4%, thus making Constable's dilatory behavior more egregious and his financial loss greater; even worse, he had not been compensated for his own out-of-pocket expenses (*CL2*, 844). As his complaint confirms, Shaw's acumen in financial matters was evolving, as Gustavo A. Rodríguez Martín underscores when citing Shaw's 1932 correspondence with his financial advisor, Stanley Clench, concerning the falling value of British currency, the establishment of a £10,000 annuity payable to his wife, and his desire to avoid "double taxation."[14] Some decades earlier, however, Shaw's mother and sister, Lucy, who had immigrated to London before him, needed him to earn a living; and Shaw struggled to do just that. The investment potential of surplus or, what Anna Kornbluh terms, "fictitious capital," the declining value of the pound, and the taxation of annuities seemed far from his mind.[15]

At this point, one might regard Shaw's early years of penury and frustration in London as unremarkable; after all, it might be argued, generations of Irish and other immigrants have suffered the same set of grinding deprivations—and many still do. Millions of desperate people have fled and, sadly, continue to flee their home countries, as Shaw did, hoping to escape the "failure," "poverty," and "obscurity" that awaited young men in Dublin only to experience more virulent strains of each in their new home (*I*, xxxvi). Yet, unlike many immigrants unable to speak the language of their new home or woefully ill-suited for the challenges of a modern economy, Shaw was entirely capable of assimilation, even if this capacity occasioned awkward, even painful social engagements. More seriously, as Anthony Roche observes in discussing Shaw and Oscar Wilde's early years in London, as immigrants they both depended on others' "continuing goodwill" and, in the last analysis, never occupied "a position of stability or security."[16] What makes Shaw's story more unique—and what adds complexity and texture to the etiology of "chronic impecuniosity"— is that his successful acquisition of money was often not an entirely happy experience either. This is not merely my opinion, but Shaw's as well. In his 1914 lecture for the Fabian Society "The Idolatry of Money and How to End It," for example, Shaw notes that he has "had no money, and I have had more than I wanted. ... I am a much less happy person, but I am a much more virtuous person." Here, Shaw, sardonically prodding at one supposition upon which the "idolatry" of money is based, appears to accede to the fallacy that "income is a measure of virtue," but as his 1905 Preface to his second novel, *The Irrational Knot* (1880) makes exceptionally clear, he could not in fact countenance the notion:

> It is the secret of all our governing classes, which consist finally of people who ... are unalterably resolved, in the first, to have money enough for a handsome and delicate life, and will, in pursuit of that money, batter in the doors of their fellow-men, sell them up, sweat them in fetid dens, shoot, stab, hang, imprison, sink, burn and destroy them in the name of law and order. And this shows their fundamental sanity and rightmindedness; for a sufficient income is indispensable to the practice of virtue ... (*Knot*, xvi)

As important for my purposes as this indictment of the privileged, Shaw adds the proviso that whatever dubious virtue inheres in money, this applies only to "earned income" (*Lectures* 27), a topic of considerable complexity in Shavian thought, as we shall see.

Indeed, if what are commonly termed "negative affects"—shame, embarrassment, fear, disgust—are for Shaw caused by extreme poverty and the enforced performance of class affiliation, earning money from writing and other labors as a public figure were often similarly anxious, even odious, experiences. Here again, Shaw's language in characterizing both certain wage-earning work and more political public performances reveals his incipient disgust with both ventures. So, while in his October 5, 1879 letter to Arnold White Shaw conceded that "it is exhilarating to make a clever stroke" in business (*CL 1*: 23)—and while several of his characters experience this same exhilaration and concomitant boost in self-esteem after making a sudden windfall—his feelings about making money were often less refulgent, as his pointed, excessively disparaging diction reveals. In declining Elizabeth Lawson's social invitation in a January, 1880 note, Shaw, describing himself as "the most unfortunate of men," blamed his absence on a "*sordid* matter of business" that "will not be put off" (*CL 1*: 29; my emphasis). The sordidness Shaw associated with business came to define his view of money as well. In outlining how "income has nothing to do with talent, character, or anything else" in "Why We Idolize Millionaires," the second of his six Fabian Lectures of 1914, Shaw firmly distinguished the heroism of soldiers from the corruptions of money by urging his audience not to insult their valor by "talking about such a dirty thing as money" in any context that included the military (*Lectures*, 21–22).

While Shaw's decoupling of income and honorable "character" finds its most persuasive example in the selflessness of soldiers, he found a similar disjunction in his own professional life. More specifically, the pursuit of "business" encroached upon his time for writing plays, and here his cultivation of metaphor resonates importantly in forging this distinction. Recall that in "The Author's Apology" for *Our Theatres in the Nineties*, a collection of his theatre reviews written for *The Saturday Review* between January 1895 through May 1898, Shaw characterized his often iconoclastic reviews in chivalric terms as amounting to a veritable "siege laid to the theatre of the XIXth Century by an author who had to cut his way into it at the point of a pen, and throw some of its defenders into the moat" (*OT* 1: v). Earning money from other writing, however, was a far less heroic exercise, as he confided to his Viennese translator Siegfried Trebitsch some years later. Writing Trebitsch on October 7, 1903 while working on his tract *The Common Sense of Municipal Trading* (1904), Shaw complained bitterly about this abuse of his time:

> And now the worst of it is that I shall have to set to work to write a Fabian Manifesto on [Fabian Socialism] instead of setting to at a new play—or rather at the abominable book on Municipal Trading that I have to finish first. … That is the secret of the greatness of my dramatic masterpieces:

I have to work like a dog at the most *sordid* things between every hundred lines.¹⁷ (*CL 2*: 375; my emphasis)

Shaw's disparagement of toiling at "sordid" nondramatic writing was preceded by his account of addressing an audience in Glasgow, a "highly successful" oration on socialism that nonetheless filled him with "self-loathing." In this instance, his self-recrimination is not directly connected to money, but rather with the onus of performing a "stupendous earnestness" that left him "empty, exhausted, disgusted" (*CL 2*: 375). These two matters, money and social performance, are conjoined in Shaw's letter to Trebitsch, as they were in earlier letters, and evoke aspects of the "chronic impecuniosity" that motivated a social pretense without the accompanying material wealth to make the charade convincing, at least to Shaw.

Without belaboring the point further, I want only to observe that Shaw's earning "lots of money" is hardly an uncomplicated matter. Elmer Rice's incredulity at how "preoccupied" Shaw and other distinguished writers were with "merchandising their wares" hints at additional layers of complexity that demand closer inspection, as do Rodríguez Martín's characterizations of Shaw's "fixation" with money and his management of his financial affairs as a "lifelong habit that pervaded his public and private lives."¹⁸ Preoccupation, "fixation," and the notion of money's "lifelong" insinuation into one's private life—these gesture toward the interpretive potential of a more deliberate parsing of the relationship between money (including surplus money functioning as capital) and Shavian subjectivity. This potential begins with the realization that, for Shaw and many of his characters, money possessed an affective valence (disgust, feelings of emptiness and, in moments of triumph, elation) that transcends ideological differences between European modernists and their Irish counterparts. In other words, money and affect are imbricated in Shavian thought *and* Shavian psychology, and both pertain to Shaw's alternative invocations of, on the one hand, an idealized knight who ferociously jousts with defenders of an aesthetically bankrupt theatre and, on the other, a mangy and despised "dog" who scratches income out of execrable commercial writing assignments.¹⁹ At the same time, and complicating matters even further, this opposition is almost always susceptible to deconstruction, because the theatre and Shaw's writing for it exist, succeed or fail, in a world of commerce. At times, it seems, chivalric action and commercial motivation are inseparable.

In supplying this necessarily brief consideration of Shaw's vexed relationship to money, its affective implications and psychical consequences, I must at the same time admit to my promiscuous use of such terms as "affect," "emotion," and "feeling." A more precise lexicon will be required to map the various representations of these in Shaw's writing, and more needs to be said, too, about the quite different, but related, matter of a "material psychology." In this latter endeavor, I want to acknowledge the work of such scholars as Richard Farr Dietrich and Arnold Silver, which has not received the attention it deserves in promoting psychology as an interpretive *entrée* into Shavian thought more generally and his early fiction more particularly. In *Bernard Shaw's Novels: Portraits of the Artist as Man and Superman* (1996) and two influential articles—"Shavian Psychology" (1984) and "Shaw and Yeats: Two Irishmen Divided by a Common Language" (1995)—Dietrich develops insights, some of them unorthodox ones, that are of great value to my project. In the former article, for example, Dietrich emphasizes that "Shavian psychology was parallel in important respects" to Freudian thought and finally constituted "an alternative" to it.[20] As Peter Gahan observes, underscoring Shaw's own admission in a 1916 review of Julius West's *G.K. Chesterton: A Critical Study*, Shaw paid Freud a "serious if disrespectful attention" and, as I touched briefly upon in my "Acknowledgements," expressed "ambivalence" about his psychoanalysis. This is actually putting the matter politely considering that in the same review he indicted Freud as having "neither delicacy nor common sense."[21] In particular, Shaw "intensely disliked" the concept of depth psychology—going so far as calling psychoanalysis a "craze" in his 1921 Preface to *Immaturity* (xviii)—and, as Dietrich explains, tended to "project psychological issues as cultural issues,"[22] an assertion consistent with the idea of affect as a kind of surface phenomenon deeply connected to—and often catalyzed by—the events that comprise social life.

In the latter article, Dietrich collapses the notion that Shaw was a "bloodless, mechanical man" compared to W.B. Yeats, contending that he developed a "characteristic affective approach" to his characters, particularly thinly veiled autobiographical figures like Owen Jack in his third novel, *Love Among the Artists* (1881).[23] In doing so, Dietrich promotes a sentence in Shaw's May 16, 1907 address "The New Theology" as indicative of this approach: "I do not address myself to your logical faculties, but as one human mind trying to put himself in contact with other human minds."[24] At first glance, Shaw's exordium may seem to have little to do with the topics under consideration here; rather, he uses it to introduce his delineation of a "will or life-force" engaged in a "continual struggle to produce something higher and higher" and to advance his argument that the Judeo-Christian God who designed the universe from its beginning is being supplanted by an emergent discourse shaped by evolution and Charles Darwin's conception of natural selection. "The aim of the New Theology," Shaw emphasizes, "is to turn the process the other way and conceive of the force behind the universe as working up through imperfection and mistake to a perfect, organized being."[25]

Still, this emphasis on Shaw's "affective approach" hints at one of the aims of this study, and Dietrich's nod to another passage in "The New Theology" neatly captures this aim.[26] In the excerpt, Shaw attempts to explain the "unconscious" acceptance (his term) of religious ideation by recalling a seemingly trivial moment from his own experience in which he was oblivious to, or unconscious of, an otherwise almost mundane reality. Prior to washing his hands, he tells his audience at the Kensington Town Hall, he had rolled up his shirt sleeves and then, after completing his ablutions, he neglected to return them to their more proper order. Deciding later to take a walk in west London, he meets an acquaintance who, noting this sartorial lapse, inquires, "What on earth are you going about in that fashion for?" Shaw's immediate *bodily* reaction is revealing:

> Now, as I did not know that my sleeves were rolled up, they were not rolled up so far as I was concerned until that intrusive friend came and quite unnecessarily called my attention to the fact, covering me with blushes and confusion.[27]

This episode hints at a quite different aspect of Shaw's "affective approach" that will garner considerable attention in the readings that follow: namely, the sudden manifestation of a feeling and an accompanying bodily response. Unaware or "unconscious" of his breach of decorum ("that *fashion*"), Shaw expresses no feeling whatsoever; however, when his interlocutor calls his attention to his dishevelment in the public space of London streets, Shaw's body, particularly his face, reacts immediately and involuntarily by blushing.

Shaw's relating of this anecdote is also slightly ironic, as "The New Theology" privileges the centrality of Darwinian thought on evolution, *not* on understandings of affect, its various expression, or physical sensation. For had his lecture addressed these topics, Shaw might have alluded to *The Expression of the Emotions in Man and Animals* (1872), in which Darwin discusses such matters as the physiology and textuality of facial expressions—in the increased flow of blood in facial capillaries when blushing, for instance, or the multiple significations of an arched eyebrow—as they pertain to or reveal emotion. In this study Darwin asserts that blushing, unlike, say, weeping and trembling, cannot be induced by "any physiological means—that is, by any action on the body." Characterizing blushing as "the most peculiar and the most human of all expressions," he adds that "it would require an overwhelming amount of evidence to make us believe that any animal could blush."[28] Scientists, philosophers, and scholars from Herbert Spencer and Darwin in Shaw's day to Cary Wolfe and Cora Diamond in ours have contemplated such matters, often as they pertain to species differentiation, and these embodied phenomena constitute a fertile ground for Shaw to cultivate an "affective approach" not merely in the rhetoric of his public speeches, but also in his representation of a character's subjective reality in his drama and fiction.[29]

Shaw's blush thus underscores the need for both a more refined understanding of the relationship between social interaction and affect, on the one hand, and a more precise lexicon when discussing affect, on the other. To respond to the former need—and to view the scene and dialogue from "The New Theology" through the lens of performance theory—I want to turn to Joseph Roach's sense of *surrogation* as a tripartite process involving performance, substitution, and memory. "Performance," Roach observes, "stands in for an elusive entity that it is not but that it must vainly aspire both to embody and replace." However different, the myriad activities that might be termed "performance"—in theatrical production, in such social events as nuptials or funerals, or in competitions—connote a kind of completion: a theatrical production completes a script just as an athletic or musical performance is the culmination of training and practice.[30] Performance is, at least in one sense, an aggregation of traces and echoes of antecedent events, just as theatrical production is marked by previous iterations of the play being produced. As Roach explains in an article on performance's Orphic nature, performance implies action; it is always a "doing or a thing done," and this thing done is "authorized by something prior, even when it isn't." Performance "may or may not be conventionally artistic, but it is always social," and for this reason "the smallest practical unit of performance is two," as it is in Shaw's parable of the rolled sleeves from "The New Theology."[31] Given all of this, we might infer that his friend initially regarded his appearance—rolled sleeves and all—as a kind of performance, an iconoclastic protest, even, of gentlemanly comportment and "fashion." Shaw himself was initially oblivious to all of this until jolted back into consciousness by his acquaintance's query.

In what ways, then, is Shaw's encounter on West End London streets a "performance"? It is an event enacted before an audience, in this instance an audience of one who seems to perceive this interaction as at least partly representational: the display of rolled sleeves stands in or substitutes for a something else. As important, when his appearance is brought to his attention, Shaw is automatically and uncontrollably suffused with blushes. This is significant, for if a successful performance is an embodied practice that involves both a looking back "as well as a movement forward,"[32] then Shaw's urban stroll may be regarded as unsuccessful in terms of forward movement because it instantiates a reaction whose trajectory leads to the past. In her chapter "Shame Before Others" in *The Cultural Politics of Emotion* (2004)—and shame, embarrassment, and humiliation are related affective phenomena—Sara Ahmed explains that shame "as an emotion requires a witness"; further, in shame, "one desires cover precisely because one has already been exposed to others."[33] One might reasonably demur at this point, considering "shame" as too strong a term here and suggesting that "surprise" or "embarrassment" more accurately catalyzes Shaw's blush. Fair enough. But what exactly is being exposed? How do the rolled sleeves—an unintentional performance of slovenliness—function as a substitute? Or, stated somewhat differently, given the prominence of memory in the process of surrogation, what memories underpin Shaw's reaction? Does the episode recall an impoverished childhood, and is it thus rooted in a past that impedes psychical progress? Does it reinstate an adherence to codes of fashion that, among other things, function as an iteration of class affiliation and, as such, serve as a troubling reminder of the anxious pretenses of social belonging without the income needed to perpetuate the ruse?

Pursuing a much different project than mine here, Charles Altieri in *The Particulars of Rapture: An Aesthetics of the Affects* (2003) might have been describing Shaw, his unfortunate sleeves, and his abrupt awareness of his appearance when stating, "Many affects have power in our lives because they emerge as immediate aspects of the kind of attention we pay to the world and to ourselves."[34] Several elements of Altieri's thesis deserve further scrutiny, most particularly the shift from inattention to attention and the complementary notion of immediacy or sudden emergence. Most contributors to the growing corpus of critical literature known as "affect theory" would agree with Altieri about immediacy, and also endorse Brian Massumi's underscoring of the "event" as the catalyst of emergence: "The expression-event is the system of the inexplicable"—and of intensity. In addition, "intensity," Massumi notes, might be "equated with affect."[35] Nearly all of these insights are corroborated by Shaw's recollection of what would otherwise be an unmemorable peregrination: that is, an "event" occurs when, after meeting his friend, Shaw is advised about his unfastidious appearance. He responds immediately, if inchoately, by blushing and is left "confused" by the intensity of his own bodily reaction. Here it is worth noting, as Ahmed does in tracing elements of an opposite feeling, happiness, that etymologically speaking "happiness" claims the Middle English ancestor "hap," which denotes "chance." Feeling or affect, then, frequently stems from the "messiness of the experiential" and the "drama of contingency."[36] You are suddenly moved by a refrain in a piece of music, frightened by a shadow, elated by an unexpected victory, or confused, perhaps embarrassed, by the offhand remark of an acquaintance you happen to meet. All of these examples include contact with *things*: music, shadows, and, of course, people. Affect "is what sticks," Ahmed explains, preserving connections between "ideas, values, and objects."[37]

Altieri offers both a useful definition of affects and, relevant to the latter need mentioned above for a more judicious language of affect, a taxonomy of its varieties. For Altieri, as Shaw's blush implies, affects are "immediate modes of sensual responsiveness to the world characterized by an accompanying imaginative dimension." In this definition, not surprisingly, immediacy and bodily reaction are privileged, joining intensity ("covered" with blushes) as salient features of affects. What "accompanying imaginative dimension" is evoked in Shaw's encounter isn't entirely clear, but what *is* certain is that "confusion" accompanies his involuntary coloring. In this taxonomy, Altieri identifies four categories of affects—feelings, emotions, moods, and passions—the former two of which are of more importance to my project than the latter tandem. That is to say, feelings, or "elemental affective states characterized by an imaginative engagement in the immediate process of sensation," and emotions, or "attitudes that typically establish a particular cause and so situate the agent within a narrative and generate some kind of action or identification," are central to my undertaking.[38] In these terms, Shaw's street encounter is productive of *feeling* and, unlike, say, sadness or jealousy is not so tethered to prior narratives and occurrences. Further, the incident involving rolled-up shirt sleeves not only is "elemental" and "immediate," but also complicates the relationship between objects and sensations (Why would shirt sleeves provoke such a reaction?). Nor does Shaw's encounter imply his agency. On the contrary, Shaw is powerless to suppress his blush and the feeling responsible for it. To be sure, this feeling *may* loop back to a meaning-laden past, a deep structure or narrative which is responsible for the more complex identification Altieri associates with *emotion*. Shaw's history with his friend, with prior deprecations of his appearance, or with any of the myriad of real or perceived slights inherent to social intercourse may also underlie his feeling and uncontrollable blushing, but this is impossible to determine from the brief account he provides. Just to clarify, it is not the case that I am disinterested in mood or passion, both of which play their parts in Shaw's fiction. Rather, feeling and emotion are more centrally located in the narratives of Shaw's novels, and their prominence motivates the discussions that follow.

In these ways, Macmillan and Company's rejection of *Immaturity* in 1880 in part because of its apprehension that "most readers would find it dry, unattractive, and too devoid of any sort of emotion" (*CL1*: 27) seems inaccurate, particularly in its final criticism. On the contrary, sudden manifestations of feeling and emotions *of all sorts* occur throughout Shaw's writing, fictive and personal alike, though they might not conform to the emotional trajectories that late Victorian publishers sought when attempting to acquire marketable fiction. Heretofore, not enough has been said about the more narratively complex etiology of feeling, emotion, and their contributions to a larger Shavian psychology. At this point, it might be objected that, however performative Shaw's encounter on a London street may be, the feelings emanating from it have little to do with money or exchange. Rather, the scene evokes a relationship between feeling and the material object (shirt sleeves) but not with materialism or capital *per se*. Perhaps. Yet such examples are prominent throughout Shaw's fiction, and several will be considered in detail in the chapters that follow. More important, insofar as these incidents concern performance and the immediacy of *feeling*, however remote from issues of money or affluence they might seem, they suggest how the perennial wounds of poverty include anxiety or dis-ease about participation in the conventional rituals of social class that Shaw often found difficult.

This, in turn, means that the term "material" or even "materialist" psychology, somewhat paradoxically, has a social dimension. Through such a construction I mean to identify in Shavian thought the relationship between performance, feeling and emotion, and both money and the process of commodity exchange, including the exchange of one's labor as a commodity for wages or royalties. As Shaw very well knew—or felt—money has the capacity to exhilarate or to wound. As, again, he confessed to Arnold White in 1879, "although it is exhilarating to make a clever stroke occasionally, the everyday work is too serious, in my opinion, to be undertaken for the purpose ... of enriching an individual at the expense of the community" (*CL1*: 23). To be sure, Shaw's growing socialist perspective allowed him to recognize the ramifications of the unfettered pursuit of wealth, even if at the same time he recognized the affective dimension—the thrill or exhilaration—of doing so successfully. In Shaw's writing, money and positive feeling are yoked together as frequently as impecuniosity and negative feelings are, but this in no way should suggest that wealth always brought happiness for Shaw or all of his characters, as Sidney Trefusis, Shaw's protagonist in *An Unsocial Socialist* (1883), so strikingly demonstrates.

In this and other ways, a material psychology in which feeling, emotion, and money are foregrounded serves to complement recent articulations between economic theory and the fundamental tenets of Freudian psychoanalysis. This critical articulation begins with the premise that both psychoanalytic and economic theory hypothesizes, indeed privileges, a monadic consumer-desirer over a class-grounded subject, a premise that Marxist critiques of Freudianism, many of which are coterminous with the rise of psychoanalysis, refute in voicing their opposition to the psychoanalytic movement. In 1927, for example, the semiotician V.N. Vološinov attacked the construction of an "abstract biological person" intrinsic to psychoanalytic models of human subjectivity. Such a figure, he contended, "does not exist at all"; on the contrary, "outside society and, consequently, outside objective socio-economic conditions, there is no such thing as a human being." His ferocity is entirely consistent with Dietrich's hypothesis of a Shavian psychology projecting outward to larger social and institutional structures:

> *Only as part of a social whole, only in and through a social class, does the human person become historically real and culturally productive.*[39] [emphasis in original]

More to the point of the performative dimensions of Shavian psychology, for Vološinov emotion and feeling are irrevocably tied to larger social formations and rituals, including social class. This constitutes the basis of his strenuous objection to Freudianism, as the italics in the original imply: "*Processes that are in fact social are treated by Freud from the point of view of individual psychology.*"[40]

Yet in his representation of human subjectivity, Shaw, the outspoken Fabian socialist, allows for the subject's *less* social and more individual affective reactions, especially where capital is concerned. That is to say, while poverty exerts what are at times devastating self-disparagements and paralyzing social anxieties, the acquisition of not merely money but wealth holds the potential to revise the human subject's sense of self-worth, even if like the Lacanian mirror stage this sense of self is factitious. But this is hardly surprising, as scholars have recently and productively addressed the ways in which Freudian psychoanalysis borrows from economic discourse contemporaneous with its emergence. In a seminal article that traces these appropriations, Richard T. Gray summarizes this network of influence:

> ... even in its earliest formulations Freud's psychoanalytic project was underwritten by economic categories both on the substantive level of theoretical blueprint and its rhetoric. The curious reciprocity between economic argument and economic language is a constant and pervasive feature of Freud's thought and work.[41]

As Gray emphasizes, Freud conceived of the libidinal economy in the context of scarcity—a defining dimension or, rather, *the* defining object, of economics—and, therefore, as a kind of "balance sheet." Similarly, interleafing economic and psychical entities in their intellectual work, late nineteenth-century economists such as Carl Menger and the English marginalist William Stanley Jevons conflated feeling with such matters as money and capital: "pleasure, pain, labour, utility, value, wealth, money, capital are all notions admitting of quantity."[42] All, in other words, can be illuminated by scientific analysis so long as the metrics are sensitive enough to provide accurate measurement.[43] If value and money are knotted in a skein with pleasure and pain—if, as Shaw asserted in 1905, "Economic science is concerned with nothing less than a calculus of human welfare and human desires"[44]— then exchange, too, arises from this dynamic. In other words, if the pleasure principle impels organisms to seek "excitations in the external world that will fill existential needs and eliminate internal stimuli,"[45] then the drive is implicated in a process of exchange that resembles the circulation and consumption of commodities (which include both things and, as we shall see, performances). Because a commodity, to be useful, must possess properties that gratify a human need, some connection—real or imputed—must exist between the psychical and commercial domains. "In short," Gray concludes, "economic value for Menger is always predicated on scarcity, and Freud incorporates this doctrine into his theory of the psychic economy."[46]

So does Shaw. The well-known and well-traveled term "psychic economy" to which Gray alludes, however, will not quite suit my purposes here, which is why I want to replace it with "material psychology." As Anna Kornbluh observes in *Realizing Capital: Financial and Psychic Economies in Victorian Form* (2014), "psychic economy" is a "notion so ubiquitous, a conceit so familiar, it ranks as one of modernity's reigning tropes." This "casual ubiquity," she points out, "warrants no explanation; it aptly encapsulates the structure of subjectivity and opportunely portends the structural continuity between individuals and sociopolitical macroeconomics."[47] As she earlier delineates, the idea that "subjectivity is fundamentally economic" and the "economy is fundamentally psychological" gained prominence among Victorian thinkers well before the young Shaw arrived in London. She charts its rise from such various events as financial crises in the 1820s, the 1833 Bank of England Charter Act's "erasure of strictures on usury and authorization of paper banknotes," later financial crises in the 1830s and 1840s, Limited Liability legislation and Joint-Stock Companies licensure in 1856, and much more.[48] However, although indebtedness and credit play minor roles in what follows, my interests only tangentially pertain to matters derivative of an ascendant Victorian "financialization" that greeted Shaw in the 1870s: lending practices, stock speculation, futures contracts, and other workings of "fictitious capital." Similarly, "structural continuity" and homologies between models receive little attention here. The adjective "material," perhaps, could be replaced by another modifier such as "materialist" but, however imperfect, this verbiage is intended to suggest a focus on, well, "real money" and everyday expenditures—on more tangible transactions more immediately felt by subjects—*not* on the workings of "fictitious capital." My use of "material psychology" also signals my efforts to avoid the freight that "psychic economy" carries with it and not to repeat "casual evocations" of the term that, as Kornbluh reasonably complains, "abound in contemporary critical discourse."[49]

Even this goal, as I have implied, tends to run against the grain of common understanding, as critics frequently invoke Shaw's indifference to or ambivalence about an emergent psychoanalysis at the turn of the century.

For Shaw in "The Sanity of Art," psychoanalytic tenets, particularly as Max Nordau in *Degeneration* manipulates them to bolster his "vivisection" of art and artists at the fin de siècle, amount to a "mock scientific theory picked up secondhand from a few lunacy doctors with a literary turn" (*MCE*, 332, 330). Much like his "fixation" with money, Shaw's impatience with psychoanalysis persisted throughout his long career. Humorously and somewhat self-consciously moved both to comment on his shortcomings as an autobiographer in his "Apology" for *Sixteen Self Sketches* and seize an opportunity to deride psychoanalysis, Shaw suggests that "Perhaps our psycho-analysts may find in such dull stuff"—the fragments of his life contained in the pages that follow—"clues that have escaped me" (*SSS* 7). Later, when summarizing the shame he felt during his unhappy school days, shame that amounted to "more or less a psychosis," he mockingly cheers, "Finally, a point to be scored by our psycho-analysts" (*SSS* 25). Accepting such wryness as gospel, some writers have severely or entirely discounted the potential of psychology and psychoanalysis in reading Shaw. But like Dietrich, who attempts to derive a psychoanalytic or more broadly psychological theory from Shaw's work, I hope to undertake an analogous enterprise, also demonstrating why all of this matters to a reading of Shaw's *oeuvre*, particularly his novels. The brief exposition that follows is offered as a prologue to, and an example of, such a reading.

Money, Affirmation, and Value: Shaw's "Theatre of the Future" as Testamental Text

"Since [*Worstward* Ho] allows us to put together a table of contents for the entirety of Beckett's work, it is entirely apposite to treat this text as if it were, above, all, a network of thought or shorthand. ..."—Alain Badiou, "Being, Existence, Thought: Prose and Concept" (2003)

Judged by almost any standard, Shaw's "The Theatre of the Future," published in *The Grand Magazine* (February, 1905), is an odd story. The oddities begin in the story's inaugural sentence with the introduction of Gerald Bridges, the eventual catalyst for shaping a "new" theatre that, in the end, resembles the old London theatre against which, as a critic for *The Saturday Review* a decade earlier, Shaw had inveighed. What, a reader might reasonably ask, qualifies Shaw's expatriate protagonist, returning to England in the spring of 1910 after a 22-year residence in Argentina, to influence the theatre in even minimal ways other than the blunt force of the four words that open the story's second paragraph: "Bridges was a millionaire" (*Short*, 55)? The unlikeliness of such a theatrical neophyte transforming the contemporary stage is just one of the story's many curiosities which I hope to unpack while also suggesting, perhaps even more oddly, that "The Theatre of the Future" functions as a kind of "testamental text" in Shaw's corpus. That is to say, much as Alain Badiou privileges *Worstward Ho* (1983) as a "testamental" or "recapitulatory text" that "takes stock of the whole of Samuel Beckett's intellectual enterprise,"[50] I want to suggest that "The Theatre of the Future" constitutes both a forecast of and a prescient "shorthand" for Shaw's understanding of human subjectivity. In doing so, this otherwise unremarkable story advances issues particularly germane to the readings of Shaw's work in this book: performance and the substitution inherent to it, the etiology of feeling or affect—both wounds and exhilarations—and the "enormous importance" of money, as Shaw once described it, to the psychical life of the human subject (*Knot*, xii). In "The Theatre of the Future," Shaw yokes intense feeling to performance, to conceptions of value, however misguided, and to a materiality for which money functions as a signifier; as such, it offers a précis of a Shavian psychology rather different from better-known explanations of human subjectivity at the turn of the century—but, in several respects, not *that* different. For, like Freud and Simmel, Shaw braids together the symbolic economies of the material and the psychical, thus positioning himself centrally in *fin de siècle* thought on this precise articulation.[51]

While the bulk of "The Theatre of the Future" concerns both bizarrely exaggerated and more mundane business practices—particularly those related to the operation of commercial theatre—Shaw's story, other than the exposition in its opening paragraph about the delights of London in the spring, doesn't begin in a West End theatre or with a star-actor's tour of threadbare provincial venues. Instead, it provides a sketch of how Bridges, after a long hiatus in Buenos Ayres, returned to England as a millionaire-aficionado of Elizabethan and Jacobean tragedy, a passion that emerges only after he has secured his fortune. Such a turn of events, it must be said, is impossible to predict from Bridges' adventures in South America. Convinced that he suffers from a respiratory ailment for which a sea voyage might prove salutary, Gerald travels on his uncle's cargo boat and, soon after arriving in Buenos Ayres, foolishly acquires a small agency destined to fail. His impetuous investment was "so unworthy of a youth of the smallest sharpness that Gerald's uncle jumped at the opportunity of disowning him," with the result that the "poor dupe," lacking the "gumption" to ameliorate his situation, could only wait for the inevitable result of his miscalculation: "imminent destitution" (*Short*, 55). Miraculously, he languishes in this state of financial limbo for only three minutes, when a "Yankee" enters his office inquiring about picrate of selenium, a commodity about which Gerald was entirely ignorant. The procession of visitors continues an hour later, when three German businessmen come seeking the same thing, followed by a local farmer eager to disburden himself of a stone he suspected might be worth something to Gerald—and it is. After paying the farmer a modest sum, he is able to sell this mass of selenium to eager buyers at an enormous profit, making "more on that single deal than he could have earned in two years at the bank" (57) where he was formerly employed. This business novice, disowned by his uncle and nearly ruined, instantly becomes wealthy, joining a roster of Shavian protagonists who, once orphaned or poor, eventually rise to affluence. Andrew Undershaft in *Major Barbara* is the most obvious of these self-made men, but many other successful entrepreneurs populate Shaw's writing, from Ned Conolly in *The Irrational Knot* to the underwear magnate John Tarleton in *Misalliance* (1910), Alastair Fitzfassenden in *The Millionairess* (1936), the "proletarian"-born and "famous lucky financier" Buoyant in *Buoyant Billions* (1948) (*CPP* 1: 765), and the erstwhile tramp Bossborn in the unfinished "comedietta" *Why She Would Not* (1950).

For my purposes, what is especially resonant about Gerald's providential rise is not so much the "torrent of gold" that poured into his "empty pocket," but rather both the manner in which he acquired his wealth and the psychical impact of his good fortune (*Short*, 58). A "born amateur," he would likely have remained a modestly remunerated bank employee all his life had he not "blundered into the exact spot" (58)—at the precise moment—where a fortune might be made. Gerald, however, didn't regard himself as unambitious, bumbling, or just plain lucky. Instead, believing he had "'made' the difference" between the cost of the mineral and the price of its sale "by his own business ability," he began "*to see himself in a new light*" [my emphasis]. He had *earned* this enormous profit, or so he thought; and, given this misapprehension and revised sense of self-worth, he was "convinced that he had 'built up' his business by his own industry and astuteness." As a result, when a German chemist later invented a process that rendered selenium worthless as a commodity, Gerald deemed the sudden collapse of his enterprise as "no discredit whatever on his ability"

(57). But there is more. He "saw his business go as he had seen it come, without emotion," in large part, Shaw's narrator confides, because he cared little for either picrate of selenium or money "any more than for any other necessary convenience of a comfortable life" (58). He was similarly indifferent about other people, but, again oddly, grew to *feel* quite differently about a "hobby" that evolved into a "passion": reading plays. With gold in his pocket and a new passion, Gerald, the beneficiary of amazingly good fortune and possessive of a new sense of self-worth, returned to London.

His revised sense of self seems clear and predictable enough, but why does Shaw freight the narrative with descriptions of Gerald's lack of affect? Why cite examples of Gerald's variegated lassitude: "He did not care even for money"; "He had never cared enough for any woman to get married"; "He had not cared enough for England or any other place to desert Buenos Ayres for a single month…" (*Short*, 57)?[52] It should be added that Gerald's lack of feeling or emotion is hardly unique in the corpus of Shaw's short fiction. Zeno Legge in "The Miraculous Revenge" (1885), to take one example, begins his first-person account with this description of his uncle, the Cardinal Archbishop of Dublin: "He is, like most of my family, deficient in feeling, and consequently cold to me personally" (*Short*, 29).[53] While Zeno seems to crave attention—from his uncle and especially from the "shrewd, and yet so flippant!" Kate Hickey, an Irish beauty he meets and falls in love with in County Wicklow (40)—Gerald never does. Instead, his voracious, albeit shallow, reading of drama serves as a partial compensation for this weary lack of interest and engagement; specifically, "He loved rhetorical balderdash: it gave him an impression of greatness that nothing else could" (58). Conversely, "He could not stand modern naturalism and realism, nor even much of the translations of Goethe" (58), genres and writers lacking the verbal flourishes of a Shakespeare, Otway, Webster, or Chapman. One answer to the questions with which this paragraph begins, then, is that Gerald's indifference to money, women, and England is countered not merely by his *love* for rhetorical excess, but by the feeling created by texts and, later in London's West End, performances which impress upon him a sense of greatness analogous to the "new light" within which he saw himself.

This makes the account of Gerald's sophomoric readings and heartfelt approbation of largely tragic drama all the more intriguing. For much as he had when relating the story of his fantastic ascent to wealth, Shaw's narrator underscores Gerald's intellectual limitation and lack of probity:

he never went to the theatre in Buenos Ayres; he was incapable of distinguishing the "cheapest platitude from the deepest and surest stroke of character dissection" (*Short*, 58); and he "quite seriously believed that Webster's imagination was gigantic and Chapman's elevation sublime" (58). In other words, money and drama both catalyze in Gerald feelings he cannot access from any other source; and both, as we shall see, serve as affirmations of worth or value, including self-value. The problem is, the London theatre Gerald discovers upon his return to England has little to do with sublimity or senses of greatness. Set in 1910, five years into the future, "The Theatre of the Future" actually describes two theatres: the vulgarly commercial one Gerald finds upon his arrival in the West End and the one he helped shape, which, not surprisingly in the story's final moments, turns to Shakespearean historical drama for its repertory. However, before taking our seats in the stalls and settling in for an evening of Shakespeare or the enthralling political conspiracy of Otway's cabalists in *Venice Preserved* (1682), we might pause to consider the relationship between the story's London theatres and the prolegomenon that precedes their description. Why introduce an absurd depiction of the theatre's vulgar commercialism with seven paragraphs detailing a character's unlikely ascent to wealth in Argentina? Assuming that the last of these paragraphs serves to delineate Gerald's love of plays, thereby creating some transition between Buenos Ayres and London, rocky South American ranches and London playhouses, what do the preceding paragraphs achieve? Why employ them as an introduction to a commercial theatre that has devolved into a venue of ostentation and vulgarity?

The answer is because theatre, like money, links commerce and human subjectivity via substitution; and, because one aspect of theatrical performance is its ability to complete something antecedent to it—the written script—it has the capacity to satisfy need, even desire, much as commodities do. Recall Richard Gray's formulation that, to function successfully as a commodity, an object must be regarded as possessing properties that satisfy human need; further, "human beings must acquire intellectual insight into the causal connection between this need and the object's ability to satisfy it."[54] However, just as so-called "buyer's remorse" afflicts consumers unhappy with a purchase they have made—disappointed, perhaps, that the thing does not fulfill a need or complete them as expected—the same can be said of theatrical performance. It is, in many respects, a kind of commodity, a fact that Shaw underscores in Gerald's first demoralizing survey of London's theatre district. As he walks westward from the Strand, he notices that "many of the old theatres were gone" and the "very newest theatre" was literally surrounded by shops (*Short*, 59). Further, these playhouses could scarcely be distinguished from cathedrals or museums, a design practice that, as Shaw's narrator quips, has led two architects to suicide and one to murder. But the plays in Gerald's imaginary theatre, plays by Otway, Webster, and Chapman that exude greatness, are neither sterile museum exhibitions nor the stuff of dry religious rituals. Nor can these tragic dramas and the theatre that mounts them be viewed as another shop that hawks, hence *devalues*, plays as if they were mere retail goods for sale.

However, that is exactly what this cityscape implies. Equally important, Gerald's dismay over this discovery hints at the subjective or *immaterial* basis of value that Georg Simmel explains:

> Valuation as a real psychological occurrence is part of the natural world; but what we mean by valuation, its conceptual meaning, is something independent of this world; is not part of it, but is rather the whole world viewed from a particular vantage point.

Value is "not a quality of objects," Simmel continues, but originates in *perceptions of* objects and the magnitude of their attributes.[55] It is, as Marx recognized in the first volume of *Capital*, "an abstraction that exceeds the exigencies of mere reality," a kind of "ersatatz grounding for the logical non-groundedness of exchange."[56] Moreover, value exists temporally in the *futur anterior*, "retroactively actualized, performatively enacted."[57] Its provenance resides in the human subject's ineffable sense of such qualities as "greatness," the attribute Gerald cherishes in the rhetorical effusions of tragedy. This means that the "intellectual insight" responsible for the calculation of value might potentially mask the ways in which the acquisition of commodities—or enjoyment of performances—may not originate in rational decision-making or satisfy needs so much as they induce the consumer *to believe that they will*. Paramount among these perceived values is affirmation. Whether the thing affirmed is an ineffable sense of greatness or the brilliance of a young entrepreneur is less significant than the fact that such values are presumed to inhere in the desired commodity or performance.

However unconventional "The Theatre of the Future" might be in fusing its two seemingly incongruous halves—a South American rags-to-riches sketch coupled with an excoriation of extant London theatrical practices—into a single narrative, there is nothing anomalous about Gerald's response to what he finds in London. Indeed, characters in Shaw's fiction frequently attend the theatre, opera, and music recital; and, like Shaw himself, they are often underwhelmed by the experience. Or, rather, performance does not satisfy needs which reside, at times, closer to desire than to mere customer satisfaction with, say, a can opener or tee shirt. Shortly after arriving in Dublin in "The Miraculous Revenge," for example, Zeno Legge resumes an "eternal search" that "drives" him in ways he does not fully understand first to the streets and then to the auditorium:

> I went to the theatre. The music was execrable, the scenery poor. I had seen the play a month before in London, with the same beautiful artist in the chief part. Two years had passed since, seeing her for the first time, I had hoped that she, perhaps, might be the long-sought mystery. It had proved otherwise... (*Short*, 29)

Similarly, the beautiful young woman who narrates Shaw's 1887 story "Don Giovanni Explains"—a woman who observes that the "proof of her prettiness" is confirmed by the fact that men "waste a good deal of time and money in making themselves ridiculous" about her—is deflated by a performance of the opera, one that "mutilated and maltreated" Mozart's work (*Short*, 95, 97). On the train home, however, a more enthralling performance occurs as the ghost of Don Giovanni appears to her, overpowering her emotionally with "his surprising flow of language" (102) and personal story to the point that her "hair had been trying to stand on end" (112). Ghost or dream figure, this Don Giovanni elicits feeling and intense sensation that the "conceited Frenchman" with a "toneless, dark, nasal voice" playing him in the opera could not (96). The completion she and Zeno sought—existing proximate to "long-sought" mysteries associated with desire—could not be realized by the theatres they patronized.

Nor could Gerald's passion. In fact, just the opposite affect—his disgust with and aversion to what he sees in the West End—grows in intensity as the theatre's inability to correspond to (form an equivalence of) his sense of drama's greatness becomes more apparent. Venturing inside a lobby and overhearing a negotiation between a manager and an unhappy playgoer, he learns that plays performed at these venues, not unlike spectacular entertainments in Las Vegas's most lavish hotel-casinos today, serve primarily to entice audience spending on other commodities.

Shaw's narrator identifies East End houses as refining an economic model in which theatres increase the profitability of an entrepreneur's other investments, thereby reducing melodrama—such theatres' most enduring attraction—to little more than a "loss leader" in shops: an item reduced in price to draw customers. In this scheme, drama, among other entertainments, draws playgoers to working-class houses like the Britannia Theatre and Saloon in Hoxton; and while there, they spend money on drinks, meals, and other commodities:

> [F]ortunes were made in Hoxton out of owning one theatre and ten public houses—not counting bars before and behind the curtain—long enough before it was accidentally discovered at the west end that Savoy suppers paid better than Savoy Opera. (*Short*, 65)[58]

In today's Las Vegas, casinos exploit this same revenue model. To be sure, some audience members actually buy tickets to see spectacular Cirque de Soleil shows or superstar singers, but many do not; instead, high rollers receive "comped" tickets in an effort to encourage them to spend money on other, more profitable amenities: gourmet meals prepared by celebrity chefs, high-end shopping, and—of course—gaming. Like high rollers at today's Bellagio, Caesar's Palace, and MGM Grand, socialites in "The Theatre of the Future" occupy reserved seats at the theatre owner's expense, expecting "money flung about" whenever they want anything (62). This includes in Shaw's story conveyance to the theatre by a furnished "motor," and not just any vehicle will do; further, as the angry Mr Glossop complains to a house manager, once wealthy playgoers arrive at the theatre, flowers, coffee, and more should be provided *gratis*. A modest honorarium might also be considered to compensate the socialite for his time. In this theatre for the "vulgarly ambitious commercial and social adventurist," a phrase I have lifted from Shaw's *The Common Sense of Municipal Trading*,[59] spectacle has been relocated from the stage to the stalls where costume and social standing have become *de rigeur*; by contrast, what transpires behind the proscenium is just a "little show" (62).

Glossop, however, remembers a time when playgoers paid for their own seats at "the first rate west end houses," required no social introduction, and, shockingly, "wore pretty well anything they liked" (*Short*, 63). There and then, they could thrill to the talents of actors of "good standing" like Henry Irving appearing in plays by Shakespeare and starring in the roles in more modern plays that accompanied his Hamlet, Shylock, and Benedick in repertory.[60] Now, gadflies like Glossop are far more concerned about the socially performative appurtenances of their attendance than the quality of drama being staged: how audience members dress, how social elites are compensated, what amenities they enjoy. Stunned by this conversation, Bridges is repulsed by the implications of these overheard negotiations:

> Gerald Bridges, listening to this conversation … found his hobby revolting against these two men with an intensity which revealed to him for the first time how deep a hold the theatre had upon him. (68)

If there were ever a Shavian passage to be advanced as a specimen for deconstruction, this might be it. Here, "hobby" scarcely captures Gerald's passion—and feeling. As Shaw's narrator explains, because drama and theatre had "always been a fairyland" to him, he is "repulsed" by the discussion of such prosaic matters as a house's financial viability (68). Absorbed by drama's "art and poetry and fascination," he "instinctively" banished such considerations as paying "rent" and catering to audience members from his "fairyland" and its "deep hold" on him (69).

One of the most striking aspects of Gerald's reaction to Glossop's philistinism is its sheer *intensity*; his disgust is so overwhelming as to prompt an epiphany that illuminates the depth of his feeling, and this from a man who cared so little for everything else—except, of course, his "pet delusion" that he had "made" his own fortune, not fallen into it. Believing that "he could do anything" (*Short*, 70), a greatness not unlike that of the rhetoric he valorized in Tragedy, Gerald sets out to reform the theatre through one simple revision of extant practice: namely, require playgoers to buy their own tickets. All that remains to do is hire an acting manager, secure a venue and plays to produce, and advertise his new Cash-For-Admission-Theatre (C.F.A. Theatre). This last project also allows Shaw an opportunity to lampoon the fatuity of contemporary social drama when Gerald posts the following announcement in the popular press:

> The manager of the C.F.A Theatre regrets to have to announce that his attempt to procure a new play introducing a married woman in love with her own husband, and without a past, has been wholly unsuccessful. An appeal to our leading dramatic authors to write such a play has elicited a unanimous refusal…. (77)

Because these "leading dramatic authors" feared that the presence of a married woman on stage without a past—a woman unlike, say, Arthur Wing Pinero's Paula Tanqueray or "Notorious" Mrs. Ebbsmith—would appear "abnormal" and appeal directly to "morbid tastes" (77), no playwright would dare hazard such a creation. Lacking a new drama, Gerald turns to Shakespeare's *Henry VI* plays, which also instantiate his return to wonder. His acting manager Wilkinson, in the story's closing moments, corroborates the existence of this feeling by noticing that while every seat in the house was taken—the production, in other words, was an unqualified commercial success—Gerald remained "just like a little child about the theatre still."[61] The opening of *Henry VI, Part One*, in short, was just as enthralling as ever, as the actor delivering the lines made "no attempt whatever to degrade them into prose":

> Hung be the heavens with black! Yield, day, to night!
> Comets, importing change of times and States,
> Brandish your crystal tresses in the sky—(82)

"The Theatre of the Future" probes the complicated farrago—a good Beckettian term[62]—that is depth of feeling and materiality, tracing the relationship between success in business and the ascription of value in the human subject. Wildly successful in Buenos Ayres and confident about his abilities, Gerald could do anything. His wealth affirmed his value to himself, just as the poetry of *1 Henry VI* restored value to the tawdry commercial theatre that Gerald despised.

Shakespeare's plays, then, like money, *affirm* value, in this instance the value of the theatre Gerald has subjectively constructed as an emblem of greatness. Also, as numerous critics and theoreticians have argued, at base the theatre itself functions as a site of affirmation, irrespective of the style, genre, and staging of the plays it produces. Weary of critics who advance a "two-bit, dinner-party vision of despair" in their readings of Samuel Beckett, for example, Badiou argues that the "indestructability of possibilities" is "affirmed by Beckett" in many of his texts often mischaracterized as depressive or inherently pessimistic.[63] For Jacques Derrida, Antonin Artaud's "Theatre of Cruelty" signifies "affirmation itself in its full and necessary rigor." In this assertion, Derrida follows Artaud, who defines the Theatre as "the affirmation of a terrible and, moreover, implacable necessity."[64] Stating the matter even more emphatically, Derrida argues that the very "essence" of western theatre is affirmation, even if the radically reconceived theatre for which Artaud advocates would abolish the stage, reposition the spectator in the center of performed action, and replace spectacle with "festival."[65]

Affirmation is equally central to many critical exfoliations of tragic drama, the genre for which Gerald harbors such deep feeling, although commentators may differ on the question of what precisely the form affirms. For Joseph Wood Krutch who, not unlike Gerald, had little interest in modern realism, "No increased powers of expression, no greater gift for words, could have transformed Ibsen into Shakespeare," precisely because the materials out of which the latter crafted his drama—"his conception of human dignity, his sense of the importance of human passions, his vision of the amplitude of human life—simply did not and could not exist for Ibsen."[66] More recently, Tragedy and affirmation function as a motif in the opening chapter ("A Theory of Ruins") of Terry Eagleton's *Sweet Violence: The Idea of the Tragic* (2003), as Eagleton readily admits in responding to critics who accuse him of "setting the value of pessimism too briskly aside." Eagleton finds this "an odd upbraiding, given that far too much of *Sweet Violence* is devoted to poking fun ... at those critics of tragedy who regard it as the most robustly affirmative of forms, just the right cure for a bout of the blues."[67] In "A Theory of Ruins," Eagleton catalogues various hypotheses about Tragedy and affirmation that he later collapses: Tragedy with a capital "T" is "life-affirming," for instance, and its representation of "dignified endurance" instantiates an "exultant self-affirmation." Given this logic, critics must "dismiss as non-tragic works which do not affirm freedom, and where destruction is not part of an evolutionary process leading to a new life."[68] In short, for Eagleton's opponents, Badiou's Beckett, and Derrida's Artaud, theatre means affirmation, and such a claim insofar as Tragedy is concerned is, at base, an expression of value: the value of human industry and endurance, or of committed struggle. For Eugene O'Neill, as Eagleton notes, Tragedy may be the only thing that makes an "individual life" significant.[69] For Badiou, Beckettian affirmation has less to do with individual life than with an admirable indomitability and the constant possibility of change embedded in the event.[70] The tragic theatre, the Theatre of the Absurd, Artaud's Theatre of Cruelty—all provide affirmation and, like commodities, possess value insofar as they map onto the very subjective operations in which value and desire originate in the first place.

In Shaw's writing, however, there is another affirmative, if problematic, value machine that hums along in nearly continuous operation as well:

money. Yet this operation insofar as drama and theatre are concerned is inherently problematic because money, on the one hand, has the power to erode distinctions between Gerald's conception of greatness and mere dross for sale in London's West End but, on the other, it can revise the very definition of what constitutes important drama. Shaw drolly comments on this latter possibility in *Sixteen Self Sketches*: "… nobody taught me to write my plays, which were denounced as no plays until they made so much money that the fashion changed, and I was hailed successor to Shakespeare" (*SSS* 70). This makes the retrospective Shaw of 1949 rather different from the younger man 45 years earlier laboring like a dog to produce that "abominable" tract on Municipal Trading so as to earn enough to be able produce his "dramatic masterpieces." Then, the brilliance of every hundred lines of genius was dimmed by the need to earn his bread through "sordid" commercial writing. Years later, what does it mean that the "successor" to Shakespeare ascends to this title by virtue of creating dramas that make "so much money" they permanently alter theatrical tastes?

While the significance of the ledger sheet seems obvious in the collaborative enterprise of professional theatre—and while financial success may even define the term "play," as Shaw observes about his rise in stature as a dramatist—what forces are at work in the more mysterious process of the assessment of self-worth? As I will discuss in more detail in the following chapter, Simmel provides several possible answers to this question: the relationship of value to desire, the separation of subject and an object of enjoyment, the manner in which the object of desire is located outside of the subject and the value that inheres to their reunion, and much more. Such phenomena, however, might also be said to underlie the audience's rapt attention to the opening lines of *1 Henry VI* at the culmination of "The Theatre of the Future." As Shaw's narrator describes, "Sh-sh-sh-sh-sh!" echoed throughout the audience as the curtain rose and the play's opening lines came "wailing from the stage" (*Short*, 82). It is hard not to detect a note of sarcasm in the participles Shaw's narrator employs: "the first lines came rolling" as the actor began "wailing"; but no matter. In what amounts to an oxymoron that epitomizes the story and much more, the theatre is "child's business" (82). It is fairyland and business at the same time, immaterial and psychically resonant, yet irreducibly material—and social—at the same time. As such, it emblematizes the Shavian psychology I am attempting to theorize and deploy in readings of Shaw's writing—from his earliest novels and short fiction to his last plays and later prose.

A Closing Note on Money: Profectitious, Adventitious, and Otherwise

"But when I say a thing I mean it; when I feel a sentiment I feel it in earnest; and what I value I pay hard money for. Thats the sort of man I am." (*CPP* 3: 80)—Sir George Crofts, *Mrs. Warren's Profession* (1894)

In the above discussion, I have tried to outline those dimensions of affect and value connected fundamentally to a Shavian psychology that recognizes both the individual and social origins of feeling, emotion, and the bodily responses that they instantiate. I have also attempted to suggest the complexities of temporality inherent to both human affect and this psychology: a blush can arise almost instantaneously, as we have seen, but what prior event or memory may underlie this involuntary reaction or connect feeling to a deeper, narratively more complex emotion like jealousy or guilt? In the above discussion, the phrase "chronic impecuniosity," however imperfect, conveys some of these complications: one is impecunious in the moment, but as this condition grows "chronic" it obtains in the moments that follow as well, in some cases metastasizing into an ongoing anxiety. The phrase marks a poverty, therefore, that is both material and subjective and, equally important, it is inherent to the genealogy of negative affect. By contrast, it might seem that money (and its possession) is a more transparent entity: money is money, we might say, yet this may not be quite accurate. "Shaw wrote mainly for money," Declan Kiberd observed and I cited earlier, but does this observation effectively conclude the topic? We've already seen that Shaw has disparaged money as "dirty" and that the pursuit of it can be "sordid," but it might be tethered to other psychical realities as well.

Sir George Crofts, Shaw's "gentlemanly combination of the most brutal types of city man, sporting man, and man about town" (*CPP* 3: 40) in *Mrs. Warren's Profession*, and Vivie Warren's reaction to him provide us with intimations of these possibilities. In the epigraph taken from the play, Crofts makes a clumsy attempt at courtship, and its self-aggrandizement aside—in how many sentences does the pronoun "I" appear *six times*, as it does in Croft's first sentence?—the implication of these remarks parallels Georg Simmel's thesis about value's subjective provenance. What "I value," Crofts emphasizes, not a value about which consensus or corroboration exists, can be exchanged for "hard money." In Crofts' formulary, the realms of "sentiment" and "earnest" feeling thus find expression through the materiality of *hard* currency. Here, money connects directly to value, which itself serves as a tangible substitution for his *feeling* about the worth of the commodity purchased. Expressed in a more Eliotic fashion, in this metaphor, money serves as the objective correlative of a softer, more subjective sense of value and the "earnest" (deep, serious, real) feeling it evokes.

However, Crofts' lines yield even more interpretive potential than this, as they are delivered in the context of money given in marriage—in this instance, the monetary gain that Vivie would accrue by marriage to a "gentleman"-capitalist she finds odious. After all, as Crofts avers in pressing his case, he is a "safe man from the money point of view," in part because he is "richer today" than when he "first came into property"; further, being 25 years Vivie's senior, he would "take care" that she should be "well off" when he is gone (*CPP* 3: 80–81). Here, money is both "hard"—material and objective when functioning as currency used in exchange—and definitive of a "point of view." His comments to Mrs. Warren in the play's opening act prepare the audience for the finally unpersuasive climax of his argument: "I'd die before her and leave her a bouncing widow with plenty of money. Why not?" (*CPP* 3: 59). Indeed, why not? Because Shavian women often bridle at the assumption that, for them, marriage is an institution akin to a business, the only business in which the standard bearers of polite society feel they should be involved. In introducing herself to the presumptuous reader who thinks he knows all about her, the young narrator of "Don Giovanni Explains" contemptuously remarks that "nobody will admit that I have any other business in the world than to make a good marriage" (*Short*, 95). Having absolutely *no* interest in becoming Lady Crofts, Vivie objects to this conscription as well; and, given the logic of Shaw's play, were she more inclined to seek a husband—her mother's business partner, or anyone else for that matter—she would become mired in an institution that too often resembles prostitution. As Bernard Dukore observes, *Mrs. Warren's Profession* explicitly "links prostitution with capitalism in an exploitative world that resembles a brothel"; and this implicit exploitation similarly defines both of Vivie's marital possibilities: if the penniless Frank Gardner were to marry Vivie, he would "become her matrimonial prostitute" insofar as her money would provide the couple's sole means of income; if Crofts were to marry her, Dukore notes, "she would become his."[71]

The implications of both arrangements return us, however indirectly, to my earlier claim that "The Theatre of the Future" acts as a shorthand for concerns that surface and resurface in Shaw's writing. One of these, I think, is the variegated nature of money itself; that is, what Crofts dubs "hard" money in which desire and value are concretized is more mottled and conceptually porous than it might seem. Just as wealth instantiates a potentially wide array of both positive and negative feelings—self-satisfaction and occasional exhilaration, envy and revulsion—it is hardly surprising that money itself can be regarded as, alternatively, desirable or abhorrent. How one acquires money is equally complicated. Vivie's dismissal of Crofts' proposal of marriage, for example, is paralleled by her disdain for "wasters," which is in effect an indictment of the idle rich who luxuriate in wealth they did little to earn:

> Vivie [*with intense contempt for them*]. If I thought that *I* was like that—that I was going to be a waster, shifting along from one meal to another with no purpose, and no character, and no grit in me, I'd open an artery and bleed to death without one moment's hesitation. (*CPP* 3: 57)

Moments later, speaking with her mother, she reiterates her contempt both for Crofts and undeserved wealth when she is horrified by the thought that she might have the "contaminated blood of that brutal waster" in her veins (*CPP* 3: 63). By contrast, envious of Crofts' and Mrs. Warren's wealth, Frank challenges Vivie by asking why they should "take any grind when they can afford not to" (*CPP* 3: 57), here collapsing a distinction that Shaw often takes great pains to delineate between money inherited or given ("profectitious" money), on the one hand, and money earned, won, or even accidentally stumbled upon ("adventitious" money) on the other, as it is by both Gerald and theatre owners who "accidentally" become aware of the profitability of Savoy suppers in "The Theatre of the Future." For her part, Vivie despises wealth acquired absent the qualities of individual industry and "grit"; for his part, Shaw was not always so sanguine about earning money. It is better than enduring grinding poverty, perhaps, but "earning lots" does not necessarily guarantee happiness or feelings of contentment.

This distinction is subtly gestured to in "The Theatre of the Future." Recall that shortly after arriving in Buenos Ayres and recklessly purchasing the agency, Gerald Bridges was "disowned" by his uncle, which is as much to say that the money he possessed was no longer profectitious: that is, his reserve of funds was no longer akin to that of a young woman's dowry provided by a male relative, typically a father or an older relative. As

Immanuel Kant outlines in *The Philosophy of Law* (1796) while reviewing Roman civil law, a "profectitious dowry" describes money given by the father to his son-in-law and therefore delimits the amount legally recoverable by the father in the event of the marriage's failure and his daughter's return to him. Money acquired by any other means—work, chance, even accident—is deemed "adventitious."[72] This distinction, so slight in the "The Theatre of the Future" that it is intimated only in the space of a relative clause—"The transaction was so unworthy of a youth of the smallest sharpness *that Gerald's uncle jumped at the opportunity of disowning him*" (*Short*, 55, my emphasis)—would scarcely be worth mentioning were it not for the principles of characters like Vivie Warren *and* the topic's reemergence in several chapters of Shaw's *Sixteen Self Sketches*, among other texts. In addition, as in his "Apology" for the volume, Shaw confides that "all my happenings have taken the form of books and plays. Read them, or spectate them; and you have my whole story" (*SSS*, 6), it seems advisable to take him at his word and briefly track the distinction in his writing.

Here, "distinction" is not quite apt. Stated more strongly, in *Sixteen Self Sketches* Shaw is focused so sharply on inherited and earned wealth—on the implications of profectitious and adventitious money—that it rises to the level of near obsession. Not surprisingly, therefore, this issue informs both the genealogy of Shavian ruminations on money *and* the intensities of feelings his characters experience, particularly in his novels. In the perverse world in which he grew up, described so candidly in "My Mother and Her Relatives" in *Sixteen Self Sketches*, Shaw witnessed the inevitable and calamitous consequences of false senses of gentility and social class. In his account, his mother's grandfather introduced the first perceived "stain" on the family "pedigree" by making a fortune at his Dublin pawnshop, a means of income he contrived to keep secret so as not to unsettle his position as a country gentleman and subject his family to social disapprobation (*SSS*, 9). Given this destructive ideology, with its false sense of social position and self-induced blindness about financial reality, Shaw stands by helpless as his mother's unfortunate marriage to his father descends into a "hell" of "shabby-genteel poverty" (12). In the chapter "Shame and Wounded Snobbery: A Secret Kept for 80 Years," a portrait of Shaw's youth that will grow in importance later in this study, Shaw adds texture to this portrait of subjective torment by recounting an episode from his boyhood that he found so "repugnant" it had to be concealed in an "abhorred secret" (20). What was the episode? His family's injunction about consorting with classmates who were the sons of "petty shopkeepers and tradesmen"; that is, sons whose fathers worked for a living were deemed inferior to his irresponsible father "whose bills were never paid punctually" (22, 23). Numerous passages in *Sixteen Self Sketches* develop Shaw's juvenile sense of acute "shame" that originates in this paradox, and—again—these inhere in the concept of a "chronic impecuniosity" that is relentless in its capacity to wound.

More, much more, of this later. For now, I hope it will suffice to reassert that money—and its representing of a myriad of equivalencies and values—is inextricably linked to feeling, to psychical wounding and its opposite in Shaw's writing. Characters such as Vivie Warren *feel* its ramifications acutely, which is precisely why her verbal assault on "wasters" like Crofts and her mother is delivered, as Shaw's stage directions proscribe, with "*intense contempt*." To be sure, Mrs. Warren's victory, if it can be called that, in restoring some sense of a relationship with her daughter, is a partial one at best; but it would perhaps be a Pyrrhic one were it not for her ability to convince Vivie that her wealth is, to some extent, earned, not merely given by the perverse "generosity" of a man like Crofts. This distinction matters, as do even smaller ones within the ambit of the adventitious. For there is, on the one hand, admirable adventitious money and, on the other, money that creates a false sense of mastery and achievement, the wealth that Gerald Bridges stumbled upon, for example. There is poverty, shabby-genteel and otherwise, that prompts just the opposite feeling. Also, one result of this panoply of feeling with which money is implicated is a searching discourse at the turn of the century by Shaw's contemporaries—writers, philosophers, economists, and psychoanalysts—within which Shavian thought and writing might be productively contextualized. One of the important things that we will discover while conducting this work, I think, contrary to the thrust of the sentence with which this chapter began, is that unlike today's academy where such discrete configurations or disciplinary subfields as affect, economic, and psychoanalytic theory exist, at the *fin de siécle* of the nineteenth century marginal economics, Freudian psychoanalysis, and the study of affect were, to an appreciable extent, *not* separate and separable theoretical discourses. Indeed, the languages of all three permeate late Victorian and early twentieth-century examinations of human subjects, the commodities they consume and values they represent, and the larger political economy under capitalism within which they struggle. All three inform what some scholars have termed the "economico-psychic subjectivity" that drives modern realism and a "new secular and disenchanted object world of the commodity system" we associate with modernity.[73] The recovery of this very subject and the conjoined psychical and material discourse Bernard Shaw and his contemporaries produced is the immediate project of the chapter that follows and, to a great extent, that of this entire book.

NOTES

1. It is hardly debatable that these two texts are indeed the masterworks of their authors. In *Freud: A Life for Our Time* (New York: W.W. Norton, 1988), Peter Gay terms *The Interpretation of Dreams* "the centerpiece of Freud's life" and notes that Freud himself called the book his "most significant work" (4). In his introduction to the English translation of Simmel's *The Philosophy of Money* (London and New York: Routledge, 2011), translator and editor David Frisby, albeit not so absolutist in his pronouncement as Gay, privileges the text as possessing a "structure that is absent" from his other "major works" (5). Nevertheless, both texts drew sharp criticism from many of their authors' contemporaries, and Frisby suggests that Simmel's later and "more fragmentary" volume *Sociologie* (1908) had more immediate impact than *The Philosophy of Money* (14). The significance of both texts, however, would seem unimpeachable.
2. See Joseph Roach, *Cities of the Dead: Circum-Atlantic Performance* (New York: Columbia University Press, 1996), 7–17.
3. Here, like Roach, I am borrowing "critical genealogy" from Jonathan Arac, who uses the term to describe a project that "aims to excavate the past that is necessary to account for how we got here and the past that is useful for conceiving alternatives to our present condition" (qtd. in Roach, 25).
4. In a letter to Harris's widow on October 17, 1931—her husband's biography of Shaw was published in late November of that year—Shaw complained that "Frank knew hardly more about my life history than I knew about yours; and the mixture of his guesses with the few things I told him produced the wildest results" (*CL* 4: 262). Perhaps so, but the similarity between Harris's emphasis on the relationship between poverty and negative feeling, particularly shame, and Shaw's account in *Sixteen Self Sketches* seems both striking and obvious, an indication of Shaw's direct influence on Harris's narrative.
5. Frank Harris, *Bernard Shaw: An Unauthorised Biography Based on Firsthand Information* (London: Victor Gollancz, 1931), 66. All further quotations from Harris's biography will be followed by page numbers in the text.
6. See Michel Foucault, "Nietzsche, Freud, Marx" (1967), in *Aesthetics, Method, and Epistemology*, ed. James D. Faubion (New York: The New

Press, 1998). "By involving us in a task of interpretation that always reflects back on itself," Foucault remarks, these trans-historical thinkers have in effect "constituted around us, and for us, these mirrors in which we are given back images whose perennial wounds form our narcissism today" (272).

7. Friedrich Nietzsche, *On the Genealogy of Morals and Ecce Homo*, ed. Walter Kaufmann (New York: Vintage, 1989), 70.
8. Harris notes that "a kind of proud impecuniousness ... can be more humiliating than poverty" (36); Shaw alludes to his "continual dread of doing the wrong thing" in his Preface to *Immaturity* (I, xviii).
9. Harris, 57. See also Michael Holroyd, *Bernard Shaw, Volume 1, 1856–1898: The Search for Love* (New York: Random House, 1988), 3–21. Holroyd's account of Shaw's father George Carr Shaw emphasizes both his "thriftlessness" and the family's larger charade of "social pretensions" noted by earlier biographers.
10. Harris, 35. Here again, Harris's comment is consistent with those Shaw makes in *Sixteen Self Sketches*, in this case "How I Became a Public Speaker," where Shaw claims never to have taken "payment for speaking," not because of any magnanimity or scruple about doing so, but because by declining a fee he could secure "perfect freedom of speech"—he could declaim on any religious or political matter he wanted, regardless of any controversy attached to the topic—and also rebut any insinuation that he was a "professional agitator" (60). In the "Introduction" to Shaw's "Six Fabian Lectures on Redistribution of Income" reprinted in *SHAW: The Journal of Bernard Shaw Studies* 36.1 (2016), 10–52, Peter Gahan presents another view of Shaw's willingness to accept honoraria for public speaking. Gahan refers to Shaw's 1914 Fabian Society series of lectures as "highly successful—both financially and in terms of publicity" (10). Further quotations from these lectures, abbreviated *Lectures*, will come from this source and be followed by page numbers in the text.
11. See Shaw's June 10, 1919 letter to Bradford Merrill in *Collected Letters 3*, 616–17.
12. Elmer Rice, *The Living Theatre* (New York: Harper & Brothers, 1959), 4. Rice professes his admiration for Shaw and describes the "cataclysmic effect" *Plays Pleasant and Unpleasant* had on him in *Minority Report: An Autobiography* (New York: Simon and Schuster, 1963), 85.
13. Declan Kiberd, *The Irish Writer and the World* (Cambridge: Cambridge University Press, 2005), 273.
14. See Gustavo Rodríguez Martín, "Bernard Shaw Adjusted for Inflation: Evolution of Wealth," *SHAW: The Journal of Bernard Shaw Studies* 36.1 (2016): 88. The letter in question can be found in *CL4*:300 prefaced by Dan Laurence's note that Shaw made the request in response to the declin-

ing value of British currency and lagging sales of his books in Depression-era America.
15. See Anna Kornbluh, *Realizing Capital: Financial and Psychic Economies in Victorian Form* (New York: Fordham University Press, 2014), especially, 4–20. As Kornbluh notes, "fictitious capital" resided at the heart of the Victorian "financial revolution and the astronomical growth of the credit economy" (4).
16. Anthony Roche, *The Irish Dramatic Revival 1899–1939* (London: Bloomsbury/Methuen Drama, 2015), 13.
17. Shaw might also be charged with disingenuousness (or vicious self-mockery) in this instance as well, because while he characterized *The Common Sense of Municipal Trading* (Westminster: Archibald Constable & Company, 1904) as an "abominable book," in his "Preface" he parries the notion that its subject is a "dry one." Quite the opposite, he claims, "It is, on the contrary, one of the most succulent in the whole range of literature" (v–vi).
18. Rodríguez Martín, 88.
19. Here, I am alluding to the work of, among others, Karen Horney in books like *Our Inner Conflicts: A Constructive Theory of Neurosis* (New York: W.W. Norton & Company, 1945). In her chapter "The Idealized Image," Horney refers to a person "building up an idealized image of himself because he cannot tolerate himself as he actually is" (112). The opposite image, apparent in Shaw's letter about writing for money, is connected to self-loathing as the subject begins to "despise" himself. At the same time, as Nelson Ritschel demonstrates in *Bernard Shaw, W.T. Stead, and the New Journalism: Whitechapel, Parnell, Titanic, and the Great War* (London: Palgrave Macmillan, 2017), Shaw "endeavored to provoke public debate and social change, while matching or even defining the highest ideals of New Journalism" (4). Pursuing "truth and reason" as a journalist, Shaw used this medium to pursue a "more socially just society" (8). His divided reaction to commercial writing, including several journalistic projects, may be regarded as yet another paradox in a man who exhibited no shortage of such internal conflicts.
20. Richard F[arr] Dietrich, "Shavian Psychology," *SHAW* 4 (1984): 149.
21. Peter Gahan, "*Jitta's Atonement*: The Birth of Psychoanalysis and 'The Fetters of the Feminine Psyche,'" *SHAW* 24 (2004): 140. In *Shaw's Shadows: Rereading the Texts of Bernard Shaw* (Gainesville: University Press of Florida, 2004), Gahan also explains that, in spite of his "ambivalence toward Freud and his theories, Freud provided one of the best examples of the type of scientist that Shaw would champion …" (106).
22. Richard Farr Dietrich, *Bernard Shaw's Novels: Portraits of the Artist as Man and Superman* (Gainesville: University Press of Florida, 1996), 12.

23. R[ichard] F[arr] Dietrich, "Shaw and Yeats: Two Irishmen Divided by a Common Language," *SHAW* 15 (1995): 69. Shaw's occasionally derisive comments about Freudian psychoanalysis will be discussed in a later chapter.
24. Dietrich, "Two Irishman," 69.
25. Bernard Shaw, "The New Theology," in *The Critical Shaw: On Religion*, ed. Michel Pharand (n.p.: RosettaBooks, 2016), 38, 39.
26. Shaw, "The New Theology," 39.
27. Shaw, "The New Theology," 28.
28. Charles Darwin, *The Expression of the Emotions in Man and Animals*, 200th Anniversary Edition, ed. Paul Ekman (1872; Oxford: Oxford University Press, 2009), 310. Darwin's study is filled with photographs of human faces and readings of their expressive potential. See, for example, "Special Expressions of Man: Suffering and Weeping," which includes plates of the faces of infants and adults and readings of such matters as eyelids, mouths, exposed teeth, and so on (146–75).
29. In his introduction to the first edition of *The Expression of the Emotions in Man and Animals*, Darwin discusses Herbert Spencer's *Principles of Psychology* (1855) and his analyses of human expression including fear and laughter (16–17). In the first chapter of the text, Darwin alludes to Spencer's efforts to distinguish emotions and "sensations" (33). My allusion to Wolfe and Diamond refers to the volume *Philosophy and Animal Life* (New York: Columbia University Press, 2008), by Stanley Cavell, Diamond, John McDowell, Ian Hacking, and Wolfe.
30. Roach, 3.
31. Joseph Roach, "Performance: The Blunders of Orpheus," *PMLA* 125 (October 2010): 1078, 1081. Roach's reference to performance as a "doing" or "thing done," as he acknowledges, comes from Elin Diamond's *Performance and Cultural Politics* (1996).
32. Roach, "Performance," 1082.
33. Sara Ahmed, *The Cultural Politics of Emotion* (New York: Routledge, 2004), 105, 104.
34. Charles Altieri, *The Particulars of Rapture: An Aesthetics of the Affects* (Ithaca: Cornell University Press, 2003), 10.
35. Brian Massumi, *Parables for the Virtual: Movement, Affect, Sensation* (Durham: Duke University Press, 2002), 27.
36. Sara Ahmed, "Happy Objects," in *The Affect Theory Reader*, eds. Melissa Gregg and Gregory J. Seigworth (Durham: Duke University Press, 2010), 30.
37. Ahmed, "Happy Objects," 29.
38. Altieri, 2.
39. V.N. Vološinov, *Freudianism: A Marxist Critique*, trans. I.R. Titunik (1927; New York: Academic Press, 1976), 15.

40. Vološinov, 24.
41. Richard T. Gray, "Accounting for Pleasure: Sigmund Freud, Carl Menger, and the Economically Minded Human Being," *PMLA* 127.1 (January 2012): 123.
42. Here Gray is quoting from Jevons' *The Theory of Political Economy* (1871), 124.
43. As I will discuss later in Chap. 4, in some respects following Anna Kornbluh, like the marginal economists Freud regarded such intangible entities as feeling as potentially measureable. Later in his career, however, in *Civilization and Its Discontents* (1930), he admitted that such psychical phenomena were difficult to measure and this difficulty troubled him.
44. Quoted in Pater Gahan, *Bernard Shaw and Beatrice Webb on Poverty and Equality in the Modern World, 1905–1914* (London: Palgrave Macmillan, 1917), 4. This line comes from a lecture that Shaw delivered at the London School of Economics in December, 1905, and is part of Gahan's introduction to Shaw's interest in economics, 1–10.
45. Gray, 125.
46. Gray, 126.
47. Kornbluh, 137.
48. Kornbluh, 2–3.
49. Kornbluh, 140. Here, Kornbluh also alludes to Freud's own reservations about the status of "economy" in psychoanalytic discourse, referencing his comment that the term amounted to a "rather vague expression" and recalling his use of admonitory "scare quotes" and qualifications when discussing it.
50. Alain Badiou, "Being, Existence, Thought: Prose and Concept," in *On Beckett*, eds. Nina Power and Alberto Toscano (Manchester: Clinamen Press, 2003), 81, 80.
51. My use of the phrase "symbolic economies" is intended to echo the title of Jean-Joseph Goux's *Symbolic Economies: After Marx and Freud*, trans. Jennifer Curtiss Gage (Ithaca: Cornell University Press, 1990).
52. It should be noted that emotional coolness or lack of affect forms a veritable motif both in biographies of Shaw and in Shaw's early writing. The principal exponent of such coolness is Shaw's mother, and Bridges is hardly the only figure so described in Shaw's short fiction.
53. It is within this context of affectual aridity that Zeno's disparagement of his former companion Bushy as "not a man of feeling" accrues added meaning (*Short*, 32).
54. Gray, 126.
55. Simmel, *The Philosophy of Money*, 62. All further quotations from this book with be followed by page numbers in the text.
56. Kornbluh, 7.

57. Slavoj Žižek, *The Parallax View* (Cambridge: MIT Press, 2006), 52. Joshua Clover discusses this aspect of value in "Value/Theory/Crisis," *PMLA* 127 (January 2012): 107–14.
58. The commercial activities of East End theatres in the later nineteenth century have been discussed by many scholars. See, for example, Jim Davis and Victor Emeljanow, *Reflecting the Audience: London Theatregoing, 1840–1880* (Iowa City: University of Iowa Press, 2001).
59. Shaw, *The Common Sense of Municipal Trading*, 11. Here, Shaw is attempting to describe the people best-and least-suited for positions as municipal managers, the former of which do not harbor "dreams of vulgar ambition" or indulge in the "excitements of financial speculation" that partially define their commercial counterparts. Moreover, in making the demands of theatre managers that he does, Glossop resembles the social and commercial adventurer who, unlike municipal managers, is highly invested in a social drama of affluence. In outlining the advantages that municipalities have in recruiting superior talent despite the limitations of salary they can offer, Shaw alludes to the expenses that commercial managers incur in keeping up "appearances": equipages, servants, a residence in a fashionable neighborhood, and so on (10–11). Municipal managers, by contrast, do not feel required to play such lavish parts.
60. See Stephen Watt, *"Something Dreadful and Grand": American Literature and the Irish-Jewish Unconscious* (New York: Oxford University Press, 2015), especially 100–111. For his repertories, Irving routinely reprised characters from more modern plays who were either emotionally disturbed—Mathias in Leopold Lewis's *The Bells* (1871) and the title character of Dion Boucicault's *Louis XI* (1855)—or tragically martyred like the title character of W.G. Wills's *Charles the First* (1872).
61. Discussing *Major Barbara* in *Bernard Shaw and Beatrice Webb on Poverty and Equality in the Modern World, 1905–1914*, Gahan comments that "the play is self-reflexively concerned about itself as drama, and indeed about the *power* of theatre" (12). Throughout his book, Gahan subtly returns to Shaw's belief in this power, and this moment from "The Theatre of the Future" provides further evidence of this belief.
62. In *Worstward Ho* (1983), Beckett's narrator refers to the "farrago from eye to mind." This "old tandem," constituted of "things and imaginings," pertains directly to the material psychology described in this essay.
63. Badiou, *On Beckett*, 4, 62.
64. Jacques Derrida, "The Theatre of Cruelty and the Closure of Representation," in *Writing and Difference*, trans. Alan Bass (Chicago: University of Chicago Press, 1978), 232.
65. Derrida, 264.

66. Joseph Wood Krutch, *The Modern Temper* (New York: Harvest Books, 1929), 80–81.
67. Terry Eagleton, "Commentary," *New Literary History* 35 (2004): 152.
68. Terry Eagleton, *Sweet Violence: The Idea of the Tragic* (London: Blackwell, 2003), 1,6.
69. Eagleton, *Sweet Violence*, 25.
70. The "event" and the relationship between "Being" and the "encounter" are complicated matters not particularly relevant for our purposes here. See "Being, Existence, Thought: Prose and Concept," in *On Beckett*, esp. 89–90.
71. Bernard F. Dukore, *Money & Politics in Ibsen, Shaw, and Brecht* (Columbia and London: University of Missouri Press, 1980), 34, 35.
72. There is an echo of Roman law in *Mrs. Warren's Profession* when Frank explains to Praed that his "Roman father had to pay my debts. He's stony broke in consequence…" (*CPP* 3:45).
73. Joe Cleary, "Toward a Materialist-Formalist History of Twentieth-Century Irish Literature," *boundary 2* 31.1 (2004): 213.

CHAPTER 2

The Materialist Dream Theatre: Affect and Value, Freud and Simmel

> *"Company at table or table d'hôte ... spinach was being eaten ... Frau E.L. was sitting beside me; she was turning her whole attention to me and laid her hand on my knee in an intimate manner. I removed her hand unresponsively. She then said: 'But you've always had such beautiful eyes.' ... I then had an indistinct picture of two eyes, as though it were a drawing or like the outline of a pair of spectacles....."*
> (SE 5: 636–37)
> —Sigmund Freud, *On Dreams* (1901)
>
> *"A psychological process by which ... indifferent experiences take the place of psychically significant ones, cannot fail to arouse suspicion or bewilderment.... What takes place would seem to be something in the nature of a 'displacement'—of psychical emphasis, shall we say?—by means of intermediate links.... Displacements of this kind are no surprise to us where it is a question of dealing with quantities of affect or with motor activities in general."* (SE 4: 176–77)
> —Sigmund Freud, *The Interpretation of Dreams* (1900)

This first epigraph above constitutes the entirety of Sigmund Freud's account of one of his own dreams in the slender volume *On Dreams*, published a year after the appearance of his masterwork, *The*

© The Author(s) 2018
S. Watt, *Bernard Shaw's Fiction, Material Psychology, and Affect*,
Bernard Shaw and His Contemporaries,
https://doi.org/10.1007/978-3-319-71513-1_2

43

Interpretation of Dreams, in 1900. His motives for recounting it are both rhetorical, insofar as he believed that his readers needed to be firmly disabused of the misconception that "dreams scarcely reach the level of being psychical phenomena at all" (*SE* 5: 634), and illustrative, as he modeled for them the interpretive methods of "free association."[1] In fact, from the outset of *On Dreams* Freud attempts both to refute a myriad of fallacies concerning the origins and importance of dreaming, and to display the operations of a process he had delineated at considerable length in his earlier work. At times, the aims of the two projects merge. So, for example, the meticulous operations of free association implicitly repudiate the presumption that some details in dreams are either irrelevant or too unimportant to consider; the serving of spinach or the *non sequitur* about his eyes in this dream account, however seemingly minor, cannot therefore be immediately dismissed. Stated another way, as Cannon Schmitt does while characterizing the argument of Georg Lukács's 1936 essay "Narrate or Describe?", dream-narratives as parsed by free association resemble the dense significations of narration: "Narration admits of no filler. Description, by contrast, is all filler.... Description treats as mere backdrop or setting that which, in narration, would be freighted with consequentiality."[2] In dreams, in part because of the mechanisms of the dream work and the "quantities of affect" to which Freud alludes in the second epigraph, there is little "filler." *Any* dream element, such as those in Lukács's narration, may resonate with affective intensity, even as Freud identifies "the inhibition of affect" as the "*second consequence of the censorship of dreams, just as dream-distortion is its first consequence*" (emphasis in original; *SE* 5: 468).

Freud urges his readers to be equally attentive to "ideas that occur" while discussing dreams and to do so without "any premeditation," asking them to "continue pursuing the trains of thought which will emerge" even to the most seemingly insignificant detail (*SE* 5: 636). He is adamant about this "inviolable rule" (*SE* 15: 115),[3] a fact registered in his insistence that the dreamer take notice of "*whatever occurs to his mind without any exception* and report it to the physician" (emphasis in original; *SE* 5: 635). By engaging seriously with all the associations that surface in unpacking the imagery of which dream narratives are constructed, however disagreeable or seemingly trivial, some will be seen, upon reflection, to be "clearly connected with the pathological idea" which was the dream element's origin or starting point (*SE* 5: 636). Freud was well aware, of course, that some phenomena in dreams originate in more than one "idea"—in fact, in several places he asserts that *all* such elements have multiple origins—hence his elaboration in several chapters of *The Interpretation of Dreams* (hereafter abbreviated as *Interpretation*) of overdetermination and of the frequent appearance of composite pictures in the characters who populate dreams.[4]

Freud's deployment of free association in investigating the sources of his own dream reveals details relevant to my purposes here. Consistent with his privileging of day residue and the recent waking experience of the dreamer, an emphasis he promotes from the earliest chapters of *Interpretation*,[5] Freud initially connects this dream's setting—"*Company at table or table d'hôte*"—to an event the evening before. Leaving a small party, he and a friend shared a cab home, and his friend paid the fare. As Freud reports, the cab had installed a taximeter that displayed a 60 heller (6 d.) charge before they had even begun to move, motivating his retort to his companion about owing money already, which he later associates with the accumulation of debt at a *table d'hôte*. (Although Freud doesn't cultivate this association, it seems reasonable to infer that the *table d'hôte* in his dream conflates the space or site of a communal table at a hotel restaurant with the *prix fixe* commonly charged for a full course meal served there.) From this association, a torrent of thoughts ensues: "My debt seems to be growing too fast," "I'm afraid of getting the worst of the bargain," and I "must keep my eye on my own interests." The display on the taxi's meter, in short, kept "reminding [Freud] of what I owe" (*SE* 5: 637). This series of deliberations leads him to memories of a *table d'hôte* at a resort in the Tyrol mountains two weeks earlier when he became mildly irritated that his wife was not being "sufficiently reserved" toward people sitting nearby with whom he had no desire to interact while, at the same time, ignoring him. Here, as in the cab ride, he felt he might not be getting the best of the bargain, in this case the value of his wife's company and attentiveness to him.

What is significant in this example—or one inference we might make from Freud's commentary—is not so much his creation of a chain of explanatory associations from the thought underlying the dream narrative, but the fungibility of feeling (spousal attentiveness) and material indebtedness in these associations.[6] From this and other dyads—recent event and deeper memory, communal table and *prix fixe*, monetary debt and human feeling—Freud constructs an archive of relationships within which he refines his reading. Frau E.L., for instance, who places her hand on his knee "in an intimate manner," is the daughter of a man to whom Freud was once indebted; and her compliment of his eyes, as he construes it, conveys the accusation that "'People have always done everything for you for love: you have always had everything *without paying for it*'" (emphasis in original; SE 5: 638). Parrying this aspersion, Freud counters that he has always "paid dearly" for any accommodation he has enjoyed; he has earned it, in other words. This dream, then, melds the socially performative dimensions of hotel dinners with both sexual *frisson* and deeply held anxieties about debt, the expenditure of money, and his wife's attentiveness. In fact, as I shall discuss in more detail, many of the dreams that Freud analyzes not only link monetary value and feeling, but also take as their *mise en scènes*, as this dream does, social spaces and events such as parties, dinners, visits to the theatre, and so on. In doing so, the affective dimensions of social encounters, many of which are concerned with a class affiliation inscribed by wealth and so much a part of the "chronic impecuniosity" of Shaw's adolescence and early years in London, return as motifs in dream narratives, adding performative dimension to definitions of a "material" psychology.[7]

Freud's dream of the *table d'hôte* also reveals the operation of condensation in the dream work, a process evident in many manifestations of affectual intensity in Shaw's fiction as well. Consistent with his earlier descriptions of this process, later in *On Dreams* Freud asserts that "each element in the content of a dream is 'overdetermined' by material in the dream-thoughts; it is not derived from a *single* element ... but may be traced back to a whole number"—and these may not necessarily be "closely related to each other" (emphasis in original; SE 5: 652). The cab's taximeter with its indication of a fee already owed, the *prix fixe* at a communal table that means diners will pay for something such as spinach whether they like it or not, the comments of the daughter of a person to whom Freud once owed a debt—these are all compacted by the dream work. Yet, however fictive or bizarre the dream's narrative and *mise en scène*, the affect these produce, specifically, recalling Charles Altieri's taxonomy of affects, the *feeling* these evoke, is very real. The latter epigraph above thus addresses a very real quality of dreams parsed in great detail in Part Two of *Interpretation*: the importance of displacement and transference not only to the processes of the dream work as it arranges psychical material pictorially, but also to the ways in which both contribute to the transvaluation of feeling in dreams. From the earliest pages of *Interpretation*, when alluding to Havelock Ellis's commentary on memory in dreams, for example, Freud acknowledges the curious fact that "the trifling, the incidental, the 'forgotten' impressions of daily life" frequently appear in dreams, and this leads him to ask, "Why does consciousness so often in dreams receive the impression of *indifferent* mnemic images?" (*SE* 4: 19). One answer is that an "indifferent moment" from the day's residue often incites intense feelings because of its link to an antecedent event lingering in the "remotest corners of the chambers of one's memory" (*SE* 4: 20). The process of free association is calibrated to bring such shrouded connections between proximate and temporally remote experiences into the light of analysis.

Stated somewhat differently, in the early chapters of *Interpretation* and through his analysis of several dream narratives, Freud discovered that although the manifest content of dreams may foreground seemingly unimportant details of lived experience—elements from waking life that engendered indifference at best—their interpretation frequently uncovered an "*important* impression" of something that "justifiably stirred [his] feelings" (emphasis in original; *SE* 4: 174). A few sentences later, he puzzles over this fact and wonders, "Why is it, then, that, though the occasion of my dreaming was a daytime impression by which I had been justifiably stirred, I nevertheless actually dreamt of something indifferent?" (*SE* 4: 174). Some 300 pages later, he hazards an answer to the question:

> Analysis shows us that the *ideational material has undergone displacements and substitutions, whereas the affects have remained unaltered*. (emphasis in original; *SE* 5: 460)

In other words, the dream work achieves strategic disjunctions—Freud captures this notion in, among other phrases, "dream distortion"—whereby the ideational material, at times heavily modified, is no longer "compatible with the affect, which is retained, unmodified" (*SE* 5: 461). In addition, while the analogy is hardly perfect, I want to return to Shaw's "unconsciously" rolled sleeves alluded to in "The New Theology." As you will recall, their inadvertent display while Shaw strolled in London led to a friend's admonition about appearing in public in "that fashion," which produced Shaw's suffusion of blushes. Whatever memories and substitutions subtend his blush—and whatever "consequential" ideation underlies Shaw's shame or embarrassment—his reaction hardly matches something as "trifling" as rolled sleeves. Are such moments of affective intensity, therefore, as overdetermined as some dream images, traceable to several origins including the perennial wounds of adolescent poverty and acute shame?

Whatever the case, this walk in London and Freud's analysis of his dream of the *table d'hôte* might facilitate our engagement with Shaw's fiction and its adumbration of a material psychology. The latter, for example, underscores the frequency with which debt, value, and money appear in dreaming; that is to say, when self-censorship is no longer so vigilant as it is in waking life—when the dreamer's ideation is subject to a less vigilant suppression—dream narratives frequently contain material and *materialist* issues. These pertain to the dreamer's evolving sense of self, much as Gerald Bridges revised his self-assessment after acquiring new found wealth in "The Theatre of the Future." This self-evaluative process typically engenders related questions: What does my wealth say about me? Did I earn it through my own merits or actions? The procedure can also take a more self-critical turn, as in Freud's dream: Am I getting the best bargain? Am I in another's debt? Am I embarrassed by my lack of wealth? Such questions can be based on the substitution of material concerns for amatory ones and, perhaps most important, in formulations of value, producing intense feeling regardless of the absurdity of events that comprise the dream narrative (even after the modifications of secondary revision produce something more comprehensible). It is to such matters that I now turn, first as discussed by Freud and then by other contemporaries, Georg Simmel in particular, in an effort to construct an archive at the fin de siècle within which to assess Shaw's contributions to this discourse.[8] Throughout, I hope to underscore the processes by way of which affect, especially feeling, and value are implicated with each other—and with money.

Freud, Money, and Existential Anxiety: Performances of Value with a Shavian Prologue

> The Domesday Clearances filled your pockets with gold to console you for the horror and remorse of your dreams…. It is from you that we shall exact compensation: aye, to the utmost farthing. You are conspiring here with these capitalist bloodsuckers to rob us again of the value of what you have already stolen…. We shall expose you. (*CPP* 5: 586)
> —Aloysia in *On the Rocks* (1933)

Even in a play such as *On the Rocks*, with its often parodic commentary on a faltering capitalism, an enervated aristocracy, and alienated labor,

Shaw finds ways of mapping his dialogue on to many of the affective and material concerns that Freud outlined in *The Interpretation of Dreams*, *On Dreams*, and elsewhere. This may seem mildly surprising, given Shaw's well-known antipathy toward psychoanalysis, from his lampooning in "The Sanity of Art" of Max Nordau's reliance upon the "sham science" of psychology in *Degeneration* (1892), an attack on modern culture premised heavily on contemporary psychological thought, to his disparagement of Freud in particular and wry commentary about psychoanalysis more generally some half a century later in *Sixteen Self Sketches*.[9] Continuing in this critical vein in *On the Rocks*, Shaw affords his protagonist, the troubled British Prime Minister Sir Arthur Chavender, opportunities to take sharp jabs at psychoanalysis. Verbally sparring with the vivacious Aloysia Brollikins who, in the play's later moments, announces her accession to an "evolutionary appetite" driving her to marry Chavender's eighteen-year-old son David, Sir Arthur rejects her claims that his son "never loved anyone but his sister" and, worse, that he "hates his mother":

> He had no right to tell you that he hates his mother, because as a matter of fact he doesnt [sic]. Young people nowadays read books about psychoanalysis and get their heads filled with nonsense. (*CPP* 5: 610)

Given the tumultuous action of the play, Sir Arthur's exasperation is understandable: the country's social fabric has been torn by poverty and unemployment which, in turn, have sparked strikes raging outside his window; he has suffered a nearly debilitating breakdown that sent him to a mountain retreat and, somewhat mysteriously, motivated his daily regimen of reading Marx; his two late-teenage children are rebelling against him, and more. But his disparagement of psychoanalysis as promulgating "nonsense"—and Aloysia's response to him, which reduces Freudian thought to the Oedipus complex as she attempts to explain David's estrangement from his family—should not obscure the ways in which *On the Rocks* not only links the material and psychical in Shaw, but also parallels Freudian thought on this very constellation.

Aloysia's attack on the privileged class in the above epigraph and, in particular, her threat to exact "compensation" for the "value" it has stolen evoke the materially inflected psychology underlying the dreams of many of Freud's patients (and, as we have seen, his own as well). Moments earlier, Aloysia reveals the impetus for her indictment: the fact that the Duke's family drove "a whole countryside of honest hardworking Scottish crofters into the sea" after realizing that tenant farms weren't nearly so profitable as deer forests for wealthy hunters to indulge their passion (*CPP* 5: 585). Set in Sir Arthur's cabinet room, *On the Rocks* consists of exchanges on such subjects as this between the PM and a steady parade of visitors: the Duke and Chief Commissioner of Police; Mrs. Chavender, their two children, and her doctor; a delegation from the working-class Isle of Cats including the Mayor, a "sunny comfortable old chap" cum labor analyst named Hipney, the brash Viscount Barking representing the "riverside proletariat" (*CPP* 5: 542–43), and Aloysia, an Alderwoman; the "Cingalese plutocrat" Sir Jafna Pandranath; Conservative leader Sir Dexter Rightside and Admiral Sir Bemrose Hotspot, and others. The result is an entertaining and occasionally prescient debate about nationalization, the plight of labor, means testing and entitlement reform, the taxation of unearned income, and the workings of "trickle-down" economics, for which Sir Dexter Rightside, anticipating Reaganomics in 1980s America and Donald Trump's strategies later, makes a familiar case:

> Yes: take our last penny! And when the little that the present ruinous taxation has left us is gone; when we have closed our accounts with the last tradesman and turned the last servant into the streets, where are they to find employment? Who is to pay their wages? (*CPP* 5: 571)

Sir Dexter's screed is one of several outbursts in *On the Rocks* that foreground economic threads woven into the fabric of western modernity, then and now. Veritable leitmotifs in contemporary political discourse, the subjects of such orations and dialogical exchanges also comprise the bulk of *On the Rocks*, which at the same time also hints at the affectual ramifications of making money, possessing it, and, in the case of destitute and starving workers, going without it.

Consistent with his later denigration of psychoanalysis, in the opening minutes of the play Sir Arthur responds to his Police Commissioner's concerns about "crowd psychology" by labeling this notion as "nonsense" and "metaphysical rot" (*CPP* 5: 528). However, if psychoanalysis and crowd psychology can be dismissed so blithely, the relationship between money and affect cannot. So, while the brash "Oxford Youth" from the Isle of Cats (Viscount Barking) can upbraid Sir Arthur for never having made any meaningful sacrifice in this bleak period of economic recession—"Have you pawned your overcoat?" "Are you sleeping ten in a room?" (*CPP* 5: 545)—Aloysia can accuse him of not being able to "feel anything at all" (*CPP* 5: 548). Although no workers appear to testify to the miseries of such privation, the causal relationship between money and both feeling and deeper emotion emerges on numerous occasions. When, for example, Sir Arthur and the Duke discuss contemporary Russia and speculate about what Marx and Lenin learned from the British, the former suggests that the aristocracy might lead a reform movement to right serious socioeconomic wrongs. Dismissing this as not "a gentlemen's job," the Duke reveals his reasons for declining, one of which concerns his battered self-image:

> Third, I'm so horribly hard up for pocket money without knowing how to do without it that Ive [sic] lost all my self-respect. (*CPP* 5: 602)

Because self-image is intimately tied to materiality in Shaw early and late, the Duke's dismay again recalls Gerald Bridge's revised and diametrically opposite self-image after attaining his sudden windfall; moreover, the Duke's predicament constitutes yet another of Shaw's ongoing representations of a penniless, yet still haughty and obstructive, aristocracy.[10]

At least one character in *On the Rocks*, however, implies that wealth is no guarantor of positive feeling or self-contentment. Upon his entrance into the Cabinet Room, Sir Jafna Pandranath, described as "*too much occupied and worried by making money to get any fun out of spending it*," is greeted by Sir Dexter as if he were the very embodiment of capital: "You represent money; and money brings fools to their senses." Sir Jafna objects to this assertion in a hyperbolic and, at base, disingenuous fashion: "Money! Not at all. I am a poor man. I never know from one moment to another whether I am worth thirteen millions or only three" (*CPP* 5: 577). When one of his interlocutors suggests that he is actually worth 20 million—or perhaps as much as 50—he replies antagonistically, alleging that he is being "plundered at every turn" by an idle class of landholding aristocrats. As his attack grows more strident, so does his truculence as conveyed in what Shaw's stage directions describe as a "*shriek*": "I live, I work, I plan, I shatter my health and risk all I possess only to enrich these parasites, these vampires, these vermin in the commonwealth" (*CPP* 5: 578). Calming slightly before completely losing his temper, he continues with stentorian pique: "Make them earn their own living, damn them" (*CPP* 5: 578), an outburst that Sir Dexter ascribes to Sir Jafna's being an "emotional oriental." Civility, however, already attenuated in the scene, cannot be restored after Sir Dexter demeans Sir Jafna as a "silly nigger"

(*CPP* 5: 599), which Jafna rejoins by labeling those assembled "needy imbeciles" who have "cringed" before him only because of his money and ability to make more (*CPP* 5: 600). He then exits abruptly, slamming the door behind him.

On the Rocks, as this dialogue indicates, not only braids affect with money but also comments on profectitious and adventitious money as defined in the preceding chapter. That is to say, the play furthers the conversation about how or if one *earns* his or her money that was initiated much earlier in the Shavian canon, from his earliest fiction through *Mrs. Warren's Profession* and beyond. At several points in the dialogue, this issue is mildly debated, as when Sir Dexter, responding to Viscount Barking's comments about money allowing one not to work, asks, "Why should a man work like anyone else if he has money?" (*CPP* 5: 583). More important than this distinction in *On the Rocks*, however, is the relationship between money and *value*, not just a commodity's value but also a person's. Georg Simmel, to whose work I shall turn momentarily, makes a point apposite to this topic when historicizing such cultural constructs as *wergild* and the institution of dowries, which place a monetary value, in the former case, on a human life wrongly taken, and, in the latter, on proffering a woman for marriage. As Simmel notes, some values, however, "cannot be expressed in money terms, even though they are theoretically recognized to be the highest values" (*Money*, 399). For this reason, money, as a means of representing "the value of incommensurable things" (*Money*, 395), has historically been deemed unsuitable for settling some disputes or satisfying certain moral or religious demands. Why? Because the values invoked in some religious ceremonies and cultural practices are irreducible to any material equivalence; lacking an appropriate *currency*, there can be no exchange. As Simmel explains, as far back as ancient Greece an awareness has existed of the "intrinsic inadequacy of money" to form the equivalent of an array of entities or practices, religious atonement for instance (*Money* 396). This precise inadequacy, it seems to me, informs Aloysia's threat to expose those who would conspire to rob workers "again" of their "value."

Stated somewhat differently, her intimation of what are finally subjective valences of value gestures toward two different connotations of money. Initially invoking the more obvious of these, money as *currency*, Aloysia vows to wrest compensation from the guilty down to the last farthing for evicting peasants from their homes; for this outrage, she implies, money might well serve as a means of restitution. However, *pace* Simmel's allusions to ancient religious ceremonies, some values—or rather, in some theorizations, *all* values—exceed money's capacity to forge an equivalence or commensurability. This is so, at least in part, because value is connected to the existence of alternatives and the psychology of choosing among these; it is also imbricated in a larger context of possibilities, some of which are ideal, not material, as Jean-Joseph Goux observes: "The analysis of value can begin only when an equivalent appears on the scene."[11] So, if Aloysia's pledge to extract monetary compensation for the Duke's ordering of mass evictions is clear and direct, her accusation that the aristocracy attempted "to make us give you gilt edged securities in exchange for the land that no longer brings you in shooting rents" is another matter (*CPP* 5: 586). As labor possesses no such securities, her metaphor requires an unpacking, one possibility of which is that impoverished workers pay for the economic miscalculation of capitalists and fecklessness of aristocrats with the precious substance of their labor and hence their very being. No monetary equivalence can justly compensate them for these. In this regard, Goux's distinction between money and currency seems apt: "*Money* is a subjective notion, connected with the idea of wealth; *currency* is an objective concept, relating to the social organization of economic exchanges." For this reason, because its primary function is to facilitate exchange in the marketplace, Goux observes, currency "escapes psychoanalysis"; by contrast, because the unconscious regards money "as a symbol of … affective exchange-value," it has subjective resonances that currency lacks. As such, money possesses signifying value that may greatly exceed or fail to approach the objective worth or use-value of a purchased commodity (however fictitious or chimerical the putative use value of a commodity may be, as will be discussed in a later chapter), and this is precisely what allows it to perform subjective work beyond the more routinized functioning of currency in the everyday process of exchange.[12]

Shaw understands the signifying value of money—and so does Freud, who throughout *The Interpretation of Dreams* contextualizes value with feeling in particular. In tracing this nexus in *Interpretation* and other texts, moreover, it is almost impossible to *overestimate* the importance of affect and value to Freudian thought even though, at times, Freud himself seemed to *underestimate* its centrality to his psychoanalysis. His seminal essay "The Uncanny" (1919), for example, begins with the following disclaimer:

> It is only rarely that a psycho-analyst feels impelled to investigate the subject of aesthetics, even when aesthetics is understood to mean not merely the theory of beauty but the theory of the qualities of *feeling*. He works in other strata of mental life and has little to do with the subdued *emotional* impulses. (*SE* 17: 239; my emphasis)

It might be countered that, in fact, Freud cannot avoid an analytic calculus in which "qualities of feeling" and "emotional impulses" predominate; as a result, they have *everything* to do with his clinical practice and evolving understanding of such negative affects as anxiety, a topic of repeated concern in his writing from the time of essays he published in 1895, through his *Introductory Lectures on Psychoanalysis* (1915–17), and continuing on to *The Problem of Anxiety* (1936).[13] He says as much in his 1925 essay "An Autobiographical Study" when recalling his collaboration with Josef Breuer on *Studies on Hysteria* (1895), which, among other characteristics, "laid stress on the significance of the life of the emotions" (*SE* 20: 22). If "the problem of anxiety" is, as he describes it in his Lecture "Anxiety," a "nodal point at which the most various and important questions converge" and is therefore also a "riddle whose solution would be bound to throw a flood of light on our whole mental existence" (*SE* 16: 393), then this negative feeling or *angst* suffered by neurotics with particular intensity is equally relevant to our considerations here. So, too, are the etiologies of emotions and feelings more generally.

Neurotic anxiety is, in fact, one of two forms of the affect Freud theorizes in his *Introductory Lectures*. To this pair, I want to add a third form of anxiety, one that I believe informs Shaw's "chronic impecuniosity" and renders it far more than a synonym for "poverty." This three-part schema might begin with Freud's parsing of the term "anxiety" in his *Introductory Lectures* and his distinction between "realistic" anxiety and a far more debilitating "neurotic" strain. The former initially struck Freud as "something very rational" insofar as it constitutes a "reaction to the perception of an external danger"; realistic anxiety, he hypothesized, might even be regarded "as a manifestation of the self-preservation instinct" (*SE* 16-393-94). After considerable reflection, Freud undertook a "drastic revision" of this position, finally determining that anxiety production is never an "expedient" phenomenon and could, in some cases, be profoundly inexpedient (*SE* 16: 394). Neurotic anxiety, which can lead to, among other things, paralyzing phobias and such other negative affects as fear, is a far more severe matter as it can lead to "positively overwhelming" emotion and often accompanies "hysterical" or intensely experienced physiological symptoms (*SE* 16: 399, 401).[14] Neurotic anxiety, moreover, exists in an "obscure" psychical region that Freud traverses with some reservation, even though he also insists that anxiety and affect have never been studied or even recognized by contemporary psychology, but rather have "grown up on the soil of psycho-analysis and are native only to it" (*SE* 16: 396). When it comes to theorizing anxiety, it seems, something Freud termed an "affective state," traveling familiar conceptual ground cultivated exclusively by one's own discipline still creates uncertainty—and, well, anxiety.

To these varieties of negative affect, as I have mentioned, a third might be added, an "existential anxiety" that, like the discipline of economics, is rooted in scarcity and thus is as native to psychoanalysis as the two forms of *angst* that Freud engages in his *Lectures*. In "Accounting for Pleasure: Sigmund Freud, Carl Menger, and the Economically Minded Human Being," cited in the preceding chapter, Richard T. Gray argues for the potency of this form of anxiety, one steeped in a "kind of Malthusian pessimism that invokes the scarcity of resources as the underlying cause of human existential anxiety and as the defining feature of human interactions with the 'real' world of commodities."[15] Managing and satisfying needs, material and psychical, are enterprises challenged equally by a scarcity that promotes fierce competition; hence, both psychoanalytic and marginal economic theory rely upon similar "anthropological presumptions."[16] Chief among these is the always-fraught project of satisfying needs in the nonutopian economies—material and libidinal—in which we exist. In other words, while Gonzalo in Shakespeare's *The Tempest* imagines a commonwealth in which nature brings forth its fruits in "all foison, all abundance," this plenitude hardly matches the realities most of us know all too well. In addition, the scarcity inherent to these underpins existential anxiety, especially as it obtains in—or is an inevitable by-product of—our often frustrated pursuit of things we value. Because "all value is speculative," as Joshua Clover asserts, an exchange value in particular is "at constant risk of going unrealized—until consumed as use value and in that instant extinguished."[17]

It is therefore hardly surprising that such concepts as value and feeling appear linked in *The Interpretation of Dreams* from its earliest, most foundational chapters. Discussing the modification of ideational material in dreaming, for example, Freud references Ludwig Strümpell's *Die Natur und Enstethung der Träume* (1874), a work cited frequently in the early chapters of *Interpretation* on topics ranging from the appearance of the trivial in dreams to the causes of forgetting them.[18] In explaining the former, Freud quotes Strümpell at length:

> With the sensation of sensory functioning and of normal vital consciousness, the mind loses the soil in which its feelings, desires, interests, and activities are rooted. The psychical states, too—*feelings, interests, judgments of value*—which are linked to mnemic image in waking life are subjected to an … obscuring pressure, as a result of which their connection with these images is broken…. (*SE* 4: 54; my emphasis)

Freud's reading of Strümpell inflects his understanding of the relationship between affect and the apparently trivial details that appear in dreams, concluding that the "the fact of images being denuded of their psychical value (which in turn goes back to detachment from the external world) plays a principal part in creating the impression of strangeness which distinguishes dreams from actual life in our memory" (*SE* 4: 54). Yet even more significant for our purposes are the notions that the "judgment of value" is a "psychical state" and that dream images, however illusory, produce affects that are all too real. This latter idea leads Freud to Salomon Stricker, who identifies the opposition reality/illusion as one of the binarisms that interpretation must illuminate as it determines "what part of the psychical processes occurring in dreams is to be regarded as real" (*SE* 4: 74).

Freud responds to this question with one answer alluded to earlier: the affect produced is real, even though the ideational material related to it may be distorted by the machinery of the dream work. However, other less obvious answers to the question exist as well, one of which is intimated in Freud's citation of Belgian philosopher Joseph Delbœuf's *Le sommeil et les rêves* (1885), in which Delbœuf asserts that "Le songeur est un acteur [The dreamer is an actor]" who plays a multitude of parts, just as we do in our waking lives.[19] Given the evidence of several of Freud's own dreams and those of his patients, this thesis about the performative kernel of dreaming seems plausible, as many of Freud's own dreams involve role-playing, at times anxiety-producing role-playing connected to his interactions at social events. His dream of the *table d'hôte* provides one instance, but there are numerous others. An easily overlooked element of the much-discussed dream of "Irma's Injection," for instance, is its social and performative setting: "*A large hall—numerous guests, whom we were receiving.—Among them was Irma. I at once took her on one side …*" (*SE* 4: 107). Even Freud's "dream of the botanical monograph" concerns a kind of performance, in this case Freud as author of a monograph on a "certain species of plant" (*SE* 4: 165). Freud as a gracious host, Freud as writer, Freud as debtor as in the dream of the *table d'hôte*—in all of these cases, he is enacting a role and, in some of them, this performance includes the incurring of debt, making payment, or conforming to extant codes of social behavior. All of these roles inform his dream of the *table d'hôte*. Equally important, Freud plumbs the dream thoughts which gave rise to it and discovers a farrago of both economic and emotional contents, returning not only to the free cab ride offered by his friend, hence the issue of debt, but also to a prior experience of his having "paid out a considerable sum of money on behalf of a member of my family of whom I am fond." His conclusion? "Love that is free of cost, however, stood in the forefront of the dream-thoughts" (*SE* 5: 656–57).

Similarly present in the thoughts underlying the dream narratives of Freud's patients are issues of feeling and, inevitably, self-assessment (including self-criticism, even self-recrimination). These may manifest themselves in or be pictorialized as frustrated attempts to procure a service or purchase a commodity, as in the dreams of one patient, "an intelligent and cultivated young woman," who reported the following innocuous dream event:

> *I dreamt that I arrived too late at the market and could get nothing either from the butcher or from the woman who sells vegetables.* (*SE* 4: 183)

Freud extracted a longer narrative from the young woman in which her frustrated shopping and her being proffered inferior meat and produce, items she declined to purchase, rose to significance. As it happens, the young woman and her cook had recently arrived too late at a market to purchase anything at all, and Freud develops a complicated reading of the incident, focusing on a disagreement between the woman and the cook that included the admonition, "Behave yourself properly!" (*SE* 4: 184). In another dream, a wife and her husband disagree about having their piano tuned, the woman arguing that it would not be a "worthwhile" investment to make as the instrument was "ugly" and "disgusting." This dream, rather simply and directly, originates in a prosaic episode in the woman's waking experience from the previous day, yet Freud notes that she employed the same language in reporting her dream that she had used when voicing her reluctance to a friend to take off her jacket—"It's not worthwhile"—because she could stay for only a minute. Freud regards the sentiment as connected not merely with her intention not to stay long and socialize with her friend, but also to her desire not to be seen ("Please don't look; it's not worth while"), for he observed her clutch her jacket toward her after a button came undone and noted her repetition of the same phrase. In both dreams, then, value for money spent conveys a more intimate meaning or dilemma (*SE* 4: 185–86). In the latter dream in particular, the "worth" of tuning an ugly and disgusting "box" of a piano claims at least a partial origin in a woman's long-standing dissatisfaction with her body, a negative feeling that hearkens back to her puberty and a persistent self-criticism of her appearance.

These dream narratives and their analyses parallel elements of Freud's dream of the *table d'hôte* by emblematizing the ways in which a commodity's value, money, and a more libidinal economy can merge in dreaming. In this context, as Freud eventually determines, Frau E.L.'s aspersion about his ability to get what he wanted without paying for it can be articulated in two different, but compatible registers: "*I should like to get something sometimes without paying for it,*" or "*I should like to get some enjoyment without cost*" (*SE* 5: 650; emphasis in original).[20] Here, Freud's conclusion, much like his understanding of the marital spat over piano-tuning as a "worthwhile" investment, shows how seamlessly the language of commodities and value can be transposed into the syntax of pleasure or desire, or into a metrics of self-appraisal in which real feeling and emotion are incited. Moreover, albeit originating in more or less innocuous incidents from waking life, all of these dreams demonstrate how role-playing and social performance inform dreams. "*Le songeur est un acteur,*" and very often the roles dreamers assume are minor ones—dissatisfied consumer, bickering housewife, or unhappy diner at a *table d'hôte*—originating in more psychically resonant memories (from early childhood, for instance). Regardless of the role's size, however, the dreamer performs it in a social theatre—frequently a materialist theatre of monetary transactions—before an audience of others or an "other," and this performance catalyzes a wide variety of affects. Some are pleasurable, while others reveal the scar tissue of anterior and, in some cases, perennial wounds.

In a few instances, many or all of these elements—social performance, cost or price, and value, including self-worth or the value of others—collide in an unusually resonant dream narrative. Such is the case with the specimen dream with which Freud concludes his delineation of the operations of the dream work in *On Dreams*, a dream to which he returns some fifteen years later in his *Introductory Lectures*. His patient, a young woman who has been married for several years, claims to love her husband and hold him in the highest regard. Freud's initial rendering of the events in her life that underlie the dream begin with the woman's recent awareness that a female acquaintance (Elise L.), who "was almost exactly her contemporary," had become engaged. This precipitated the following dream narrative:

> *She was at the theatre with her husband. One side of the stalls was completely empty. Her husband told her that Elise L. and her fiancé had wanted to go too, but had only been able to get bad seats—three for a 1 florin 50 kreuzers—and*

of course they could not take those. She thought it would not really have done any harm if they had. (*SE* 5: 669)

In his analysis, Freud trains his attention on seemingly negligible matters, the absurdity of a couple attempting to buy *three* tickets to attend the theatre, for instance: Why would they require the extra ticket? Another is the cost of the tickets themselves, although the appearance in dreams of highly specific sums of money is not, in Freud's experience, unusual. In *On Dreams*, for example, the dream account that precedes this one concerns a daughter taking three florins and 65 kreuzers from her mother's purse to pay for an item that cost much less, and Freud surmises that this sum, obviously far more than the equivalent of the desired commodity, substitutes for something of more value to her, time ("time is money"). In this instance, three florins, 65 kreuzers equal 365 kreuzers and finds a parallel with 365 days in a year (*SE* 5: 669), and this length of time was a meaningful factor in the dreamer's life. In the latter dream of attending the theatre, the price of the tickets is exactly 100 times less than the amount (150 florins) of a gift the dreamer's sister-in-law had recently received from her husband. Soon thereafter, her sister-in-law hastily decided to purchase jewelry with her husband's unexpected largesse, an impulsive action that accrues meaning as the dream analysis evolves.

The empty theatre seats in this dream, as Freud eventually comes to understand, are an overdetermined image originating in thoughts related to both value and haste. For on an earlier occasion, acting hurriedly much like her impetuous sister-in-law, the dreamer quickly purchased tickets only to discover upon later entering the auditorium that it was only half full and not sold out as she had feared, a miscalculation her husband seemed to take delight in teasing her about. There had been no reason to hurry to purchase tickets, just as there was no reason for Elise L. to settle for "bad seats" in the dream; or for the dreamer's sister-in-law to rush out to purchase jewelry. As Freud considered these dream images and the antecedent events with which they are associated, it was difficult to ignore both the dream's relationship to other women's interactions with their husbands or fiancés—those of the dreamer's sister-in-law and the bride-to-be, Elise—and their literal connection to money: an exceedingly generous gift in the former case, over-priced tickets for "bad" seats in the latter. Further, Elise L., nearly the same age as Freud's patient who, again, had been married for several years, was in no hurry to find a spouse, just as in the dream she was unwilling to accept poor seats for her money.

Remembering that Freud deploys this specimen text in *On Dreams* to summarize his hypotheses about the operations of the dreamwork, particularly displacement and condensation, his analysis of the dream thoughts that give rise to this dream seems reasonable, however inconsistent it might be with his analysand's claim to love and respect her husband:

> Now for the dream-thoughts: 'It was *absurd* to marry so early. There was *no need for me to be in such a hurry*. I see from Elise L.'s example that I should have got a husband in the end. Indeed, I should have got one *a hundred times better*' (a treasure) 'if I had only waited. My money' (or dowry) 'could have bought *three* men just as good.' (*SP* 5: 670; emphasis in original)

Given the patient's earlier profession of love for her husband, as Freud explains just a few pages later, this analysis reveals the fact that, once identified, some dream thoughts will prove so disagreeable to the dreamer that she might "dispute energetically" their very existence (*SP* 5: 672). It is precisely for this reason that the dreamwork distorts as it produces content, in essence disguising those origins of dream content that the dreamer would find abhorrent.

However, Freud was not quite finished with this dream or its cloaked features, and he revisits it in two of his *Introductory Lectures*. In Lecture VII, "The Manifest Content of Dreams and the Latent Dream-Thoughts," Freud revises the "nomenclature" he has employed in describing the unusual substitutions that occur in dreams and their relationships to dream thoughts: "Instead of speaking of 'concealed,' 'inaccessible,' or 'ungenuine,' let us adopt the correct description and say 'inaccessible to the dreamer's consciousness' or 'unconscious'" (*SE* 15: 113). This revision is hardly surprising, for by this time (1916) the concepts of repression and the unconscious were rising in prominence in his thought. Nearly a decade later, Freud underscored this emergence in succinct and clear terms in "An Autobiographical Study":

> … [T]he study of pathogenic repressions and other phenomena which have still to be mentioned compelled psycho-analysis to take the concept of the "unconscious" seriously. (*SE* 20: 31)

In the young wife's dream of the theatre visit, the substitutions in question—impetuously purchased tickets serving as proxies for husbands—link directly to dream thoughts under repression and denied by the woman.

Also, in Lecture VII, Freud provides additional evidence for this reading of substitutions, evidence he did *not* supply 15 years earlier. The tickets his patient hurriedly purchased for a performance that drew only half an audience, tickets she had felt some anxiety about being able to procure, were actually made more expensive because she was obligated to pay an additional early booking fee. Freud's assertion of the substitution of hastily acquired tickets for hastily acquired husbands is further supported by yet another detail absent from the earlier account. In *On Dreams*, he reported that the young woman had simply "received news" that Elise L. was engaged to be married; in Lecture VII, however, he specifies that "*Her husband had in fact told her that Elise L.... had just become engaged*" (*SE* 15: 122; my emphasis), thereby linking her husband to her friend's announcement. Freud's aside that she had been married for "many years" is also made more exact in his later lecture: although still a "young woman," she had been married for "nearly ten years" (*SE* 15: 123), long enough to harbor doubts about her decision and weigh the possibility that she had acted precipitously.

Lecture XIV on "Wish-Fulfillment" thickens the description of both this dream and its analysis. At the same time, it supports the analogy between dreaming and acting by recalling the process of *surrogation* introduced earlier and its three component parts: performance, substitution, and memory. During the theatrical *performance* of a play, the process works something like this: an actor *substitutes* for a character, and the audience's response to the enactment may be enriched by its *memory* of other actors' assumptions of a role, of the other notable roles a particular actor has played, and of the repertory of plays in which a performance is contextualized. To borrow a trope from theatre critic Marvin Carlson, the live performance of a play is "haunted" by these memorial potentials, especially if the play occupies a prominent place in the acting repertory and the actors in the production are well known.[21] In the case of this dream, the half-empty dream theatre may be as "haunted" as Carlson's stage. Freud gestures to the workings of surrogation by acknowledging that "marrying" is "clearly replaced by 'going to the theatre'"; therefore, buying theatre tickets too early is "an immediate substitute for 'marrying too early'" (*SE* 15: 220). However, for young women, the connection between the theatre and marriage may be mapped to even more remote memories (and desires), as Freud implies when adverting somewhat awkwardly to "simple-minded" girls said to regard marriage as a means to attend the performances of certain plays that, as single women, they were prohibited from seeing. For this reason, Freud speculates that a scopic desire—a desire to see forbidden things that recalls the childhood desire to view the intimacy of one's parents, contents subject to vigilant repression—may inhere in the ambition to marry early; thus, "a visit to the theatre" becomes both an "obvious" substitute for marriage itself and a means of fulfilling an anterior desire (*SE* 15: 220). Performance, substitution, memory—all of the elements of surrogation are evident in Freud's analysis, which also foregrounds the relationship between value, money, and feeling. "Our dreamer," Freud observes, "was not always so dissatisfied with her early marriage"; in fact, "she had been proud of it and regarded herself as at an advantage over her friend" (*SE* 15: 220; my emphasis). This last observation confirms the manner in which the dreamer's conscious estimation of her marriage and her husband's worth both inflects her own self-assessment and resides within the broader contexts of alternatives and choices she was afforded.

Then, there is the presence of memory. Throughout his analyses, Freud evokes the pressures of memories, both those of recent events in the dreamer's life and their efflorescence from repressed contents originating much earlier. As Freud delineates in such places as Lecture XIII "The Archaic Features and Infantilism of Dreams," the "remarkable amnesia of childhood" is hardly defined by a total absence of memory; on the contrary, "out of the void of memories" from early childhood, "there stand out a few well-preserved recollections" (*SE* 15: 200). Insofar as contemporary or recent incidents—and the real feeling or emotion they produce—emanate from anterior memories, we might return to the Foucauldian trope initiated in the previous chapter and speculate that some of Freud's, his patients', and Shaw's *perennial wounds* are, more precisely, wounds of memory, a topic to which I will return. At this point, I hope it might prove sufficient to turn to Paul Ricoeur's final masterwork *Memory, History, Forgetting* (2004), particularly his discussion of two of Freud's most influential essays "Remembering, Repeating, and Working-Through" (1914) and "Mourning and Melancholia" (1917). Concepts central to these essays such as traumatic memory transposed into a compulsion to repeat in the former title and collective memory in the latter are not so germane for our purposes—although they are not entirely irrelevant—as Ricoeur's observation that both phenomena allow us to speak "legitimately" of a "*wounded*, even of a *sick* memory."[22] If this were not the case, a process such as mourning, one aim of which is to liberate the ego from the pain of a grievous loss, would be a merely superfluous custom; there would be no wound to heal. There is work, indeed painful work, associated with a remembering that allows the ego to work through loss. Forgetting, of course, would be vastly less agonizing, but some injuries cannot be so easily healed.[23]

The materialist dream theatre is always already informed, even determined, by the past and by memory; and the performances of value staged there often require actorly or other substitutions. Equally important and recalling Freud's reference to the work of Ludwig Strümpell in *The Interpretation of Dreams*, if "feeling, interests, and the judgment of value" are all "psychical states" tied to particular mnemic images, then they are also variously situated within markets (libidinal and commercial) and connected to objects of desire (bodies and commodities), and money, which may function as the master role-player of all, the character actor *par excellence*. In *Symbolic Economies: After Marx and Freud*, Goux provides a short list of interchangeable substitutions compiled from Freud that includes excrement, gifts, money, child, and penis; he also unpacks the homology between money and the phallus (after the phallic stage) and the deployment of gold as a "material representative of general wealth."[24] In any given circumstance, money can be interchanged with any of these: it can symbolize the wealth and social standing of gold, the power and privilege of the phallus, the filthy aspect of excrement ("dirty money"), or the generosity of a gift. In the dreams examined above, several of these equivalences emerge: money as more valuable than a worthless (execrable?) box of a piano or tied to the gift of a taxi ride. The most compelling substitutions in Freud and Shaw's theatres of value, as I shall outline, involve people—a young wife's confused estimation of her husband couched as hastily purchased tickets for a half-filled theatre, or an uncomfortable diner at the *table d'hôte* cast as a ne'er-do-well in the aspersions of a woman, or the radically devalued (and expendable) workers represented by Aloysia Brollikins in *On the Rocks*.

"Theres Money in Me, Madam, No Matter What I Go Into": Georg Simmel, Marginalist Economics, and Shavian Notions of Value

Early in Shaw's *Misalliance* (1910), John Tarleton, eccentric founder of Tarleton's Underwear, makes the claim about having money inside him while responding to his daughter Hypatia's incredulity that he might "chuck" 35 years of business success, as he threatens to do, and pursue something else.[25] "Theres money in underwear," she remonstrates; "theres none in wild-cat ideas" (*CPP* 4: 130). Tarleton queries this logic, it seems, throughout the play. Moments earlier, for example, he objected strenuously to any intimation that the underwear itself was responsible for the family's considerable fortune: "Anybody can make underwear. Anybody can sell underwear. Tarleton's Ideas: thats whats done it" (*CPP* 4: 129). An avid reader who once harbored literary ambitions, Tarleton had fantasized about a career in writing, a fantasy exploded by what he terms the "biggest tragedy of modern life": namely, the fact that his business ventures kept making money. Escape became impossible, and "Prometheus was chained to his rock" (*CPP* 4: 134, 135). However self-imposed, the chains appear to slacken—or so the smitten Tarleton hypothesizes—when possibility comes crashing down from the sky into his backyard in the form of a small plane and its beautiful passenger, Lina Szczepanowska.

Like Ibsen's Solness inspired by Hilda Wangel in *The Master Builder* (1892), Tarleton becomes infatuated with Lina who, in very short order, moves him both to pursue an awkward flirtation and to pose one of the play's central questions: "All this damned materialism: what good is it to anybody?" (*CPP* 4: 159). The answers are various, and some are clearly negative: his business and the wealth it generates serve as a "roasting jack" reducing his son Johnny, a 30-year-old businessman, to little more than a "turnspit" (*CPP* 4: 115); his money has moved his daughter to concede, "Well I cant be poor" and, as her mother observes, limited her daughter's choices in finding a suitable marriage partner (*CPP* 4: 143); and the social performances that accompany wealth have induced Mrs. Tarleton to assume the airs of a duchess, an impersonation she struggles to sustain. Even Lord Summerhays, playing the fop character from the Restoration stage by foolishly pursuing the much younger Hypatia, knows enough to provide the faux duchess with sage counsel on this very point: "Even queens drop the mask when they reach our time of life" (*CPP* 4: 121). Materialism, in short, has brought considerable wealth to the Tarleton family, but so long as the money resides inside them, they struggle to be happy—or free. Also, if the money is indeed *in* Tarleton and his family, how separable can materialism be from their subjective lives or very identities?

As I have implied, although afflicted by psychically debilitating poverty earlier in his life, particularly in the years he struggled to find publishers for his novels and walked London streets in threadbare trousers and broken boots, Shaw was acutely aware of money's ambivalence, and his characters reflect this awareness, reveling or, alternatively, languishing in their wealth. Anticipating Sir Jafna's unease in *On the Rocks*, an anxiety rooted in money, Tarleton in his clumsy wooing of Lina in *Misalliance* concedes that he can never be free of his image as a "ridiculous shopkeeper," just the kind of man Lina could never really desire. He adds, "I have to look at him in the glass while I'm shaving. I loathe him because he's a living lie" (*CPP* 4: 159). Still, he wants to make a "fool" of himself with Lina, who quickly adds him to her list of male suitors. "I keep a list of all my offers," she notes, rationalizing her list-keeping with a line of special relevance to the aims of this chapter: "I like to know what I'm considered worth" (*CPP* 4: 160). Less concerned with the larger economic issues that spark the at times heated exchanges of *On the Rocks*—labor strikes, nationalization, rates of taxation—*Misalliance* nonetheless raises questions equally crucial to modernity and to what Joe Cleary, as mentioned in the preceding chapter, terms its revised "economico-psychic subjectivity": What is the value of a person? What constitutes value in the first place?

Many of Shaw's contemporaries were vitally engaged with these very questions, the latter in particular, and as Shaw concedes in "Biographers' Blunders Corrected" from *Sixteen Self Sketches*, his own understanding of value evolved considerably in the 1880s. He points admiringly to Philip Wicksteed's revisions of Marx's theory of value, implying their fundamental importance to his evolving education:

> I never threw Marx over. In essentials I am as much a Marxist as ever. But when Philip Wicksteed, converted by Jevons, attacked the famous value theory of Marx and I had to defend it because nobody better was available, I knew nothing of abstract economics.
>
> For some years I hammered away at the subject, sitting under Wicksteed at a private society to which he lectured on the Jevonian theory.... I found that ... as to abstract value theory Marx was wrong and Wicksteed right. (*SSS* 81)

As Michael Holroyd explains in his biography, in this passage Shaw is alluding to regularly held sessions of a small group of friends and acquaintances, several of them economists, at the home of stockbroker H.R. Beeton between 1885 and 1889. The group convened frequently to discuss economics, and many of the meetings were led by Wicksteed, the results of which, as Holroyd notes quoting Shaw, were his "education" and "conversion" to a more capacious view of a commodity's value than its representation of the labor involved to produce it.[26] The "gospel according to Saint Marx," as Hesketh Pearson described the economic theory lustily imbibed by Shaw after hearing Henry George lecture in 1882, underwent the significant revisions of marginalism when taken up by a new evangelist.[27]

Several issues inhere in this topic, one of which is the manner in which the discourse of marginalist economic thought informs both Freud and Shaw. That is to say, consistent with Richard Gray's thesis that Freudian psychoanalysis shares much with Carl Menger's (1840–1921) marginalism—more reciprocally, that marginalism depended on "arguments derived from psychology" and, in turn, Freud relied on "language and themes drawn from economics"[28]—I want to suggest that Shaw was similarly influenced by this body of thought, even if his formal acquaintance with it might have come after finishing *An Unsocial Socialist* in mid-December, 1883 and responding in print to Wicksteed's October, 1884 critique of *Das Kapital*. While the case for the *direct* influence of marginalism on Shaw's novels is thus difficult to prosecute, I hope to demonstrate instead that his fiction anticipates his more formal education on its principles. In addition to referencing Menger's writing, Gray identifies one of the texts that shaped Wicksteed's thought and, by extension, Shaw's, William Stanley Jevons's *The Theory of Political Economy* (1871), stressing the "propinquity of Jevons' utilitarian take on economics with Freud's basic conception of psychology."[29] Illustrative of this point, in *The Theory of Political Economy* Jevons devotes a chapter to a "Theory of Pleasure and Pain," meditating upon the "pleasure derived from the possession of an object, and the pain encountered in its acquisition"; speculating about the intensity of anticipation that possible possession of the object elicits and the manner in which anticipation influences the "accumulation of stocks of a commodity to be consumed at a future time"; and outlining other dimensions of the affectual dimensions of commodity acquisition.[30] Equally important, Jevons's understanding of consumption privileges an economy that sounds as much libidinal as commercial: "… the demand for, and the consumption of, objects of refined enjoyment has its lever in the facility with which the primary wants are satisfied." His conclusion insofar as value is theorized underscores its dialogical core:

> This, therefore, is the key to the true theory of value. Without relative values in the objects to the acquirement of which we direct our power, there would be no foundation for Political Economy as a science.[31]

Here, Jevons achieves two key elisions: first, *value* is imbricated within the relative *values* we project onto the objects we acquire; and second, an *object's* value is impacted by the range of alternative *objects* to which we direct our attention, each of which might satisfy our desires.

This conjunction of the material object and individual desire makes value a more complicated concept than, say, price, elasticity, or supply and demand, the concepts to which some commentators have reduced Wicksteed's (and, by extension, Jevons's) theories.[32] Announcing the goal of *The Common Sense of Political Economy* as the exposition of the marginal theory of economics, and alluding to Jevons, Léon Walras, and Carl Menger,[33] Wicksteed, like Jevons, routinely crosses what now might seem to be established disciplinary boundaries between economics and psychology. Indeed, in an almost uncanny way, Wicksteed's language in describing the administration of domestic resources—the ways in which the heads of households, usually mothers, spend their money and maintain their budgets—anticipates that of Freudian psychoanalysis. He begins his consideration of value by asserting that, in some ways, the economic world which we navigate daily resides beyond our "conscious" control.[34] Moreover, anything "that changes the value or significance of any application of energies or resources," may "affect the purchase of any single article at a market stall."[35] To continue the analogy with Freudian psychoanalysis, this "single article" in the marketplace functions much as an object of desire in the dream theatre; as such, the process of its selection can be distinguished from such forces as instinct or *drive* that push for satisfaction irrespective of the specificity of objects. Jacques Lacan underscores this very point in his *Four Fundamental Concepts of Psycho-analysis* (1977): "*As far as the object of the drive is concerned, let it be clear that it is, strictly speaking, of no importance. It is a matter of total indifference.*"[36] By contrast, in the calculation of value an object is assessed in a larger, more discerning context, and desire—not merely brutish instinct raging to be satisfied—is one of its crucial components.

Tethered to desire, under certain conditions such objects may also engender discomfort; and, in delineating the common sense of political economy, Wicksteed resorts to a lexicon of desire, satisfaction, and pain. In choosing between things, he observes, consumers often determine "not which of two satisfactions we would rather forgo, but which of two pains or miseries we would rather escape"; similarly, the positive satisfaction gained by acquired objects must be measured against the negative satisfaction one hopes to avoid. A commodity's price, therefore, is not merely reducible to money: "Insensibly," Wicksteed summarizes, "we have passed from the confined conception of price as so much money, to the generalized conception of price as representing the terms on which anything we may want be had or anything we shun avoided."[37] Herein resides the explanatory potential of margins. Marginal significance, marginal consumption, marginal values—these and other "marginal considerations" concern a "slight increase or diminution of the stock of anything which we possess or are considering"; and our marginal desire "for more of anything is measured by the significance of a slight increment added at the margin of our present store."[38] From this sense of margins, one might infer the difference—or, more accurately, chasm—between a utopia marked by super-abundance and a modernity of scarcity, for the more we add to the storehouse of a thing, the less marginal utility an additional unit of that same thing will possess.

Although Shaw frequently discussed money—his ignorance of its power as a young man, his disdain for certain income-earning journalistic assignments, his ambition to secure a lucrative agreement for the production of this or that play—his commentary on *value* is not nearly so prolific. However, such commentary, that in *The Intelligent Woman's Guide to Socialism, Capitalism, Sovietism, and Fascism* (1928), for example, demonstrates the influence of marginalism. After explaining the use of money as a "necessary tool" in exchange, one vastly more expedient than the proffering of donkeys or potatoes for fares on buses,[39] Shaw hints at the complexity of the attribution of value:

> All this is as easy as ABC. What is not so easy is the question why the donkey should be worth, say, three-quarters of a sovereign (fifteen bob, it would be called at this price), or, to put it the other way, why fifteen bob should be worth a donkey. All you can say is that a buyer at this price is a person with fifteen shillings who wants a donkey more than she wants the fifteen shillings. (*Guide*, 252)

"The matter of value grows more complicated when contextualized with other commodities that might be acquired for the same money, for while the donkey represents "just a donkey and nothing else," Shaw notes, the 15 shillings "represents fifteen shillingsworth [sic] of anything you like, from food and drink to a cheap umbrella" (252). The donkey's *value*, therefore, is relative to the *values* of these other goods as assessed in the consumer's psychology of choice.

Moreover, this value is inflected by supply, but also by a commodity's marginal utility, as Shaw takes some pains to explain. Switching from donkeys to butter, he notes, "It is easy to say that butter is cheap when it is plentiful and dear when it is scarce" (252), but that assumes that the value of the currency used is stable (what Shaw deems the most important duty of a nation's government). Equally important, continuing to mine his trove of examples from domestic economy, Shaw argues that if a manufacturer of needles makes ten times more product than anyone wants, "then their needles will fetch nothing as needles because no woman will pay anything for the one needle she wants if there are nine lying about to be had for nothing" (257). The tenth doughnut, the tenth soft drink, the tenth ham sandwich—desperately hungry or thirsty people will pay dearly for the first or second of these, but after consuming them another choice might prove of more value: an antacid, for instance. Value relates to supply, as Shaw clearly understood, but a myriad of other factors make its calculation more than an "easy" task.

Without getting too far ahead of myself, it might be added that in *The Philosophy of Money* Georg Simmel meditates upon both utility and scarcity, arriving at a similar and more psychically resonant analysis of the relationship of value to both. Simmel notes that, in general, to be of value an object is thought to possess at least some utility; by comparison, scarcity is a "relative" and "quantitative" factor, signifying only the relationship between the object in question and a "total available amount" of it. Quickly, however, he discounts the explanatory power of utility, observing that we "desire, and therefore value economically, all kinds of things that cannot be called useful or serviceable without arbitrarily straining ordinary linguistic usage." Given this perspective, the concept of "utility" may merely be another term, perhaps even a diverting euphemism or rationalization, for "desire" itself (*Money*, 96). This is hardly surprising, given that in Simmel's *Lebensphilosophie*—or philosophy of life—"subject and object" occupy an epistemological and ontological "common ground"[40]

In any event, from the marginalist perspective value exists within a complex "psychology of choice" and its ever-vigilant monitoring of anticipated pleasure or pain, positive and negative satisfaction. As such, value represents neither the labor required to produce a commodity nor the price charged to acquire it. Nor is it reducible to money. Value emanates from an economy of desire; consequently, providing an accurate cartography of every psychical highway or avenue it travels, every backroad it might be found with its motor humming, is a daunting undertaking. For, although one can reliably predict where the circuit of desire might end—in the meeting of subject and object—determining the origin(s) and itineraries of the journey is another matter. At base, it might be argued, the process of making such determinations resembles the analytical work of excavating the latent content or repository of thoughts underlying the manifest content of dreams in Freudian psychoanalysis. In their articulations of the commercial marketplace with the operations of human desire, both Jevons and Wicksteed intimate this interpretive labor conducted at the intersection of economics and psychology.

However, perhaps no one at the *fin de siècle* of the nineteenth century addressed these matters more meticulously and capaciously than Simmel in *The Philosophy of Money*. As David Frisby recalls in his introduction to the English translation of the text—first published, again and curiously enough, in the same year as Freud's *The Interpretation of Dreams*—the genealogy of this study includes both Simmel's delivery of a paper entitled "The Psychology of Money" in 1889 and his address some seven years later to the Society of Austrian Economists whose ranks included Carl Menger.[41] Rather surprisingly, it would be 78 years before *The Philosophy of Money* received its first translation into English, one of several reasons why Elizabeth S. Goodstein characterizes it as a leading candidate for the title of "the twentieth century's most significant mostly unread theoretical text."[42] This history of neglect is being revised, however, by scholars working in a wide number of fields, and in a very modest way I aspire to be one of them by urging its complementarity to the material psychology of Freud—and Shaw—and summarizing its contribution to an intellectual formation at the close of the nineteenth century which included economics, psychology (including affect study), and performance. Without expanding upon Freud and Simmel's shared presumption of a so-called "deep structure," for example, Frisby gestures toward this notion by identifying the starting point of Simmel's analysis of the workings of money as the "surface level of economic affairs" or, alternatively, "the details and superficialities of life." Only after examining these, Frisby notes, can a "guideline" be dropped into the "ultimate depths" (latent content?) of meaning. Economics, psychoanalysis, sociology, cultural criticism—the "philosophy of money," insofar as it informs notions of value in a modernity in which a monetary economy was ascendant and, more particularly, insofar as it inflects the interior life of the modern "economico-psychic" subject, inevitably requires the disciplinary insights of all of these.[43] As Simmel emphasizes, "objective value" is more than a metric invoked in exchange; it also amounts to a "psychological fact," one "that can no more be altered than can reality itself" (*Money*, 65).

The thoughtful, multidisciplinary reflections on this "psychological fact" in *The Philosophy of Money* allow John Tarleton's claim that "There's money in me" to be unpacked in several ways, an opportunity which is hardly surprising given the expansiveness of Simmel's thought. Yet, as I have suggested, and unlike his two better-known contemporaries, Simmel has only occasionally been remembered outside of small circles of highly specialized academicians working mainly in sociology. Introducing one of the earlier American studies and selected translations of his writing, and paradoxically intimating one reason for his relative neglect, editor Kurt H. Wolff alludes to the "catholicity and originality of his intellect," collecting in his anthology discussions of everything from Simmel's treatment of the Kantian question "How Is Society Possible?" to his brief essays on the formal aesthetics of handles and the expressiveness of the human face.[44] In the inaugural pages of her study *Georg Simmel and the Disciplinary Imaginary* (2017), Goodstein endeavors to explain the enormous irony that a writer as prolific as Simmel, author of more than two dozen books and hundreds of articles and someone who today would be labelled a "public intellectual," could remain so marginalized. This is especially puzzling given the wide influence not only of *The Philosophy of Money*, but also of Simmel's *Sociology* (1908), commonly regarded as a founding text of formal sociology.

One seemingly absurd explanation for this neglect is that, like money itself and its analysis, Simmel's thought spanned a multitude of discourses and disciplines, perhaps too many. Like Shaw, Simmel wrote about the arts, on Goethe and Rembrandt for instance; like Shaw the journalist, Simmel also contributed to widely read periodicals and, in Simmel's case, an avant-garde art magazine; like Shaw's, his public speaking—more specifically, his lectures at the University of Berlin—attracted large crowds.[45] Both men wrote admiringly, even rapturously, about the Italian actress Eleonora Duse (a figure to be taken up in a later chapter), Simmel in one of his 25 brief "snapshots" published between 1897–1907 along with poems, short stories, fables, and other forms of writing.[46] This breadth of interest—his very substantial writing on philosophy, sociology, and cultural criticism, on the one hand, and his forays into fashion, gambling, and other "feuilletonistic fluff" (Goodstein's striking phrase) on the other— struck some academicians as too eclectic, too *undisciplined*. "Georg Simmel's marginality began during his lifetime," Goodstein writes, "with an academic career that combined international fame with a long series of rejections and professional slights at the hands of the German professoriate."[47] In these latter respects, his dilemma resembles the plights of his contemporaries. Shaw, particularly between 1876 and 1885, was no stranger to professional slights, collecting some 60 rejections for his novels from publishers and, as characterized by Pearson, growing "hardened" by his "persistent failure to obtain a word of encouragement."[48] Similarly, as he recalls in his "Autobiographical Study," Freud felt that he had "no followers" for most of the decade of the 1890s after his split with friend and collaborator Josef Breuer: "I was completely isolated. In Vienna I was shunned; abroad no notice was taken of me" and, as he noted resignedly, *The Interpretation of Dreams* scarcely received a review.[49]

Simmel's professional frustration during his lifetime, however, was more longstanding than Freud's or Shaw's, and disciplinarity, not just a catholic multi-disciplinarity, may also be a contributing factor in this. That is to say, today we almost automatically—and correctly—regard Freud as a psychoanalyst and Shaw as a playwright, even as we recognize their contributions to intellectual conversations well beyond these arenas. Simmel is a different matter. Although often lionized as the father of "formal sociology," Simmel himself bridled at this recognition, as he complained in an 1899 correspondence with French academic Célestin Bouglé: "It is altogether rather painful for me that abroad I am only known as a sociologist—whereas I am a philosopher, see my life's vocation [*Lebensaufgabe*] in philosophy, and only pursue sociology as a sideline" (qtd. in Goodstein, 41).[50] Unpacking this unusual disclaimer, Goodstein observes that his oeuvre is "situated at what were during his lifetime relatively permeable boundaries between philosophy and social science." As a result, it is "misleading to think of Simmel either as a sociologist who also philosophized or as a philosopher who happened to participate in the emergent discipline of sociology."[51] That is to say, in Simmel and Shaw's time boundaries between academic disciplines did not exist with the force and clarity in evidence today as inscribed by specific journals, curricula, professorships, and the turf wars endemic to a higher education obsessed with tuition revenue. Yet another factor in Simmel's uneven reception— and in his inability to secure a university professorship until 1914, four years before his death—may have been that, like his contemporary Max Nordau as described by Shaw, Simmel was possessive of a "cosmopolitan sensibility" and cultivated a "cosmopolitan approach" that some of his peers used as a rationalization to conceal their anti-Semitism.[52]

Although he would hardly have been the only victim of the misguided belief in Germany that a "Jewish threat" imperiled the contemporary university, there is little question that anti-Semitism contributed to his difficulty obtaining the professorship he richly deserved.[53]

This history and Simmel's long overdue recognition aside, his work can inform our reading of Shaw. One Simmelian way of understanding Tarleton's claim in *Misalliance*, for example, is also more obviously Freudian than Wicksteedian (if such an adjective can be admitted): that is to say, because value is inextricably linked to desire, human subjects are completed by an object of desire. Yet, before "quarrying" (Frisby and Goodstein's metaphor of choice) *The Philosophy of Money* for veins of insights to deploy in a reading of Shaw's characters (and of Shaw himself), I want to admit to mobilizing Simmel's text in a way to which Goodstein quite reasonably objects. That is to say, she mounts a persuasive case for regarding *The Philosophy of Money* as not only a work of modernist philosophy, but also as one that provides a "unified account of a fragmented reality" shaped by "the modern money economy." As such, and even though it has been hailed as "the founding text of the sociology of modernity," this sociological project is finally "ancillary to its philosophical objectives."[54] In a section of her book devoted to "Reading Simmel's *Philosophy of Money*," Goodstein expands upon these philosophical ambitions, one of which is to integrate attention to "the phenomena of everyday social and cultural life with nuanced reflection on their philosophical and historical significance."[55] Gleaning or "quarrying" *The Philosophy of Money* for single observations thus may have the deleterious effect of obscuring this more holistic project, as it also minimizes the import of Simmel's last chapter "The Style of Life." Here, unlike Nordau in *Degeneration*, Simmel does not bemoan the exhausting pace of modernity, allege its production of hysteria, or diagnose a debilitating fatigue endemic to modern cities in particular; nor does he accuse the period's most significant figures— Henrik Ibsen, Friedrich Nietzsche, and, worst of them all, Richard Wagner—of degeneracy.[56] Rather, he considers the ramifications of money's hegemonic rise and its installation "as a purpose," its distortion of *collective* cultural values, the rise of occupations that lack any specific content "except making money" (agents, traders, and so on), and more (*Money*, 365–70). As illuminating as these analyses of money and modernity are—and as useful as they might be in deciphering the workings of the neoliberal and global economic governance that defines our own century[57]—their consideration here would distract us from the project of engaging the operations of money and value in Shaw's depictions of the modern subject.

Tarleton gazing into a mirror in *Misalliance* and seeing not an ego-ideal, or his ideal ego,[58] but a figure he despised, underscores the significance of the subject-object relationship in Shavian thought, as it is in Simmelian and Freudian theory. In Chap. 2 of *The Philosophy of Money*, "Value and Money," Simmel describes the primitive "state" at the beginning of "mental life" in which "the Ego and its objects are not yet differentiated" (66); later, the "I" recognizes objects external to itself, and at this moment "subject and object are born." Similarly, in "Libido Theory and Narcissism" Freud speculates that preceding the birth of the object and "object-libido," narcissism or the ideal ego finding gratification in himself defines the psychical state of things: "… It is probable that this narcissism is the universal and original state of things, from which object-love is only later developed" (*SE* 16: 416). The space between subject and objects of desire prefigures the distance between subject and commodity, with value contingent upon both this distance and the object's resistance to possession. However, this is only one nexus between Freud and Simmel—and Shaw. As Lacan, following Freud, posits the complete indifference of the *drive* to its objects, Simmel also distinguishes between desire and what he terms "demand" or the "crude impulse," which "wants to release itself towards an object and to be satisfied…. [It] pays no attention to its bearer on one side or its object on the other" (68). Value is "reinstated as contrast, as an object separated from the subject"; the "possibility of desire is the possibility of the objects of desire," and objects are "not difficult to acquire because they are valuable, but we call those objects valuable that resist our desire to possess them" (69). (Think here of Lina's disruption of Tarleton's world and her function as resisting his resurgent desire.) Subtending the surface of exchange, therefore, resides a determinative subjective history:

> Exchange presupposes an objective measurement of subjective valuations, not in the sense of being chronologically prior, but in the sense that both phenomena arise from the same act. (85)

Finally, Simmel's thesis that "*every* valuation is supported by an elaborate complex of feelings which are always in a process of flux, adjustment and change" (my emphasis, 91) complements Freud's ideas about objects—at times, seemingly trivial ones—and affect production in dreams.

Although insights like this these map more readily onto Freud's psychoanalysis than Wicksteed's marginalism, most are compatible with marginalism (which is not surprising given the reciprocal relationship between these discourses). Even Simmel's diminution of the concept of utility, which he subsumes under the larger psychical umbrella of desire, parallels the tenets of Jevonian and other marginalist economics. So, too, is Simmel's understanding of the role of "sacrifice," a kind of synonym for Jevons and Wicksteed's conception of pain, in the calculation of value: Value is determined not by the relationship to the demanding subject, but by the fact that this relation depends on the cost of a sacrifice ..." (85); in this way, subjective appraisals mimic the operations of economic systems (or vice versa), balancing sacrifice with gain. Yet, in a manner even more elaborate than the discourse of marginalism which frequently illustrates concepts by juxtaposing *fin de siècle* economic practices with those of earlier periods, Simmel wields a vast knowledge of exchange in primitive societies and earlier epochs in European history in his analysis of value and the hegemonic rise of a "money economy."[59]

Simmel's historical knowledge of money and value creates yet another context for parsing characters' introspections in *Misalliance*, in this instance not Tarleton's claim that money is in him, but rather Lina's insistence on learning what she is worth. In his fifth chapter on "The Money Equivalent of Personal Values," Simmel considers three historical instances in which money served as an equivalence for the worth of a person: wergild, slavery, and marriage, the last use including societies in which men were expected to provide emoluments to the families of their brides and, alternatively, those in which dowries were paid by the father of the bride ("profectitious" dowries). Wergild, or the atonement of murder by monetary payment, is of less relevance for our purposes, although it does provide an historical instance of a person's worth being equated with a specific monetary sum. Simmel notes that in Anglo-Saxon England 2700 shillings was legally required as compensation for the murder of a king, far more than the 200 shillings demanded for the killing of an ordinary freeman. Yet if such historical facts and specific cultural practices may seem tangential to our purposes, Simmel's inferences from them are not. For wergild "illustrates that the tendency to reduce the value of man to a monetary expression is so powerful that it is realized even at the expense of objective accuracy." This tendency "not only makes money the measure of man, but it also makes man the measure of the value of money" (385).

And women, too. Purchasing women, or the mandate in some cultures that purchase was a prerequisite for marriage, in one sense testifies to their intrinsic value, as men sacrificed a portion of their material wealth to secure a partner in marriage. However, this value is dubious. Citing analogies between this practice and prostitution, analogies that Shaw exploits in *Mrs. Warren's Profession*, Simmel delineates the ways in which such practices diminish women, reducing them to objects and marriage to the sexual act. The "terrible degradation" of prostitution, Simmel writes, is "most clearly expressed by its monetary equivalent," insofar as in prostitution a woman "surrenders her most intimate and most personal quality" for a "totally impersonal, purely extraneous and objective compensation" (408). He is quick to add, however, that such a critical view is in no way universally endorsed, as in ancient Asia "girls of all classes prostituted themselves in order to obtain a dowry" and suffered no loss of reputation as a result (411). By contrast, in contemporary society money and women's sexual "honour" are linked in a different relationship. Wergild became impossible when the value of human life rose and that of money declined; similarly, as the "special significance" of individuals ascended in western mores, the relationship between money and marriage changed with it (411). Herein resides a kind of paradox: as the money economy grew more pervasive in western modernity, its power to form an equivalence—or its use as a codicil in the marriage contract—declined. Money became, in short, inadequate, for while it may exist *in* people like Tarleton, it was incommensurate in terms of assessing the value *of* people. Yet this incommensurability in no way diminishes the pervasive effects of money on both modern culture and the modern subject. Again, although Simmel in the best traditions of modernist writers, thinkers, and artists was attempting "to foster new modes of human self-understanding adequate to a world in radical—aesthetic, cultural, political—flux,"[60] my focus is trained, for the most part, on the internal worlds and feelings of Shaw and his characters.

Just as value, wealth, and self-assessment inform *Misalliance*, they permeate the canon of Shaw's writing and emerge in his own views of marriage as well. Vivie Warren is repulsed by the idea that marriage to Crofts would, one day, make her a wealthy widow; and the beautiful young woman who narrates "Don Giovanni Explains" begins her narration by ridiculing the relationship between money and marriage. The "proof" of her prettiness and marital eligibility, as I have mentioned earlier, is that men "waste a good deal of time and money in making themselves ridiculous about me" (*Short* 95). As she grew accustomed to her suitors' silliness, she began to realize that this spectacle had more to do with the men's childishness—their delight in being tickled irrespective of the source of the pleasant irritation—than her own allure. In addition, while the topic of marriage and money is foregrounded in such later plays as *The Millionairess* and *Buoyant Billions*, it is equally prominent in Shaw's view of his evolving relationship with Charlotte Payne-Townsend, whom he met in late January, 1896, a time in his life that Michael Holroyd describes as "the perfect moment." As is well known, Charlotte came to London with the considerable wealth of her Derry family, a wealth to which Shaw alluded in correspondence with friends, but in which he claimed to take no interest. In a October 6, 1896 letter to William Archer, he characterized Charlotte as "my Irish lady with the light green eyes and the million of money" (*CL* 1: 676). In the same letter, he describes his relationships with actresses Florence Farr and Janet Achurch, conceding that until he turned 29 he was simply "too shabby for any woman to tolerate" him (*CL* 1: 677), implying that the impecuniosity responsible for his seediness had been ameliorated. In his correspondence with Ellen Terry some few weeks later, he reiterated his feeling about marriage and money: "Love falling in love—but, mind, only with her, not with the million."[61] In a November 16 letter, he playfully boasts about his salutary effect on Charlotte's health, who experienced pangs of anxiety and disrupted sleep before meeting him. Sensing an opportunity for humor, Shaw asks Terry whether Charlotte should be charged 5000 pounds a year and her hand in marriage for these remedies. He answers his own question with a mild chiding of his celebrated interlocutor: "What kind of swindler and fortune hunter do you take me for?" (*CL* 1: 702). Returning to the topic of marriage and money over a half-century later in *Sixteen Self Sketches*, Shaw recalls that "Not until I was past 40 did I earn enough money to marry without seeming to marry for money" ... (115). The relationship between marriage and money that Simmel traced through a variety of cultures had changed, but it had not disappeared. Shaw felt its pressures acutely, as do several characters in his novels, most of them women.

His disinterest in Charlotte's fortune notwithstanding, Shaw, like Tarleton, had money *in* him. Even as he implied to Archer that his period of abject poverty was well behind him, the fear of poverty still haunted him. This emerges in a startling admission to Terry in a letter of November 30, 1896 after engaging in a flurry of activity that included the completion of a draft of *The Devil's Disciple*:

> I finished my play today—what do you think of that? Does that look like wasting my time? Three acts, six scenes, a masterpiece all completed in a few

weeks, with a trip to Paris and those Ibsen articles thrown in [on *Peer Gynt* and *Little Eyolf*] ...

[But] now that the play is finished (in the rough) I shall try to earn a little supplemental money—not that I really want it; but I have always been so poor as to coin that nothing can persuade me now that I am not on the verge of bankruptcy. (*CL* 1: 705)

If Shaw did not "really want" or *need* money in 1896, he didn't in 1912 either. Holroyd emphasizes Shaw's enormous success with *Fanny's First Play*, which opened in April, 1911 at the Little Theatre before moving to the Kingsway Theatre on January 1, 1912 and enjoying a 622-performance run. But well before the play closed, his and Charlotte's wealth proved sufficient in the summer of 1911 to finance a 16-week recuperative holiday—Shaw was suffering from exhaustion—in which the couple and their driver visited some 40 towns in the Alps, Dolomites, and elsewhere.[62] Shaw began *Androcles and the Lion* in January, 1912 and completed a draft of *Pygmalion* in June, shortly thereafter resuming his correspondence with Mrs. Patrick (Stella) Campbell professing both his admiration of her and his desire that she play Liza. Yet even in this playful, affectionate correspondence, Shaw's concerns about money surface. In a letter on August 19, 1912, he reveals his advice to the producer of *Fanny's First Play*, who had a contract to stage Harley Granville Barker's *The Voysey Inheritance* that he needed to honor, to close his still very popular play at the cost of his own income. He reassures Stella that he is nonetheless as "anxious as anyone can be to have a lucrative success with *Pygmalion*," and then jokingly adds, "As the gentleman in *Bleak House* says, il fo [sic] manger."[63]

By 1912, Shaw was not so impecunious as to be concerned about eating, and his use of the term "anxious," as opposed to an innocuous term like "eager," is more indicative of his efforts to recruit Stella Campbell than it is revelatory of his "existential anxiety." Still, his admission to Ellen Terry that *nothing* could convince him that he had escaped destitution—income from a long-running play or the financial wherewithal to take extended holidays—confirms the fact that, like Tarleton in *Misalliance*, money and the feelings associated with having it or losing it are indeed *in* him. And one could ask, "Why wouldn't they be?" If accomplishing nothing else, Simmel, Freud, and the marginalists delineate the myriad ways in which commodity consumption, value, and materialism—and money itself—insinuate themselves into our psychical lives, waking and dreaming.

The "style" of modern life, Simmel writes, "in so far as it is dependent on the relationship between objective and subjective culture, is tied up with money transactions." Moreover, for Simmel one ineluctable force obtains in the modern moment: the "superior power of the culture of objects over the culture of individuals" (*Money* 508). How could Shaw be any more impervious to this force than anyone else?

Epilogue: On Shaw's Dreams

Of course, he wasn't. In *Sixteen Self Sketches* Shaw acknowledges an "economic link" between several of his most celebrated characters—Cashel Byron, Sartorius, Mrs. Warren, and Andrew Undershaft—and, specifically, this commonality is that all of them prospered through "questionable activities" (the interrogation of analogies between prize fighting, slum tenement ownership, prostitution, munitions making, will have to wait for another occasion). More to the point, Shaw asks, "Would anyone but a buffleheaded idiot of a university professor … infer that all my plays were written as economic essays, and not as plays of life, character, and human destiny like those of Shakespear or Euripides?" (89). The answer must be an emphatic "no," for even the most intellectually challenged member of the professoriate, when sober, can distinguish plays from essays. Rather, as Freud and Simmel demonstrate, "life"—psychical life as well as social and cultural life—is vitally informed by "economic" matters; consequently, "plays of life" must inevitably include the realities of economics, even if the thrust of the economic does not drive a play's conflict, but is limited in scope only to the ambition of an Undershaft or Sartorius.

Money plays a part in this character construction and in the material psychology that this chapter has attempted to describe. Also, as was the case with Freud's dreams and those of his patients, money eventually found its way into Shaw's dreams, perhaps more often than sex did. While summarizing his sexual experiences to Frank Harris in a letter of June 24, 1930, he frankly reports his "very unfrequent [sic]" and "involuntary incontinences" in "dreamland" (*SSS* 113).[64] In a more frequent and recurrent dream, Shaw anxiously returned to his unhappy days as a clerk with an estate agent while working as a teenager in Dublin:

> I sometimes dream that I am back in that office again, bothered by a consciousness that a long period has elapsed during which I have neglected my most important duties. I have drawn no money at the bank in the mornings,

nor lodged any in the afternoons.... Whole estates must have been sold up, widows and orphans left to starve, mortgages foreclosed, and the landed gentry of Ireland abandoned to general ruin.... I generally wake in the act of asking my principals, with the authority which belongs to my later years, whether they realize what has happened, and whether they propose to leave so disgracefully untrustworthy a person as myself in a position of such responsibility. (*SSS* 36–37)

Several elements of Shaw's dream resemble those of Freud and his patients. The temporal condensation of Shaw's dream, for example, and his querying of his principals with an authority he acquired in his later years parallels the temporal compressions of the dream of Elise L.'s trip to the half-empty theatre. The prominence of money, mortgages, and other debts, along with the potentially disastrous consequences of Shaw's inaction, are reminiscent of the accusation in Freud's dream of the *table d'hôte* of his failure to pay for things.

The most significant elements of Shaw's dream, however, are its recurrence, its performative dimension, and its production of negative affect. That is, when he notes that the dream "generally" concludes—or, alternatively, that he typically awakens at the same moment in the narrative—he is confirming that this dream has visited him on numerous occasions. More important, the climactic appearance of his principals seems crucial, for in the dream Shaw is performing his gross incompetence in front of others, much as several dreams Freud recounts occur at dinners or receptions where he plays various social roles. Most crucially, the dream concludes with Shaw's sharp self-recrimination as "disgracefully untrustworthy." This feeling contrasts with those that accompany his other memories of his time as a budding businessman when he gave himself "certain airs" and, when traveling on business for his firm, did so "first class" with little challenge to the amount of expenses he accrued. Behind or beneath this performance of the rising young titan of business resided a nervous youth worried about his possible incompetence. As he admits while ventriloquizing Harris in "How Frank Ought to Have Done It" later in *Sixteen Self Sketches*, Shaw was "an incorrigible and continuous actor, using his skill deliberately in his social life" (124). But it was an uneasy talent. The dream, like his fear of social encounters and his later anxiety that the wealth he had amassed could not ensure his financial solvency, was *in* him. And thus in this latter way, like Tarleton in *Misalliance*, money was in him as well.

Navigating an ever-expanding money economy and living a frenetic urban reality may make such dreams inevitable. It may also be the case that at the end of the nineteenth century thinkers such as Freud and Shaw were, as Elizabeth Goodstein describes Simmel, "hypersensitive urban subjects."[65] Both Freud and Shaw harbored special affection for their mothers and were emotionally more distant from their fathers; both loathed life in Vienna and Dublin, preferring, respectively, the woods and fresh air of Freiberg and the beauty of Dalkey, south of Dublin, where Shaw could "see such pictures as no painter could make for me" (*SSS*, 72). In fact, somewhat uncannily, as elderly men both vividly recalled what Shaw described as the "one moment of ecstatic happiness in my childhood" at sites removed from the grinds of urban modernity: Shaw in *Sixteen Self Sketches* and Freud in 1931 at the unveiling of a bronze tablet at his birthplace. Both also endured years of poverty as they attempted to carve out professional lives: Freud's poverty prevented him from pursuing academic publishing for some five years between 1886 and 1891—"assuring" his "material existence" and that of his family were more important—and Shaw's poverty has already been discussed.[66] For all of these reasons, both inhabited in their dreams an irreducibly materialist theatre, where value, feeling, money, and the social consequences of wealth frequently occupied the limelight. Much the same might be said of the protagonists of Shaw's first two novels, particularly Robert Smith of *Immaturity*, to whom I now turn.

Notes

1. When Freud returned to the topic of dreaming later in his career, he frequently deployed a similar rhetorical strategy of refuting prevalent misconceptions about dreams, their origins, and their relationships to other phenomena. Such is the case, for example, in his 1922 paper "Dreams and Telepathy" delivered to the Vienna Psychoanalytical Society. All quotations from Freud's works come from *The Standard Edition of the Complete Psychological Works of Sigmund Freud*, 24 vols., trans. James Strachey (London: The Hogarth Press and the Institute for Psycho-analysis, 1953). Quoted excerpts will be followed by volume and page numbers in the text.
2. Cannon Schmitt, "Interpret or Describe?" *Representations* 135 (Summer 2016): 104. This article appears in a special issue of the journal on "Description across the Disciplines" and contains a valuable meta-narrative on reading methodology. One of Schmitt's juxtapositions of narration with description hints at the point I am attempting to make about the ways in

which dream narratives as interpreted by Freud match the semiotically rich quality of narration as theorized by Georg Lukács, the subject of Schmitt's argument: "Animated living narration; static, dead description: that of the 'fat and the living' to 'the thin and the dead'" (104).
3. Freud continued to insist on this level of attentiveness and expansive sense of inquiry in exploring the thoughts underlying dream contents. In Lecture VII on "The Manifest Content of Dreams and the Latent Dream-Thoughts" in his *Introductory Lectures on Psychoanalysis*, for example, he is adamant that the dreamer "must not hold back any idea from us," which includes not only seemingly unimportant details, but also "disagreeable" truths that a patient might be reluctant to report (*SE* 15: 115).
4. Freud identifies the overdetermined nature of both images and affects often in *The Interpretation of Dreams*. In reflecting upon the significance of "trimethylamine" in the so-called "Dream of Irma's Injection," for instance, he recognizes that "so many important subjects converged upon that one word" (*SE* 4: 117); and, in his chapter "Affect in Dreams," Freud concludes that "it appears that affects in dreams are fed from a confluence of several sources and are over-determined in their reference to the material of the dream-thoughts" (*SE* 5: 480). Freud adduces examples of composite pictures in several chapters, some of the most useful occurring in "The Work of Condensation" (*SE* 4: 292–93) and later (*SE* 4: 320–22).
5. See "The Relation of Dreams to Waking Life" (*SE* 4: 7–10), where Freud refutes an earlier generation of commentators who regarded dreamers as "removed" from the "world of waking consciousness" (7).
6. It is hardly accidental that "fungible" originates in the Latin *fungi*, to perform. Substitution in exchange is a kind of performance of equivalences, Crofts' "hard money" in *Mrs. Warren's Profession* for whatever he values, for example.
7. Biographers routinely describe Shaw's difficult early years in London. Hesketh Pearson, for example, depicts his "indescribable seediness" in the later 1870s and early 1880s. This abject poverty was accompanied by his anxiety about social encounters, an anxiety that motivated both his study of books of etiquette and his membership in The Zetetical Society, a debating club where he could practice his public speaking. See Pearson, *Bernard Shaw: His Life and Personality* (London: St. James's Library, 1942), 62–74. Growing up in the Leopoldstadt section of Vienna, a Jewish district, Freud also experienced the results of considerable financial difficulty. Peter Gay in *Freud: A Life for Our Times* (New York: W.W. Norton, 1988) notes that the "majority" of residents "huddled in badly overcrowded, unprepossessing quarters. The Freuds were with that majority" (13). Freud acknowledged that in those days his family lived in "very straitened circumstances" (qtd. in Gay, 25).

8. As I suggested in the acknowledgements to this book, not only do the dates of Shaw's, Freud's, and Simmel's births make them contemporaries, but they also share a kind of ironic kindred as all three reached their middle age near the end of the nineteenth century. Again, Shaw and Freud were born, respectively, in July and May of 1856; Simmel, less than two years later in March of 1858. By the end of the century, all three were well-published writer-intellectuals, although all three—Simmel in particular—were buffeted by criticism and were tormented by feelings of isolation. This topic is discussed later in the chapter.
9. Although he refers to contemporary research in psychology, Nordau, as might be expected given the date of publication of *Degeneration*, does not draw upon Freud's work. Instead, many of his comments on psychology, hysteria, and related topics are indebted to the research of such notable figures as Richard von Krafft-Ebbing, Jean-Martin Charcot, Alfred Binet, and others. See, for example, "Book One" of *Dengeneration*, English translation (London: William Heinemann, 1898), 1–44. Shaw's charge that Nordau was seduced by "mock scientific theory" and "sham-science" (*MCE* 330, 331) is thus not aimed at Freudian psychoanalysis. In *Sixteen Self Sketches*, however, the elder Shaw makes occasional sorties against psychoanalysis and Freud himself. In Chapter IX, "Who I Am, and What I Think," reprinted from a "catechism" he wrote years earlier, the elder Shaw provides this parenthetical interpolation: "When I wrote this in 1901, I did not believe that an author so utterly void of delicacy as Sigmund Freud could not only come into human existence, but become as famous and even instructive by his defect as a blind man might by writing essays on painting ..." (52).
10. See, for example, Mrs. Tarleton's advice to her daughter Hypatia in *Misalliance*. Recalling that she once regarded the aristocracy as a "nasty sneering lot," Mrs. Tarleton observes that it's "far worse when theyre civil, because that always means that they want you to lend them money; and you must never do that, Hypatia, because they never pay. How can they? They dont make anything, you see" (*CPP* 4: 121–22). She also confides that while her snobbish father "looked down" on her industrious husband, he was often forced to borrow money from him, a necessity that invariably "hurt his pride" (*CPP* 4: 135).
11. Goux, 22.
12. Goux, 30.
13. Freud's first three sets of lectures were actually delivered at the University of Vienna in October, 1915. In a footnote to Freud's lecture "Anxiety" in the *Introductory Lectures*, James Strachey emphasizes that "The problem of anxiety occupied Freud's mind throughout his life, and his views on it went through a number of changes" (*SE* 16: 392). This useful note directs

readers to several places in the *Standard Edition* where Freud refines his views of the topic.
14. See Lecture XXV "Anxiety," *SE* 16: 397–401. Here Freud defines three forms of neurotic anxiety, proceeding from more or less trivial phobias to anxieties of far greater import and physiological consequence including tremors, heart palpitations, and more.
15. Gray, 122.
16. Gray, 123.
17. Clover, 112. Clover quickly adds that not until "this moment, when value ceased to be, can it be priced" (112).
18. See *Interpretation* 4: 19 and 4: 44–45.
19. In Freud's "Bibliography A," this work is attributed to I. Delbœuf (*SE* 5: 689).
20. It is worth noting that in discussing *kosten*, a word that can mean both "cost" or "taste," Freud specifically mentions the serving of spinach in his dream of the *table d'hôte*. Earlier, I characterized the allusion to spinach as an aspect of narrative that, while seemingly insignificant, may accrue meaning, and in this instance it does. Freud conjectures that at such a meal a mother might need to cajole her children into tasting the spinach (in part, presumably, because its "cost" is already calculated in the *prix fixe* and to do otherwise would be to ignore or waste its "value").
21. See, for example, Marvin Carlson, *The Haunted Stage: The Theatre as Memory-Machine* (Ann Arbor: University of Michigan Press, 2001). Carlson cultivates the metaphor of haunting in particular as it relates to memory, finding memorial ghosts cultivated by prior theatre-going endemic to our responses to stage performance.
22. Paul Ricoeur, *Memory, History, Forgetting*, trans. Kathleen Blamey and David Pellauer (Chicago: University of Chicago Press, 2004), 69 (emphasis in original).
23. It is partly for this reason that Ricoeur later challenges the notion that forgetting is a sign of a dysfunctional memory: "… we shun the specter of a memory that would never forget anything. We even consider it to be monstrous." He wonders aloud if "appropriate memory" might have "something in common with the renunciation of total reflection" (413), an insight pertinent to a patient, like Freud's discontented young wife, who resists a dream analysis suggesting the low esteem with which she regards her husband.
24. See Goux, 28–29.
25. Shavians are well aware of Shaw's idiosyncratic method of punctuation, as evidenced in both the epigraph for this section and elsewhere: no apostrophe marks for contractions, for example, and a space between letters (m e)

rather than italics or underlining for emphasis. Throughout, Shaw's practices of punctuation will be retained without an explanatory note.
26. Holroyd, *Bernard Shaw: The Search for Love*, 178. Peter Gahan also discusses Shaw's regular "seminars with the leading economists of the day" and his bemused fascination with Wicksteed's "Jevonian curves" in *Bernard Shaw and Beatrice Webb on Poverty and Equality in the Modern World, 1905–1914*, 2–6.
27. See Pearson, 68–69.
28. Gray, 123.
29. Gray, 124.
30. William Stanley Jevons, *The Theory of Political Economy*, 2nd edition revised and enlarged (London: Macmillan and Company, 1879), 35, 37.
31. Jevons, 46.
32. See, for example, Holroyd, who regards Wicksteed's key contribution to value theory is his refutation of Marxist economists who "had failed to account for the obvious dependence of prices on supply and demand" (178). As *The Common Sense of Political Economy* (London: Macmillan and Company, 1910) shows, Wicksteed's conceptions of value and of marginalist economics more generally is far more nuanced than this brief summary would suggest.
33. Wicksteed, vii.
34. Wicksteed, 19.
35. Wicksteed, 25.
36. Jacques Lacan, *The Four Fundamental Concepts of Psycho-analysis*, trans. Alan Sheridan (New York and London: W.W. Norton, 1977), 168. Drive thus might be likened to a machine that is constantly turned on, which Jean LaPlanche implies when asserting that while an object may possess attributes that "trigger the satisfying action," no object "can satisfy the drive." See *Life and Death in Psychoanalysis*, trans. Jeffrey Mehlman (Baltimore: Johns Hopkins University Press, 1970), 11–13.
37. Wicksteed, 25–27.
38. Wicksteed, 40–41.
39. Through his meetings with Wicksteed and others, Shaw became acquainted with William Stanley Jevons's theories of money as a medium of exchange, a "common denominator" that can replace the supreme awkwardness and so-called "double coincidence" of a barter economy. In his 1905 preface to *The Irrational Knot*, Shaw reveals his familiarity with the work of "General Walker"—Francis Amasa Walker (1840–97), American economist and once president of MIT—who also demonstrated a keen familiarity with Jevons' theories. In the inaugural chapter of his book *Money* (New York: Henry Holt and Company, 1891), Walker reviews Jevons' several hypotheses about the functioning of money, mildly rebutting the notion that

money may serve as a "store of value" used for deferred payments (12). For a succinct discussion of money's four primary functions and insights into Jevons, see "The Money-Function," Walker, 1–23.
40. Joseph Bleicher, "Leben," *Theory, Culture and Society* 5 (2006): 343; as quoted in Henry Schermer and David Jary, *Form and Dialectic in Georg Simmel's Sociology: A New Interpretation* (Houndmill, Basingstoke: Palgrave Macmillan, 2013), 59.
41. David Frisby, "Introduction to the Translation," Georg Simmel, *The Philosophy of Money*, 1.
42. Elizabeth S. Goodstein, *Georg Simmel and the Disciplinary Imaginary* (Stanford: Stanford University Press, 2017), 137.
43. Frisby, "Introduction," 3.
44. Kurt H. Wolff, "Preface," *Georg Simmel, 1858–1918* (Columbus: The Ohio State University Press, 1959), ix.
45. In a 1963 lecture at the Leo Baeck Institute in New York City, Albert Salomon recalls attending Simmel's lectures at the University of Berlin in 1910, lectures so popular—a fact that apparently disturbed Simmel—they were held in the university's largest "classroom" (or lecture hall), which seated hundreds. The lectures were scheduled at an unattractive time specifically to keep the attendance to a number the hall could accommodate. See Salomon, "Georg Simmel Reconsidered," ed. Gary D. Jaworski, *International Journal of Politics, Culture and Society* 8.3 (1995): 362–63.
46. See "Selections from Simmel's Writing for the Journal *Jugend*," trans. Thomas B. Kemple, *Theory, Culture & Society*, 29 (7/8) (2012): 263–78. Simmel's interest in the theatre, like Shaw's, extended beyond the artistry of Eleonora Duse, and at the time of his death in 1918 Simmel had drafted a book on the sociology of stage acting which was stolen along with the suitcase in which it was conveyed and never recovered. Henry Schermer and David Jary discuss this incident in *Form and Dialectic in Georg Simmel's Sociology*, 54.
47. Goodstein, 15.
48. Pearson, 60.
49. In his biography, Gay recalls the encouragement, affection, and financial support Breuer lavished on Freud throughout the 1880s, a closeness that began to change in 1891 and by the end of the decade Freud's similar affection for Breuer had been shattered. See Gay, 67–69.
50. Schermer and Jary understand this matter slightly differently, citing a letter to Bouglé while writing *The Philosophy of Money* in which Simmel explains that he was "completely absorbed" by sociology (54). But this is so much small beer in light of their agreement with Goodstein on the "fluidity" of disciplines at the time and the fact that at the University of Berlin Simmel lectured on a wide variety of topics from several disciplines: logic, the philosophical aspects of Darwin's writing, and others. See Schermer and Jary, 50–56.
51. Goodstein, 7.

52. Simmel's lectures at Berlin University garnered an international "cosmopolitan" audience that troubled some German academics. Goodstein emphasizes his cosmopolitanism in her introductory chapter, especially 15–20. Also, as is well known, one of the negative valences of the term "cosmopolitan" is its cloaked anti-Semitism. Both Simmel and Freud experienced anti-Semitic hatred, Simmel in particular when seeking appointments as a university professor. As Peter Gay describes, borrowing from Freud's autobiographical account, Freud suffered anti-Semitic hostility in his early days at the University of Vienna, and in 1883 confronted several fellow passengers hurling ethnic slurs at him in a train car (27–28). Years later long after Simmel's death in 1918, his sociology was viewed "with suspicion" by the Third Reich, which banned his books during their rule (Goodstein, 143).

In a recent essay on Shaw's sharp review of Nordau's *Degeneration*, I discuss his characterization of Nordau as a "cosmopolitan Jew." Nevertheless, and paradoxically, Shaw also saw himself as far more cosmopolitan than nationalist. See, for example, "A Note on Aggressive Nationalism," *The New Statesman* July 12, 1913, rpt. In *The Matter with Ireland*, eds. David H. Greene and Dan H. Laurence (London: Rupert Hart-Davis, 1962), 81–84. And in his 1921 "Preface" to *Immaturity*, Shaw identifies himself as a European cosmopolitan, not an Irishman: "And so I am a tolerably good European in the Nietzschean sense, but a very bad Irishman in the Sinn Fein or Chosen People sense" (xxxviii–xxxix).

53. Albert Salomon discusses anti-Semitism at length in his lecture "Georg Simmel Reconsidered." He reminds his listeners that Simmel and his parents were baptized as Christians, a common practice among upper- and upper middle class Jews at the time, and that after later leaving the Protestant religion, Simmel never adopted the practices of Judaism. The so-called "Jewish threat" included the charges that Jewish academics sought to corrupt their youthful students and were corrosive of the "academic standards of moral and religious philosophy" (367). See Salomon, 364–68.

54. Goodstein, 140.

55. Goodstein, 149.

56. See Nordau, 34–44, and his protracted assault on Wagner in "The Richard Wagner Cult," 171–213. The opening chapters of *Degeneration* treat such topics as mass transportation, the chronic fatigue of the modern city-dweller, the frenzied pace of modern life, and the psychological impact of these developments. Shaw's take on life in the modern city was somewhat different. See Nelson O'Ceallaigh Ritschel, "Shaw, Murder, and the Modern Metropolis," *SHAW 32: The Annual of Bernard Shaw Studies*, ed. Desmond Harding (University Park: The Pennsylvania State University Press, 2012), 102–16. Ritschel recounts the circumstances of Shaw's writing the letter "Blood Money to Whitechapel" on September 24, 1888,

which connects Jack the Ripper's assaults with slum housing conditions, thus making the "comfortable classes" complicit in the commission of these savage crimes (107). For the larger context of these atrocities, see Ritschel's *Bernard Shaw, W.T. Stead, and the New Journalism*, 9–58.
57. See Austin Harrington and Thomas B. Kemple, "Introduction: Georg Simmel's 'Sociological Metaphysics': Money, Sociality, and Precarious Being," *Theory, Culture & Society* 29 (7/8) (2012): 16–20. Here, Harrington and Kemple describe Simmel's applicability in reading the pervasive effects of money in our own century: its flattening out of "customary ties of economic reciprocity," for example, and its creation not of liquefaction, but rather of rigid monetized debt relations and a "veneer of spurious moral authority" (17).
58. In *The Four Fundamental Concepts of Psycho-Analysis*, Lacan makes this distinction as it connects to the child seeing himself (or herself) in the mirror: "By clinging to the reference-point of him who looks at him in a mirror, the subject sees appearing, not his ego ideal, but his ideal ego, that point at which he desires to gratify himself in himself" (257).
59. This claim, admittedly, is slightly unfair to the marginalists. For example, in his *Money and the Mechanism of Exchange* (1900), Jevons constructs useful histories of coins, the use of metals as currency, and systems of metallic money, adducing numerous examples from ancient cultures, primitive ones, and European history, recent and more remote. See Jevons, 40–65 and 85–103.
60. Goodstein, 152.
61. Holroyd, *Bernard Shaw, Volume 1*: 435. Here Holroyd is quoting from Shaw's letters.
62. See Michael Holroyd, *Bernard Shaw, Volume 2: 1898–1918: The Pursuit of Power* (New York: Random House, 1989), 282.
63. Bernard Shaw, Letter to Stella Campbell, 19 August 1912, in *Bernard Shaw and Mrs. Patrick Campbell: Their Correspondence*, ed. Alan Dent (London: Victor Gollancz, 1952), 40–41. Stella replied gaily on August 31, "It's a real delight to read this nonsensical play of yours. But I *do* wonder what you'll do without me for Eliza" (41).
64. This letter appears in its entirety in both Harris's biography (234–38) and in *Collected Letters, 1926–1950*, vol. 4: 190–93. The former is a more fastidiously punctuated version of the latter.
65. Goodstein, 17.
66. Freud, "An Autobiographical Study," *SE* 20: 18. In *Freud: A Life for Our Time*, Peter Gay repeats the 75-year-old Freud's remarks at the unveiling: "Deep within me, covered over, there still lives that happy child from Freiberg …" (9).

CHAPTER 3

"UNASHAMED": Negative Affect, Money, and Performance in *Immaturity* and *The Irrational Knot*

In his "Preface to *Major Barbara*," Bernard Shaw engages with a topic that he spent much of his life contemplating: the power of money, which he ordained the "most important thing in the world" (*CPP* 1: 311–312). Shaw adds ideological and sociological dimension to his claim by adducing such instances of the far-reaching influence of money as its imbrication in "our social conscience"; its determinative power in shaping cultural conceptions of beauty, strength, and honor; and, most damningly, its complicity in causing poverty, what Andrew Undershaft indicts in act three of *Major Barbara* as "the worst of crimes."[1] In Undershaft's dilation of this point, poverty is implicated in, even responsible for, the blighting of cities, the spread of pestilence and disease, the erosion of the human spirit, and the cold-blooded murder of the "happiness of society." Like Freud and Simmel, whose intellectual work crosses the boundaries of psychology, sociology, and economics, Undershaft, the non academic former "east ender," identifies poverty's pervasive effects from the vantage afforded by several of these disciplines. Penetrating the very core of individual subjectivity, he contends, poverty "strikes dead the very souls of all who come within sight, sound or smell of it"; and, as hypocritically redacted in social policy, the suffering poor *force* the ruling class to defer their "own liberties and to organize unnatural cruelties for fear [the poor] should rise" against them (*CPP* 1: 434). But perhaps his most intriguing insight for my purposes—one redolent with irony as it is delivered in an ersatz Garden City that, as Susan Cannon Harris describes, has been "wholly captured by capitalism"[2]— emerges in his homily to Barbara, Cusins, and Lady Britomart in the play's concluding act in which he attributes to money the power to lift "seven millstones" from "Man's" neck: food, clothing, firing, rent, taxes, respectability, and children (*CPP* 1: 434).

At first glance, Undershaft's millstones seem little more than an eccentric congeries of biological needs (food, clothing, shelter, and energy), legal and familial obligations (the payment of taxes and the support of children) and, oddly, the feeling or status of respectability. Whether originating internally—John Tarleton's *disrespect* for his image in a mirror in *Misalliance*, for instance—or signifying the (dis)esteem with which one is held by others, "respectability" seems weirdly out of place in this list. In what body of philosophical or psychological theory is the drive for respectability equivalent to that for food and water (or libidinal gratification)?[3] More simply put, how is the impetus for respectability analogous in force to that of a biological drive? From the Lacanian and Simmelian perspective summarized in the preceding chapter, *drive* differs from desire, in part, by taking no notice whatsoever of the object satisfying it; the object of the drive, as Lacan stipulates, is a "matter of total indifference." Starving people are driven to ease their hunger by consuming whatever is available, even grass or blighted potatoes as was the case during the Great Famine in nineteenth-century Ireland; people must take in water or fluids in order to survive. Similarly, Simmel understands brute sexual instinct to take no notice of an object providing gratification, an indifference which in turn underlies his abhorrence of the "terrible degradation that is inherent in prostitution."[4] But how is the desire for "respectability" in any way analogous in force to these kinds of imperatives?

Shaw's prefaces to *Immaturity* and *The Irrational Knot* suggest, in fact, that it is not; or, more accurately, that while one *must* have sustenance and shelter, respectability is hardly worth having at all, although my later reading of *An Unsocial Socialist* will suggest that, in fact, such matters as esteem, prestige, and class affiliation motivate the actions of many of Shaw's characters. In his 1905 preface to *The Irrational Knot*, as I mentioned in my opening chapter, Shaw accuses the "governing classes," in need of wealth to sustain their "handsome and delicate" lifestyles, of not hesitating to "batter in the doors of their fellow-men, sell them up, sweat them in fetid dens" and variously abuse them "in the name of law and order" and in the practice of a perverted "virtue" (*Knot*, xvi). That, in the age of modernity, such *qualities* as virtue are superseded by *quantities* of money—and that human quality in the money economy is supplanted by the metric of "objective measureable achievement"—is hardly surprising.[5] As Shaw in similarly worded refrains repeated over 20 years later in *The Intelligent Woman's Guide to Socialism, Capitalism, Sovietism, and Fascism*, the "civilization" produced by Capitalism is a "disease due to shortsightedness and bad morals" (*Guide*, 127). "Civilization," "law and order," and "virtue" can therefore be counted among the casualties of a Capitalism run amok. Much the same might be said of respectability.

Here is where Shavian ambivalence about money emerges to reveal its Undershaftian connotation. When introducing some pages ago this startling passage from the Preface to *The Irrational Knot* about a monetized "virtue" sanctioning abuse of the underclass in the "name of law and order," I neglected the sentences that immediately precede it which underscore the relationship between poverty and affect. The paragraph in question begins with Shaw recalling his social position when writing the novel and then moves to his censure of the "world of artificial greatness founded on convention and money." Shaw reveals his antipathy for this "repugnant and contemptible" world and, not belonging to it, he lacked a "sympathetic understanding" of it (xv). His contempt and repugnance are quickly redirected, however, by memories of being a poor immigrant with uncertain prospects. As odious as fashionable society might be and as perfidious as money's role is in its operation, Shaw was compelled to confess two "*disgusting* faults" of his own: his poverty and resultant shabbiness. Then, he "had to blind himself to its enormous importance" (xii); as a result, he tolerated the "gross error" that poverty was *not* a "sin and a *disgrace*." Then, he was "indifferent to the *repulsive* fact that if [he] had fallen in love with the duchess [he] did not possess a morning suit in which [he] could reasonably have expected her to touch [him] with the furthest protended pair of tongs" (my emphasis, xvi). Repulsion, disgrace, disgust—these terms communicate the older Shaw's enunciation of the causal connection between negative feeling and money, the delineation of which emerges in his earliest novels, however uninformed about money he claimed to be.

Undershaft's list, therefore, not only raises the question of money's relationship to respectability in both social and psychical arenas, but implies the analogous relationship of affect and psychical drive. How might feeling be better understood by juxtaposing it to the drive? The operation of negative feelings in particular—fear, disgust, and shame—has also interested cultural and literary critics, who frequently turn to American philosopher and psychologist Silvan Tomkins (1911–91) to establish a foundation for their interpretive work. Much like the multidisciplinary intellection of Shaw and his contemporaries, Tomkins studied playwriting, obtained a master's degree in psychology, and earned a doctorate in philosophy, writing a thesis on value theory. However, it is his understanding of the potency of affect that attracted the attention of such theorists as Eve Kosofsky Sedgwick, Sianne Ngai, and Sara Ahmed. For Sedgwick, Tomkins' notion that the power of the drive might be muted by an affect system resonates with special importance for tracing the operations of a material psychology in Shaw's novels. She quotes Tomkins' amazement when arriving at this subversive conclusion:

> ... the apparent urgency of the drive system was borrowed from its co-assembly with appropriate affects as necessary amplifiers. Freud's id suddenly appeared to be a paper tiger since sexuality, as he best knew, was the most finicky of drives, easily rendered impotent by shame or anxiety or boredom or rage.[6]

Sounding a bit like both Freud and Simmel when theorizing the dialogical relationship between subject and object—and, at the same time, challenging the privilege of "lack" or scarcity in Freud's promotion of wish-fulfillment as the defining feature of dreaming—Sedgwick offers a deconstructive assertion entirely compatible with my aims here:

> Attending to psychology and materiality at the level of affect and texture is also to enter a conceptual realm that is not shaped by lack nor by common-sensical dualities of subject versus object or means versus ends.[7]

The latter duality describes the evolution of a money economy in modern metropolises such as *fin de siècle* London.[8] For money, a standard of measurement that obviates the need for the trading of goods in barter systems, evolved to become more than a means of exchange and, in so doing, helped shape what Simmel terms the "mental life" of the inhabitants of modern cities.[9]

Shaw's use of terms like "disgust" in his Preface to *The Irrational Knot*—and "shame" when recalling the "snobbery" of his family during his Dublin boyhood —pertains directly to Undershaft's contextualization of respectability with biological and socio-ethical imperatives. The very fact that, in his nineties, the elderly Shaw painted much the same picture of his youth that he sketched two decades earlier in the *Intelligent Woman's*

Guide attests to the enduring pain of this wound. Albeit similar, however, these accounts are not identical. In the earlier volume, Shaw mildly admonishes his father's injunction against his association with shopkeepers' sons as "silly," so much "snobbish nonsense" consistent with the project of "keeping up more expensive appearances on less money" (*Guide*, 184). By the time of *Sixteen Self Sketches*, though, silliness and nonsense had calcified into an "abhorred secret" and, like a passage in Charles Dickens to which Shaw alludes, metastasized into an "intense shame" (*SSS*, 20). In "Shame and Wounded Snobbery" from *Sixteen Self Sketches*, Shaw wonders aloud how his enrollment at the Model School afflicted him "with a shame which was more or less a psychosis" (24). The experience of this shame, moreover, was coterminous with his nursemaid taking him with her to visit friends living in tenements, expeditions that he claims led to his writing *Major Barbara*. Poverty, in other words, confronted the young Shaw on two different fronts: at home where appearances must be kept up and in trips to urban slums. Rather amazingly, after concealing his mortification for some 80 years, keeping it a secret even from his wife, Shaw declares himself "completely cured" with "not a vestige of my boyish shame left: it survives not as a complex but a habit flicked off without the slightest difficulty" (25).

"Flicked off without the slightest difficulty?" Affects like shame are hardly feelings one might cavalierly "flick off"; moreover, however memory may soften them, in the present such feelings are experienced immediately, often intensely, in response to an event or entity external to the self (even if the external entity is a reflection *of the self*). Numerous incidents in Shaw's novels testify to the drive-like power of affects and are frequently connected to money, though not always, nor are they always negative. In the inaugural chapter of *The Irrational Knot*, for example, Nelly McQuinch, Marion Lind's acrid cousin who was accused from time to time "of being a little shrew" (*Knot*, 37), meets Ned Conolly at a charity concert organized by Marion's brother, George.[10] Judging the American engineer to be "very conceited, and very coarse" (18), she wonders aloud whether Conolly, possessive of appreciable musical talents and a "rich baritone voice," was ever employed as a waiter, snidely remarking that he "looks exactly like one" (13, 19). Yet, moments later Nelly was both "much affected" by his singing of Charles Dibden's "Tom Bowling" and "indignant with herself for being so," staring "defiantly" at Conolly "through a film of tears" (20). The working-class audience for whose benefit the concert had been arranged was similarly "moved" by this ballad memorializing the passing of a loyal sailor, although Nelly's self-reproach has little to do with class consciousness. Instead, her tears express a feeling she could not suppress any more than one can stanch an embarrassed blush or the drive to satisfy a gnawing hunger.

Similarly, Shaw's disgust with his own poverty is a reaction that he is unable to quell, leading him when writing these novels into what, for my purposes, is a fecund contradiction. On the one hand, as in a play like *On the Rocks*, he seizes every opportunity to deride the enervation of Britain's wealthy or once-wealthy aristocracy and interrogate the corrupting power of money; yet, on the other, he detested poverty, especially his own "chronic impecuniosity." It *disgusted* him; he found it *repulsive*; he was *shamed* by it—and only money could provide a remedy. Juxtaposing drive to such affects, Sedgwick emphasizes that while both are embodied phenomena, drives are "relatively narrowly constrained in their aims" and are also delimited by time: the needs for air to breathe, water to drink, and food to sustain life are time-sensitive, reducible to seconds, hours, and days. By contrast, affective responses can persist for varying amounts of time and be triggered by a wide range of catalysts—a sentimental dirge about a brave and tragic sailor, a companion's cutting remark about shirt sleeves unfashionably rolled up—and, as such, they are "attached to things, people, ideas, sensations, relations, activities, ambitions, institutions, and any number of other things, including other affects."[11] As Sara Ahmed wittily observes, affects are "sticky" subjective phenomena, something especially true of disgust, when "the contact between surfaces engenders an intensity of affect."[12] For this reason, affects are often performative in the linguistic sense; that is to say, like speech acts that perform rather than describe an action—"I do" in the marriage ceremony, "It's a bet" when a wager is finalized—Nelly's tears announce her feeling the instant they are shed.

In the afterword of her book *Ugly Feelings* (2005), Sianne Ngai provides a useful counterpoint to the affect/drive dyad by comparing affect to desire and basing her argument on disgust, a feeling to which Shaw and many of his characters are especially susceptible. For Ngai, disgust is a "structured and agonistic emotion carrying a strong and unmistakable signal, while desire is often noisy and amorphous." Even when "boiled down to its kernel of repulsion," disgust marks a "fairly definite response, whereas the parameters of desire are notoriously difficult to determine and fix." Desire, she argues, is capable of being "vague" or "idiosyncratic," whereas disgust is inordinately specific. Disgust, moreover, echoing Shaw's comment about being unable to form a "sympathetic understanding" of artificial London society, blocks "paths of sympathy." The disgusting is "dangerous and contaminating"; one cannot remain indifferent to or tolerate its source. Also, precisely because disgust is both urgent and specific, it resembles the blunt impulsion of the drive more than the comparatively promiscuous operations of desire.[13]

By contrast, "respectability" is neither urgent nor specific. For Ngai, after Ernst Bloch, key differences obtain between "expectant" emotions such as anxiety, fear, and hope and "filled" ones like shame or disgust; the former, for instance, possess a far "greater anticipatory character" than the latter, connecting such feelings to a futurity quite different from the immediacy of filled emotion. Expectant emotions are connected less to specific objects or events than with "configurations of the world in general" or the "future dispositions of the self."[14] In this context, "respectability," however much it might be filled in the moment, is both an "expectant" status *and* a feeling, as one anticipates the earning of respect and, for this reason, its cathexis, its sheer force, differs from that of the drive. Happily, Undershaft's roster of millstones and respectability's proximity to the drive are not conundrums to be resolved here; rather, I am interested in the drive-like power of negative affects and their emergence in *Immaturity* insofar as money is concerned and in money's role in performing respectability in *The Irrational Knot*. As I mentioned some pages ago, both issues are presaged by Shaw's reference to self-worth in the Preface to *Immaturity*: "I knew I was useless, worthless, penniless ... " (*I*, xxx), a formulation that might be redacted to read, "I knew I was worthless *because* I was penniless." This stark expression of a material psychology necessarily collapses such "commonsensical" dualities as subject and object, making impossible any positive view of self apart from money.

This deconstruction of the dyad subject/object, much like the materially inflected dreams of Freud and his patients, implies the need for a psychology (and psychoanalysis) in which subjectivity and economics, the psychical and the material, are regarded as more or less inseparable. In this psychology, wealth—or, more often, its absence, poverty—produces an array of expectant affects—anxiety, for example—as Shaw was well aware. One striking letter to Stella Campbell in December of 1912 makes this point emphatically clear. Recently ill and in financial difficulty, Stella received numerous letters from Shaw in late 1912—and for many years thereafter, for that matter—which are remarkable for their expressions of his affection for her. One, however, on December 10, 1912 begins with Shaw's upbraiding of a bank manager who apparently allowed Mrs Campbell to overdraw her account "recklessly." Although Shaw admits that, in the banker's place, he might have been tempted to be similarly generous to her, he is adamant that, when it comes to irresponsible lending, limits must be imposed. At the same time, he suggests the subjective valences of money:

> But business is business: in practice there is a limit to all overdrafts. That limit may be approaching—may be already reached—must be near enough to cause some anxiety.... Are there friends—for pride is no use: when you *must* have money you must take it or raise it—must, must, must, must, MUST.

Such is the necessity of, and resultant drive-like push for, money. In relating his estimates of how much money she will require—for rent, Christmas "boxes," bills, nurses, doctors, and so on—Shaw, referring to Stella in the third person, arrives at the psychical nub of this "insistent problem": "How much will make her quite free from anxiety until she is up again?"[15]

Shaw's self-deprecating remark in the Preface to *The Irrational Knot*, therefore, that as a 24-year-old writing his second novel, he had to "blind" himself to the "enormous importance" of money is again not entirely accurate. For, as the above discussion intimates and the readings that follow amplify, the younger Shaw knew how poverty *feels*, how money can preoccupy thought, and how it informs social convention. By the mid-1880s, given his meetings with Philip Wicksteed and other economists—including his exposure to the marginalist theories of William Stanley Jevons and General Francis Amasa Walker—he had also contemplated money's use as currency in exchange, as capital in investment, and much more; and feeling and emotion play a part in some these processes. Shaw demonstrates in a myriad of ways in *The Intelligent Woman's Guide* and elsewhere how the naïve young writer evolved into a knowledgeable economist able to discuss such issues as the setting of interest rates, the favorable taxation laws for profits earned from investment, the strategies of "bulls" and "bears" in the Stock Market, even the tactic of what is today known as the "straddling" of stock options.[16] Shaw's keenest insights emerge in his unpacking of more basic matters like money's role in exchange. Printed on "bits of paper, mostly dirty and smelly," and "crowded with print and pictures" (*Guide*, 254), the pound notes are both mildly repellent and literally worth nothing. Rather, as Francis Walker explains in *Money* (1891), following Jevons, such "mere bits of colored paper" or coins "afford the common denominator needed for the expression of a list of values as long as the diversification of modern industry shall require."[17] With typical puckishness in the *Guide*, as I mentioned in the preceding chapter, Shaw ponders how much more convenient it is for bus passengers—and certainly for conductors, whose duties include the collection of fares—to proffer common denominators such as pence or shillings rather than cumbersome things like donkeys to pay what they owe (*Guide*, 252).

More important for my purposes, and consistent with the principles of marginalist economics, "commodities," those things acquired with bits of paper or metal, possess an affective value. In fact, Jevons defines this most material of entities in decidedly immaterial terms: "By a *commodity* we shall understand any object, substance, action ... which can afford pleasure or ward off pain."[18] Yet, and I think this bears repeating, Shaw's own commentary on the study of emotion and human psychology might dissuade one from a concerted study of these matters.[19] Introducing *Immaturity* in 1921, a novel he had written over 40 years earlier but not published until 1930, Shaw calls psychoanalysis a "craze" and reduces its complexities to "the cure of diseases by explaining to the patient what is the matter with him" (xviii). Still, he shows himself eminently capable of creating what Georg Simmel initially embarked upon before writing *The Philosophy of Money*: namely, a *psychology* of money. As I have suggested, impecuniosity plagues the younger Shaw and exercises profound psychical effects on him; similarly, the very mention of money, its budgeting and scarcity, triggers intense feelings that his most autobiographical characters struggle to control. In addition, while it retains its importance in the older Shaw's thought and play writing as well, money undergoes comic deflation and operates quite differently in such plays as *The Millionairess* (1935), the "comedietta" *Buoyant Billions* (1948), and *Why She Would Not* (1950).

What changes, therefore, in Shaw's later plays is not money's prominence, but the *feeling* it generates. The ways in which money, value, and self-worth emerge in these later works are of particular significance to my readings of *Immaturity* and *The Irrational Knot*. In the case of the latter novel in particular, one element of affect study also accrues added significance: social performance, which is also related to—and mandated by—respectability. In this regard, we might recall Sara Ahmed's thesis that an affect such as shame is bound up with a feeling of exposure, specifically, "to be witnessed in one's failure." Even when one is alone, shame produces the feeling of the presence of another or of an audience of others, before whom devastating personal inadequacies are revealed.[20] Shaw was acutely aware of the ways in which shame assumes the shape of a performance, a motif in tenement drama of the 1920s and 1930s by writers he admired such as Sean O'Casey. The twin sources of shame in such plays as *Juno and the Paycock* (1924)—or, say, Clifford Odets's *Awake and Sing!* (1935) and *Paradise Lost* (1935)—are the all-too-predictable pregnancy of an unwed daughter made public, and the distrainment of a family's property, its seizure for failing to pay the rent and humiliating display on the sidewalk for an entire neighborhood to view.[21] A public spectacle performed daily, shame is only one reason why, as Peter Gahan describes, Shaw felt an "intense aversion" to Dublin that "amounted to repugnance."[22] Perhaps this is why the seventh successful Undershaft scrawled "UNASHAMED" on his shop wall in *Major Barbara*, announcing, in effect, that the acquisition of wealth, even if it fails to bring respectability, can effectively vanquish the shame of poverty.

Undershaft's motto possesses a genealogy that includes not only Shaw's boyhood, but also the internal lives of the characters of his first two novels. For the experience of such feelings often transcends logic or the fact of being poor,[23] and it is not easily explained by way of a narrative wrested from pursuit of the pleasure principle, particularly its association with the "Family Romance." Biographers and critics alike, for example, tend to privilege Shaw's childhood experience as crucial to understanding his later attitudes and considerable repository of negative feelings. For St. John Ervine, the Shaw family's "overpowering" and delusive gentility as manifested by the condescension of Shaw's father and his mother's benign neglect of her children explains much about Shaw's internal life.[24] Such observations presage images of the more internally conflicted figure of Arnold Silver's *Bernard Shaw: The Darker Side* (1982) and other Shaws constructed by way of psychoanalysis. For Silver, "the scar tissue of Shaw's frightful and loveless childhood was still livid in the very old man," and the detritus of this injury exerts a septic effect on the "thought and feeling *beneath* the existing plays" (my emphasis).[25] Responding to both "unconscious as well as to conscious promptings," Silver's Shaw possesses "shadows and depths" that his public persona lacked; a psychoanalytically based investigation of Shaw the man, therefore, might restore to interpretive prominence "depths" heretofore unexplored in the plays and, as a result, prompt new readings of them.[26] Somewhat similarly, Jean Reynolds construes the depths plumbed by Freudian clinical practice as compatible with the Lacanian insight that the unconscious is structured like a language to interrogate Eliza's relationship with Higgins in *Pygmalion*. Thus, the instauration through language of Higgins as surrogate father is among those "deeper" issues of the play rendered more accessible through the application of psychoanalytic thought to Shaw's text.[27]

I have no quarrel whatsoever with these contentions. In my readings, however, such emphases will cede their primacy to a different interpretive formulary focused on characters' more autonomous reactions to objects and events that they encounter in their daily lives, what Kathleen Stewart characterizes as "both the pressure points of events or banalities suffered and the trajectories that forces might take if they were to go unchecked." These "circuits and flows" emanate from a "continual motion of relations, scenes, contingencies, and emergences."[28] To be sure, an affective loop may exist between surface and depths, and the intensity of feeling experienced by everyday events might be an "autonomic remainder" of the loop's functioning. Still, the "skin is faster than the word," as Brian Massumi observes, and consequently embodied responses to what are, in some cases, ordinary events reveal as much about the sources of emotion as Oedipal desire, latent contents, and language do.[29]

In what follows, then, I hope to complicate two commonly held suppositions about *Immaturity* and *The Irrational Knot*. The first, advanced by Nicholas Grene while charting Shaw's revisions of his first novel, is that "the author of *Immaturity*, as detected in the writing and re-writing of novel, stands revealed as a more human, a more vulnerable person than the relentlessly confident public performer that was to be Bernard Shaw."[30] Perhaps the most autobiographical of all of Shaw's creations, Robert Smith in *Immaturity*, exemplifies this vulnerability, as his extremely negative feelings, particularly his anxiety, are elicited by at times the most mundane of events, especially where money is involved. He is hardly alone in this regard. The second emerges from Richard Farr Dietrich's consideration of Archibald Henderson's critique that, by focusing in his novels on the excesses of London's aristocratic class, Shaw "did not know what he was writing about." Viewing Shaw's novels as "essentially a study of manners," Henderson cribbed his argument from Shaw himself, a critical tendency that Dietrich queries in *Bernard Shaw's Novels: Portraits of the Artist as Man and Superman*.[31] *Immaturity* and *The Irrational Knot* achieve both of these ends, creating psychically rich portraits of vulnerable characters dominated by money *and* lancing representations of social artifice and privilege. Borrowing a phrase from the marginalists, I would submit that money is the "common denominator" of both pursuits, as the following discussion is intended to demonstrate.

"Nobody Is Anybody Without Money, Seedystockings": Money and Feeling in *Immaturity*

Epifania Ognisanti di Parerga in *The Millionairess* directs this barb to Patricia Smith, also known as Polly Seedystockings from the signatures on the letters she exchanged with Epifania's unfaithful husband, as a rejoinder to Ms. Smith's aspersion: "What would she [Epifania] be without her money, I'd like to know?" (*CPP* 6: 229). As Shaw's dialogue in the play's opening scene implies, one answer might very well be "nothing," for "Nobody is anybody without money." This includes Epifania's estranged husband Alastair Fitzfassenden who, at first glance, appears to be an estimable *somebody*, hence an effective refutation of his wife's thesis. An amateur tennis champion and accomplished boxer, he also "stripped well, unlike many handsome men," or so Epifania reports. If these attributes were not enough, and they seem considerable both in and out of the bedroom, Fitzfassenden also benefits from "extraordinary luck": "He always wins. He wins at tennis. He wins at boxing," and he eventually won the hand of the "richest heiress in England" by turning £150 into 50,000 in six months (*CPP* 6: 211). Shaw's stage directions ambivalently describe him as a "*splendid athlete, with most of his brains in his muscles*" (*CPP* 6: 213); yet however dim, compared to such characters as Julius Sagamore and Adrian Blenderbland, who has "no business ability" yet sits on 15 boards of directors because of his father's influence, Fitzfassenden seems a formidable, even attractive, presence. He is, admittedly, far from perfect, relating in Act One how he lost the windfall he had acquired through "kiting" checks, leaving his wife responsible for a small debt, the "allowance of a worm," she was forced to settle (*CPP* 6: 228). This slip aside, Alastair hardly seems a "nobody."

It's also likely that Alastair would subscribe to his wife's thesis, as his sudden acquisition of £50,000 not only elevated her opinion of him, but also redefined his feeling about himself. Epifania describes the transformation to Adrian, who is "amazed" that Fitzfassenden managed to make so much in six months before squandering it in an imprudent investment in a circus:

> You may well look incredulous, Adrian. But he did. Yes: this imbecile made fifty thousand pounds and won Epifania Ognisanti di Parerga for his bride. You will not believe me when I tell you that the possession of all that money, and the consciousness of having made it himself, gave him a sort of greatness. (*CPP* 6: 222)

After Epifania instigates a verbal skirmish with her husband about the nefarious way in which he made his fortune, Adrian rises to offer his support to Alistair, couching his defense in terms especially relevant to an examination of affect in Shaw's writing:

> You are so rich, Epifania, that every decent man who approaches you *feels* like a needy adventurer. You dont know how a man to whom a hundred pounds is a considerable sum *feels* in the arms of a woman to whom a million is mere pin money. (my emphasis; *CPP* 6: 223)

Outlining the mechanics of check kiting to Adrian, Alastair ends his instruction by both corroborating his wife's analysis of the effect money exerted upon his sense of self-worth and reinstating the relationship between money and feeling: "… all I wanted was fifty thousand pounds; and I cleared out with that and came swanking back to claim Eppy's hand. She thought I was great. I was great: the money made me great" (*CPP* 6: 227). The money transformed him, in short, into "another man."

For the sake of accuracy, it seems necessary to revise these claims slightly: the money itself neither made Alastair great nor "transfigured" him, as Epifania observes; instead, it made him both *feel* and appear great in a performance that seems the inverse of the humiliating scenes played in the theatre of shame. That is to say, if shame involves an exposure of failure to others—a performance of inadequacy or impecuniosity enacted before the cold gaze of spectators, real or perceived—then Alastair's attainment of wealth is played out to an approving audience of one. From his earliest writing, Shaw seemed intent on exploring the relationship between feeling and money, and between *earning* money and establishing a person's worth. To take one example of the latter, in *The Irrational Knot*, Susanna Conolly and Marmaduke Lind, her lover and the father of her child, have a spat in the turbulent early stages of their relationship stemming from the rumor that he is engaged to his cousin, Constance. Denying it vigorously, Marmaduke is pressed to admit that, at the moment, he cannot "afford" to inform his father of his objections to the match; he is, as he puts it, "too hard up to quarrel with the governor." Countering that "it is not worth *my* while to waste my time on people who can't earn their own living," Susanna bolts from the hansom in which they were being conveyed, leaving her suitor "horrified—genuinely horrified" (*Knot*, 53). Money and the earning of it have a value for her, as the latter in particular has for Vivie Warren, that transcends the material.

This equation informs *The Millionairess*, even as it foregrounds money's opposite potential to induce Alastair to perceive himself as great. Later, near the end of the play, after asking Alastair why he jeers at her— "Is it just that I … cannot keep my husband, cannot keep even a lover, cannot keep anything but my money?"—Epifania attacks Patricia with a version of her by now familiar maxim, disparaging her as an "insignificant little nothingness who cannot afford to pay for her own stockings" (*CPP* 6: 270). However much Epifania seems willing to abandon this position in the play's final scene and marry the penniless doctor who has become absurdly fixated with her pulse—and however much this contrivance helps Shaw create a comic resolution to the action—the relationship of money and subjectivity developed at the beginning remains in force: nobody is anybody without money. *The Millionairess* proves this by way of *affirmation* in foregrounding Alastair's positive feelings of greatness in the opening act, as the making of £50,000 illuminates an ability neither he nor Epifania recognized before, which is then reaffirmed by their marriage.

As several titles in Shaw's corpus of plays intimate, money and its pervasive socio-psychical effects are never entirely absent from Shaw's later plays, although *Buoyant Billions*, a play that Shaw denigrated as a "trivial comedy" that was the best he could write in his "dotage" (*CPP* 1: 752), serves more as a summation of the Shavian distinction between men of commerce and men of vision than an interrogation of money's inflection of modern subjectivity. Men of vision or "world betterers," as young Junius Buoyant calls them, are fundamentally different from the "selfseekers" who pursue top-paying jobs to the exclusion of all other goals. The largely comic *psychology* of money in *The Millionairess*, we might say, gives way to a *sociology* of money in *Buoyant Billions* concerning the relationship of money to social welfare that Shavian characters from Sidney Trefusis in *An Unsocial Socialist* to Andrew Undershaft in *Major Barbara* delineate with such acuity. However, as Shaw makes clear, wealthy businessmen such as Buoyant are unlikely to take the lead in any project of social advancement, however penetrating their insight into capital and finance might be. This conviction is most succinctly conveyed by a single clause in Shaw's "Preface on Bosses" that introduces *The Millionairess* : "… the supremacy of the moneymaker is the destruction of the State" (*CPP* 6: 176), a destruction that the Buoyants are too eccentric and solipsistic to eventuate.

It will come as little surprise that the most autobiographical characters in Shaw's novels feel the impact of money with considerably more force than the thinly disguised stalking horses that populate plays such as *Buoyant Billions*. Such is the case with the protagonist of *Immaturity*, the 18-year-old Robert Smith whom Dietrich usefully describes as "plain" Robert, a character "who exists on the heroic plane only in his own mind."[32] *Immaturity* is comprised of four "books," the first of which, "Islington," serves not only to introduce Smith's moody introspection, but also to initiate his abiding concern with his finances. Shortly after arriving in London at Mrs Froster's Islington boarding house, Smith begins to unpack his belongings and considers the undertaking of two additional labors: the budgeting of his modest resources and the search for more satisfactory accommodations, the latter of which seems unnecessary after meeting a young dressmaker with a Scots accent, Harriet Russell, who lives down the hall. As he unpacks, he happens across a Bible and volume of Shakespeare he had purchased with the few "morsels of pocket money" he had "extracted by occasional importunity from his parents, who had been too poor and too careless to make him any fixed allowance" (*I*, 5). He promptly locks these possessions, an album of photographs, and his evening clothes into a drawer "which henceforth constituted his cabinet of treasures, to be opened only at such rare intervals as the danger of moths rendered advisable" (5).

Robert's next procedures might be characterized as more business like and forward-looking. These include the taking of an inventory of his "everyday apparel": a decent "walking suit" for employment purposes and one worn suit for domestic wear, a "black cut-away coat" for social occasions, an overcoat, and traveling cap. He arranges his four shirts and German paper collars, handkerchiefs, Sunday cravat, and other smaller items; and organizes his small library on a chest of drawers, including his well-thumbed edition of Byron and several pieces of piano music (*I*, 6). Next, literally within hours of arriving in London, he constructs a balance sheet of his income and expenses, wondering whether he will be able to live on his salary and additional interest income from his mother's investment in Cork property. His accounting reveals a constrained economy in which a little over £21 might be spent annually on the theatre, Christmas gifts, the newspaper, and other discretionary items. In fact, Robert is so intent on reaching an accurate assessment that he recalculates his budget, eventually satisfied with its precision and feeling a "contented laziness which usually follows the achievement of an irksome piece of business" (7). Much as Nietzsche identifies the setting of values and equivalences in the "earliest thoughts" of our species,[33] this penchant for calculation is part of Robert's psychical makeup, and throughout the novel it reemerges in revealing, if at times seemingly frivolous, ways. So, after safely depositing Miss Russell, with whom he had developed a close acquaintance, at King's Cross, Robert is "surprised to find tears in his eyes" without "feeling any preliminary access of emotion." At almost the same instant, and as a kind of defense mechanism, he notices the "grime" of the rail platform, which leads him to consider "how long it would take a single man to clean it." He "endeavored" to dismiss this "impertinent" idea and the mathematical challenges it poses, but he could think of "nothing else" until he arrived home (99).

Like Dietrich, and from scenes like these, we can conclude that there is little heroic about Shaw's introduction to his protagonist in the novel's first book, and by the end of *Immaturity* little has occurred to alter this perception. Two additional character traits emerge in the book's inaugural scene worthy of note. One is Smith's lassitude after calculating the specifics of his budget. This comparatively simple but "irksome piece of business" provides a preview of his later responses to—specifically, his feelings about—both his own financial straits and the labor of keeping books for his employer, as becomes apparent a week later when Mrs Froster appears at his door to collect the rent:

> This weekly settling of accounts was, in his estimation, the greatest trial to his feelings entailed by living in lodgings; and with a woman like Mrs Froster, who seemed to be always ill at ease, the transaction was specially awkward. (*I*, 36)

The phrase "greatest trial to his feelings" may seem hyperbolic, but there is little question that throughout the novel, and particularly in its first book, this relationship between feeling and accountancy—the connection between emotion and money—persists. As Dietrich observes, Robert hardly exhibits the romantic intensity Victorian readers sought in popular fiction. On the contrary, readers might expect Smith and Harriet, who were obviously fond of each other, to be married or engaged by the end of the novel; instead, Harriet meets a young artist, Cyril Scott, in the second book of *Immaturity*, "Aesthetics," which introduces an affluent and artificial world of contemporary art and privilege, and marries him in the third book, "Courtship and Marriage." By the end the novel's last book, "Flirtation," Smith is really "no further along" romantically or professionally, and there is no "'happily ever after' anywhere in sight."[34] Even more ironic, in the final sentence of "Courtship and Marriage," the dissipated preacher—and heartbroken admirer of Harriet—St. John Davis dies in jail after collapsing on Westminster Bridge, attacking, and then being brutalized by the police. In this "novel of manners," depictions of the privileged and affluent occasionally give way to gritty representations of the struggles of vulnerable Londoners to survive in the modern metropolis. One would hardly expect, in other words, a book entitled "Courtship and Marriage" to conclude with the announcement, "Mr Davis was dead" (333).

Arguably, the closest Smith gets to a more blissful subjective life occurs in only two instances in *Immaturity*: his momentary jubilance after leaving the employment he despises—his job as a clerk in a counting-house for Figgis and Weaver, sellers of carpets and oilcloths—and his trips to the theatre in Chapters VII and VIII of the novel's first book. The latter offer what is perhaps the most compelling evidence of Shaw's yoking of money with his protagonist's most acute feelings, both positive and negative. It is also the closest Smith approaches to desire, his close feeling for Harriet notwithstanding, even if staged only in his imagination. Detailing the first of Smith's several visits to the Alhambra Theatre to watch an Italian dancer with whom he had become infatuated, Chapter VII begins with a brief exposition of Smith's theater going history in Dublin, one limited to opera and enduringly popular romantic operettas such as Edward Fitzball's *Maritana* (1845) and Michael Balfe's *The Bohemian Girl* (1843).[35] Smith, Shaw's narrator confirms, was *not* an "habitual patron" of the London theatres (*I*, 70), yet when Harriet traveled to Richmond to visit her aunt for a fortnight holiday, he found himself at the Alhambra, buying an inexpensive ticket in a crowded section of seats and feeling "uncomfortable" in an atmosphere that was "hot, and flavored with gas, cigar smoke, and effervescing liquors" (*I*, 74). Smith's discomfiture was soon alleviated when, after a lengthy orchestral prelude, the curtain rose on a ballet, *The Golden Harvest*, in which a "transcendent being, the spirit of the harvest field," appeared, creating a sense of "elfin fancy and ethereality." The dancer's "dark bright eyes flashed in the limelight," and "cornflowers and golden ears of wheat were twisted fantastically in her black hair." His disbelief willingly and totally suspended, Smith immediately "forgot his surroundings"—oblivious to the cigar smoke and bursts of laughter from the theatre's bars—and became "infatuated" with the dancer who glided across the stage in a halo of light. When her performance was received with what struck him as tame applause, he reacted by "cursing the indifference of the herd to refined art" (76). He, by contrast, had been transported by what he had seen and was entranced by the beautiful creature with the flashing eyes.

Chapter VIII finds Smith back in the same theatre, but purposefully begins not with his spectation but with a diagnosis of his financial health. The narrator, somewhat surprisingly, relates that Smith was, at the time, in "easy circumstances. His material necessities were few ... [so] he could always calculate his expenditures." Further, because he possessed a "strong aversion to debts of all descriptions," an aversion that impels him to pay for "everything as he got it," he was able to remain more or less "free from the demoralizing influence of pecuniary embarrassment" (*I*, 80). The narration then moves from accountancy—psychical and material—to Smith's three trips to the Alhambra to see the enchanting Signorina Pertoldi in *The Golden Harvest*. But much more than perfervid spectatorship is involved. The dancer quickly occupies the "centre" of the smitten young man's "mental activity," effecting such "ruptures" of his "intellectual routine" as inducing him to purchase a treatise of Hector Berlioz on instrumentation and entertain thoughts of becoming a composer. One result of these intrusions on his equipoise is that he "deplored his own infatuation" and was moved to scrutinize it carefully (81). As he considers the ramifications of his devotion, self-criticism quickly yields to the cold calculations of his imaginative ledger book. As Shaw's narrator phrases it, Smith "was "*compelled* to reflect" on the financial consequences of his activity and to project how ruinous it would be to repeat treks to the theatre with similar frequency for the entire year. The total cost could run as high as "fifteen pounds and thirteen shillings per annum," so in addition to feeling "*ashamed*" by the "domination of a sensuous attraction," his intense feeling for the Italian dancer augured economic disaster, even "famine for himself" (my emphasis; 81). Soon thereafter, he is engulfed by more intensely negative feelings; he is "ashamed" of his infatuation and now notices the "dissipated loungers among whom he had to move in the shilling promenade at the Alhambra," who were "repugnant to him." Within a fortnight he grew ever more "dissatisfied with himself" and "disgusted at the theatre" (81–82), vowing never to return, yet at the same time "he felt a *restless craving* to return to it" (82; my emphasis). This chapter of *Immaturity*, in sum, stages not only an intoxicating ballet evocative of a young man's romantic fantasy, but a veritable showdown between desire and negative affect: in particular, Smith's acute anxiety about money.

The narrator's assurance in Chapter VIII that, at the time of his incessant theater going, Smith's finances were very much in order is also important, I think, in corroborating the power of money to displace the drive or "craving" with anxious concern about the future. That is, Shaw's narrator implicitly connects money to a sense of the future, a powerful "expectant" element consonant with the temporality of anxiety. As innumerable commentators on the nature of money agree, to be effective it must be transportable, acceptable, possessive of stable value—as Shaw insists in *The Intelligent Woman's Guide*—and more; these are precisely the features which enable exchange to occur over long distances and protracted time periods. Like anxiety, therefore, money pertains to a futurity by its very nature. In his best-selling *The Ascent of Money: A Financial History of the World* (2008), Niall Ferguson recalls an odd episode in recent history when members of the Nukak-Makú tribe wandered out of the Amazon rainforest near San José del Guaviare in Colombia. Living for centuries on trapped animals and the fruit they could gather, this indigenous tribe, according to Ferguson, had "no concept" of either money or futurity.[36] Neither the concept of money nor that of the future meant anything to them, as their hunting and gathering were driven by a quotidian need to survive. By contrast, Smith's dire calculations of his potential financial calamity caused by excessive theater going has nothing to do with his material existence in the present, a fact that underscores the force of the material and the future in his thoughts and feelings.

At the same time, it is not difficult to understand the socio-psychical origins of "plain" Smith's newfound infatuation, and these extend beyond his obvious isolation and loneliness. In this regard, he serves in these two chapters as a portrait not of the artist, but of a modern urban "Everyman." Shaw's juxtaposition of the splendor and rustic magic of *The Golden Harvest* inside the theatre, for example, with the chaotic rush of life outside it recalls numerous accounts of the objectifying experience of urban modernity. Exiting the theatre still enchanted by the dance and dancer he had seen, Smith encounters exactly the opposite scene outside it:

> Here was a confusion of swift hansoms, clamorous vendors of obscene literature, violet sellers, and crowds of men and brilliantly attired women

aimlessly wandering about ... with a background of the gas-lighted windows of *cafés*, gin palaces, tobacconists, and eating-houses where lobsters predominated redly over the other edibles. Through this tumult Smith rapidly made his way.... (*I*, 78)

Such a scene anticipates the frenetic life Simmel portrays in his seminal 1903 essay "The Metropolis and Mental Life," with its "swift and uninterrupted change of outer and inner stimuli," its "rapid crowding of changing images," and the "unexpectedness of onrushing impressions." These disruptions and floods of stimuli mark the accelerated "tempo" of a life for which the metropolitan man, the human subject, must invent such defenses as a nimble "intellectuality" of calculation, "inconsiderate hardness," and absorption in the cold objectivity of the money economy.[37] "Only [the] money economy," Simmel concludes, "has filled the days of so many people with weighing, calculating, with numerical determinations, with a reduction of qualitative values to quantitative ones."[38] This "calculative exactness," then, and Shaw's depiction of the lived reality of modern London—a city Simmel identifies in his essay as an example *par excellence* of his thesis—accompanies what is arguably the most quoted line in *Immaturity*. Contemplating the events that transpired, Smith concludes that even though he began to "crave for a female friend who would encourage him to persevere in the struggle for truth and human perfection," he "happily" found none, a failure that leads to this epiphany: "The power to stand alone is worth acquiring at the expense of much sorrowful solitude" (85).

The kind of freedom marked by modern progress, therefore, is double-edged, for as Simmel emphasizes, at times "one nowhere feels as lonely and lost as in the metropolitan crowd"[39]—or when trapped in the vicissitudes of a job like the one Smith despised. Still, as with his visits to the Alhambra, his employment eventually produces in him not only sharply negative feeling but also, upon escaping the job for a better position, temporary transports of elation. The second chapter opens with his work as a clerk in a counting-house for Figgis and Weaver, a "respectable firm to whom [Smith] attributed the most sordid views of existence." He liked work, but "hated the duties of his clerkship as barren drudgery, which numbed his faculties and wasted his time" (*I*, 11). Indeed, even in this brief introduction to his nascent professional life, Shaw's narrator stresses Smith's self-contempt for stooping so low to earn a badly needed pound a week. Smith attributed his readiness to please his employers as a sign of his own "cowardice"; he "loathed his own servility" and "felt himself the most degraded toady in the office" (11). He "resented" the psychical "trespass" into his dreams of any matter related to the office and even hesitated on Christmas Eve to accept a five-pound bonus, which he regarded as a "gratuity" (12).

After Christmas and returning to work, his outlook had not brightened. Near the end of the workday at six o'clock, Mr. Weaver, finding in a ledger evidence of Smith's industry, made a joke about the book being a handy "pocket edition." Smith laughed politely at the witticism, then excoriated himself as a "wretched sycophant" for doing so (*I*, 50). As he walked home later chafing from his labors and bruised by his self-recrimination, he asked himself, "I wonder … is there any profession in the world so contemptible as that of a clerk," comparing himself and his colleagues to a "mean and servile pack of dogs" (51). A seemingly insignificant conversation—a brief monologue by Weaver, actually—distinguishes these two iterations of self-loathing by relating what is, by now, the familiar Shavian yarn of an "imbecile" such as Alastair Fitzfassenden or a novice businessman such as Gerald Bridges in "The Theatre of the Future" making a windfall without knowing what he is doing. "I once knew a man worth a million of money," Weaver recalls, "who began life with twenty-five pound ten." The man was standing in front of the Corn Exchange one day, overheard two men "chaffering" over a "load of madder," and determined that there was money to be made in a commodity about which he knew absolutely nothing. One of the men demanded twenty-five pound four shillings, he paid it, sold it for 30 pounds shortly thereafter, and ultimately grew wealthy from even more profitable transactions, even though he "never kept a book in his life" (50). Smith disrespectfully requited Weaver's story with a barb related in an aside to a senior associate that he wished his employer had "half as much sense" as the "madder man" (51). A short time later, he experiences the epiphany about the job of a clerk being the most contemptible in the world.

His predicament is eventually remedied when, near the end of Book Two, after working three years for Figgis and Weaver, he abruptly resigns and secures a position for nearly twice the salary as secretary to Foley Woodward, an Irish M.P. in need of assistance managing the litter of correspondence he receives. Although Smith is enlivened by the feeling of an ascendant self-determination when he informed Figgis—who had reproached him for being five minutes late and advised that if he didn't like the terms he could leave—that "Your terms *do not* suit me, sir. I will leave," the exhilaration is short-lived. In a "transport of joy" after standing up to Figgis (*I*, 171), he strode by Temple Bar "free" and, in a moment of rare condescension, "pitied the lawyers' clerks who hurried past him." The streets seemed "gay," and "the sunlight and bustle of the Strand harmonized with the hopefulness and energy with which he faced the future." He wandered for about an hour in a state of "exaltation" (173), but the feeling soon dissipated. Having nothing else to do, he boarded a river boat and sailed quietly down the Thames, but it afforded little sense of calm. On the contrary, he grew increasingly gloomy about his present circumstances *and* the future:

> As he sailed down the river, he, for the first time since his defiance of Figgis, felt a shadow creeping over his spirits.... He had saved no money. He could not live on his inheritance of forty pounds a year. (*I*, 174)

His mind then raced to a consideration of occupations he might pursue—he "thought once or twice of the stage," of teaching, of going to sea, or of even becoming Madame Pertoldi's footman—but then "disgusted with his common sense" (174), he resolved to suspend his deliberations for a day and reconsider his options. His reconsideration confirmed that his 37 shillings and 6 pence would not "last him until he received his next quarter's interest" from his mother's Irish investments (177). He had to find work.

And he did, as I have mentioned, which prompts yet more positive feeling. After interviewing with Woodward, accepting the position, and agreeing to the terms of his employment, Smith leaves Woodward's house with a profound sense of self-satisfaction:

> "Well" he said to himself as he walked along, "for more than three mortal years have I toiled nine hours a day in a cheerless den amidst money grubbers for a pound a week. Now for nearly twice that money, an unfortunate Irish gentleman is glad to get me to help him...." (*I*, 188)

The irony of this passage reflects Shaw's own ambivalence about money: on the one hand, money grubbers in their pursuit of dirty, smelly pieces of paper are either loathsome creatures such as Mr. Figgis, or imbeciles who fall into wealth almost by accident; on the other, earning twice as much income from a new position is an attractive alternative and entirely different than "grubbing" for money. However tenuous the logic, the fact that he can now perform his tasks professionally in an environment conducive to feelings of self-worth, not self-contempt and disdain, makes an enormous emotional difference to Smith.

Smith's satisfaction with both his new salary and position, however, emanates from a repertory of negative feelings associated with both money and an uncertain future. His feelings, not unlike our own, surface in response to life events, good and bad, exciting and indifferent, but for Smith—and for Shaw, too, I think—these often take on a sharply negative quality when related to the scarcity of money or to the rigors of self-assessment. (It should also be observed that grubbing for money, however successful, can also elicit harsh self-censure, as Smith experienced in his clerkship and Owen Jack bemoans in *Love Among the Artists*.) While I don't wish to claim that the fear of indigence *haunts* Smith, his thoughts seem to drift uneasily and almost automatically to calculations about income, expenses, and a perilous future, as they did in regard to his theatre going. So, later in the novel at the beginning of Book Four, after working happily as Woodward's assistant, Smith finds himself momentarily abandoned as the family has left for a holiday in Ireland. Invited by his employer to take a holiday himself, he declines, the "trouble and expense of holiday making being more terrifying to his shyness and inexperience than the prospect of change of air was attractive." Indulging in the luxuries that free time affords—long walks, reading, reviewing his attempts at writing poetry—he soon grows "fearful of deteriorating through idleness"; in addition, he "reflected that he might at any time lose his place through the death or caprice of his employer" and, for this reason, decides to pursue a course of study that might enable him to sit for Civil Service examinations (*I*, 337). Although this plan is made unpalatable by his paying to attend and then abandoning a dismal preparatory class, Smith eventually passes, as we learn near the end of the novel from a letter Woodward sent congratulating him about the good news.

Immaturity, it should be noted, also reveals money's capacity to trigger positive feeling, something akin to Alistair's exuberance in *The Millionairess*. Also, just as Smith's negative feelings are more intensely personal, more tethered to a psychology of money than those accompanying the more comically detached discussions of money in plays such as *Buoyant Billions*, the same is true in these relatively rare instances of refulgence in *Immaturity*. One of the other lodgers in the Dodd's Building lodging house overseen by Mrs Froster, for example, is the dissipated Fraser Fenwick, whom Smith meets soon after arriving. He concludes that Fenwick is a "blackguard," and it is in part because of this impression that

Smith sinks into "very low spirits" and resolves to find another place of residence (*I*, 9). Later in the novel, Fenwick has succumbed to alcoholism and gambling, vices leaving him destitute and starving. He has pawned everything he owns, and Lady Geraldine Porter, who had employed and befriended his late mother, is his last hope. After finally gaining admittance to see Lady Geraldine, who had been enjoying the opulence and excess of one of the frequent gatherings of artists and socialites Halket Grosvenor hosted at Perspective in Richmond, he begins his request qua self-defense by claiming that he had at one time "earned" his money, not stolen it, an assertion she quickly rejects as fiction. She is quick to remind him that, unlike Smith's accomplishment near the end *Immaturity*, Fenwick was offered nominations for Civil Service but refused to work to pass the examinations. After enumerating his many failings, including a litany of thefts, firings, and unpaid bills, she finally relents and promises him ten pounds, also giving him a few shillings to buy something to eat. The effect of the money is transformative. Previously "frightened" in his abjection and exceptionally nervous about his entreaty of Lady Geraldine, with money in hand Fenwick now "swaggered through the verandah" and felt "buoyant as a trodden daisy" because he could now stifle his hunger "in luxury" (150). In this regard, Fenwick's response anticipates Alastair's transformation by the sudden acquisition of money in *The Millionairess* even as he also serves as a kind of foil character to Smith.[40]

Like Alastair Fitzfassenden's marriage in *The Millionairess*, marriages in both *Immaturity* and *The Irrational Knot* are irrevocably and problematically tied to money, and the connection between the institution and material wealth is plural and, at times, complex. The last book of *Immaturity* contains several examples of this complexity, as does *The Irrational Knot*, to which I shall turn momentarily. In Book Four, Fenwick returns to Lady Geraldine seeking her endorsement of his plan to marry his cousin Fanny Watkins, a prospect her father deems precipitous and unwise. Apologizing for his intrusion, Fenwick cites his sobriety, gainful employment, and recent raise in salary as reasons that Lady Geraldine should support him. He also apprises her of Fanny's recent running away from home, his pursuit of her, and their agreement to marry, making Fanny "independent" of her family. Unable to contain herself at Fenwick's insipidity, Lady Geraldine vigorously rejects his thesis:

> Independent! Eighty pounds a year is a pretty independence for the daughter of a well-to-do tradesman. She thinks she is securing her liberty, I suppose, poor little fool! (*I*, 404–05)

Taken aback, Fenwick parries her derision with "But she loves me. Really and truly she does," to which Lady Geraldine rejoins, "Nonsense! Love *you*! How long do you think she would love you on eighty pounds a year?" (405). For his part, Fanny's father, who arrives to express his opposition to the marriage, explains that he is not "bent again'" Fenwick personally; rather, he is concerned about his laxity when it comes to money. He "never learned how to put on his coin," Watkins alleges in his distinct dialect. "He'd spend as much money to be seen in a ensom keb, to save carryin a parcel, or to make a shopgirl think he was a hofficer in the Guards, as a real sharp man would have kept goin for a year on." He "aint sharp" (410).

The connection between money and marriage evolves in the final book of *Immaturity* with the budding, if misconstrued and ill-fated, relationship between Isabella Woodward, Foley Woodward's attractive daughter, and the swank-poet Patrick Hawkshaw. Believing that he was engaged to Isabella and that their impending nuptials had induced her to give him her late mother's diamonds, which he quickly pawns, Hawkshaw soon discovers that Isabella has no intention of marrying him. Their flirtation was merely a diversion for her while on holiday in a sleepy place in the north of Ireland, and her lending him the diamonds—with Smith's assistance—was simply an act of charity to help a starving artist. Initially stung by this rejection, Hawkshaw quickly concludes that the loss of "Isabella's person" would hardly cause him any "regret," but this does not allay his fears of bankruptcy and the responsibility to come up with restitution for the jewels (*I*, 378). With creditors demanding payment, Hawkshaw contrives the idea that he will "convert his misfortunes into money," which is, after all, "the privilege of a poet" (378). He will write and publish a long narrative poem about this broken relationship, sell it for two guineas a copy to 100 fortunate readers, and thereby recover the value of her diamonds and more. Achieving tremendous notoriety and motivated to print more copies of the poem at a reduced price, he buys back the diamonds and returns them to her angry father, who found the poet's "suaveness" exasperating. Most readers understood the cause of the romantic hero's heartbreak in Hawkshaw's poem to be an avatar of Isabella, a characterization that damaged her reputation, but no matter. Hawkshaw became a "sensation," in part by playing the role of a broken man attired all in black and looking woeful. When Lady Geraldine learns that Hawkshaw made "a lot of money off that book of his" and that the sentiment of his poem moved even professional editors to tears, her response is as immediate as it is lacerating: "Such maudlin imbecility is beneath even a man" (413).

While all of this is transpiring, Smith and Isabella's relationship evolves; he spends more time with her, assists in her efforts to save Hawkshaw from financial ruination, and even shares his poetry with her, a prospect that makes his knees weak and complexion pallid. By the novel's conclusion, the marital futures of Hawkshaw and Fanny Watkins remain uncertain, but Smith's are abundantly, and discouragingly, clear. For, while the flirtation between him and Isabella—or, rather, her flirtation with him—momentarily sparks his fantasy of being married to her, the very idea of such a union, her considerable beauty notwithstanding, grows less and less attractive to him: "Isabella always, Isabella everywhere, inevitable, the first face to be seen in the morning, the last at night." And worse: "Isabella in sickness or trouble, in a bad temper, in curl papers, at meals, Isabella old and decaying …" (*I*, 425). All he could do to combat these thoughts was shake his head and go to bed. Some two weeks later, taking an early morning walk, he meets Isabella on her way to church and accompanies her to the service. Afterward, she informs him that she is leaving London to visit her aunt in Derbyshire, and he responds by saying that, when she returns, he will have left her father's employment and taken a job with the civil service. Upon parting, they agree that they are not likely to see each other again over the next three months—or perhaps ever. As he moves away, Smith eagerly anticipates what will be "a long respite from further lovemaking," and this without ever "realizing the ineptitude with which he had conducted it" (431). Later that morning upon entering the Woodward house, his feelings calcify into something both more negative and final after he learns that Isabella had carelessly left his poems available for others like her sister to read:

> Finding the study unoccupied, he sat down, and with a sudden revulsion against his recent dallying resolved to tell Isabella unequivocally at their next meeting that his heart was not touched by her, and never had been, if the event of his leaving Mr Woodward's employment did not avert that encounter for ever [sic]. (433)

Isabella ultimately reaches a similar conclusion, as some months later Foley Woodward writes Smith to disclose, among other things, that she plans to marry a Mr. Saunders in the coming months.

At least one character other than Harriet, however, proceeds through "Courtship and Marriage" and "Flirtation" to the more conventional resolutions of romantic comedies. After seeing Isabella for the final time,

Smith meets a lavishly attired Fraser Fenwick at the Liverpool Street railway terminus, who announces that Lady Geraldine has "set her heart on making a match" for him and has succeeded (*I*, 432). In fact, he is on his way that very morning to be wed and invites Smith to accompany him, an invitation he cannot accept. Attired in a "glossy hat, blue frock coat adorned with a flower, white waistcoat, lavender gloves, patent leather boots, and trousers of small black and white check" (*I*, 431), this reformed, dandyish Fenwick recalls the swaggering character who was elated at coaxing money from Lady Geraldine so many pages earlier. However, Fenwick's ebullience never really transfers to Smith, from whom such buoyancy is seldom exhibited, nor does any romantic inclination. But is this really so atypical of the modernizing London in which Shaw's novel is set? For it must be said again that except for Harriet's marriage to Cyril Scott, a marriage that, as we learn in the novel's epigraph set some years later, has produced two lovely children, flirtations and courtships are routinely undone by money and a suitor's dismal prospect for future success. In this way, Simmel's critique of the modern city seems consonant with the travails of would-be lovers in *Immaturity*:

> London has never acted as England's heart but often as England's intellect and always as her moneybag![41]

Shaw's novel seems to bear this out, as Smith's anxious calculation of his scarce resources and resultant negative feeling overwhelm his "heart."

On a conscious, even philosophical level, Smith takes a measure of pride in being a figure of negation; his stance as an Agnostic, as he explains to Isabella while parsing distinctions between religious belief, Atheism, and Agnosticism, defines his position on religious matters as "pure negation" (*I*, 279). But such a stance is far more than a performance of iconoclasm or iteration of a sophisticated philosophy or metaphysic. As I have tried to demonstrate, Smith is driven toward the negative, a position inherent to Shaw's representation of urban life, which is why such feelings as disgust, revulsion, and—particularly when he is the subject of his own lacerating analysis—shame recur throughout *Immaturity*. In the novel's concluding paragraph, as Smith gazes out over the city of London, Shaw's narrator underscores this tendency:

> As Smith recrossed the bridge, he stopped and stood in one of the recesses to meditate on his immaturity, and to look upon the beauty of the still

expanses of white moonlight and black shadow which lay before him. At last he shook his head negatively, and went home. (*I*, 438)

Where money is concerned, or when Smith worries about his ability to acquire a sum of it sufficient to meet his expenses, this negativity is exacerbated and at times metamorphoses into embarrassment, self-deprecation, and repulsion; and such negative affects can constrain or even decathect libidinal drives or the "restless craving" for a woman to love. If Smith in *Immaturity* is indeed an avatar of his creator, therefore, then it is all the more apparent why the motto "UNASHAMED" so aptly describes Undershaft in *Major Barbara*—and Shaw himself.

Money and the Staging of Respectability in *The Irrational Knot*

In *The Irrational Knot* money, much like its disruptive appearances in *Immaturity*, in Freud's dreams, and in those of his patients, affects social performance, including the niggling appurtenances and role-playing that define late Victorian respectability, particularly where marriage is concerned. As such, it is a crucial factor in Shaw's representation of British aristocracy and its behaviors. In this regard, his second novel seems more accurately described than his first as a "study of manners," in part because, although like its antecedent, *The Irrational Knot* has its share of victims—one of whose life, like that of St John Davis in *Immaturity*, is sadly abbreviated by alcoholism—its narrative is focused more intently on Britain's upper class. By contrast, Shaw's representation of the privileged in *Immaturity* does not commence until the novel's second book, "Aesthetics," well after its exposition of Smith's materially inflected psychology and repertory of feelings.

"Aesthetics" introduces readers to Halket Grosvenor's lavish estate Perspective in Richmond, a site of excess and conspicuous consumption. Benefiting from "great" wealth, as Shaw's narrator notes, Grosevenor was also possessive of a "luxurious indolence" that partially explains his pattern of beginning, yet seldom completing, his own artistic works. More a patron of the arts than an artist himself, this "finished *gourmet*" and "fastidious glutton" (*I*, 105) hosts an annual Easter week gathering "devoted to an artistic congress." Throwing open the doors of his considerable estate, complete with a gallery and "handsome apartments," visitors enjoy artworks of all description, from Tintoretto to stained glass windows. The event itself is carefully staged, a performance of Grosvenor's eclecticism and frustrated artistic ambition, as Shaw's narrator describes: "Bowls, plates, candlesticks, statuettes, and etchings were everywhere. Artistic effect, consciously striven for, was apparent at every step" (108). "Bodily wants" are satisfied by the appetizing selections of numerous buffets where, if one so desires, a visitor can "gorge himself" and "be social, solitary, obscure, or conspicuous, exactly as he pleased" (109). Offering a kind of physical and affectual utopia, this scene of plenitude provides a vivid contrast to Smith's constrained circumstances; moreover, unlike the frenzy that greets Smith outside the Alhambra Theatre, its leisurely climate and the friendly, "promiscuous composition" of gatherers—save for the few attendees engaged in lively colloquies on aesthetics—produce both "harmony" and "good feeling." To be sure, "Unpleasant incidents sometimes occurred; but they were of that kind from which no society is exempt" (109). This sumptuous and artificial world, in short, could hardly differ more from the noisy, overcrowded streets and accelerated pace of the city that Smith navigates.

Unlike the opening chapters of *Immaturity* set in Smith's lodging house, its Islington neighborhood, and his "den" of loathsome employment, *The Irrational Knot*, as I mentioned earlier, begins with a concert organized by the aristocratic class for the benefit of workers and their families. For the most part, there is little in Shaw's second novel that parallels Smith's exceptionally modest living conditions, his anxiety about his budget and uncertain future, his dissatisfaction with his employment, and the abjection of Fenwick or Davies at their worst, save for the concluding chapter that details the decline and untimely death of Ned Conolly's alcoholic sister, Susanna. Instead, Shaw's narrator, in both subtle and more overt ways, focuses on the hauteur and variegated obsolescence of the privileged class, especially when compared to a "workman" and brilliant inventor such as Conolly. Indeed, the term "workman" resonates as a motif in several chapters in the novel, typically conveying a critique of the shallowness—the manners—of the enervated aristocratic class that wields the term as a marker of class difference. The institution of marriage, that irrational knot of social orthodoxy and class striation, is implicated in this critique, particularly in its perpetuation of the unsavory business of exchanging nuptial commitments for dowries. All of these factors contribute to what is, much like the uneventful conclusion of *Immaturity*, an unexpected and deflating ending guaranteed not to satisfy the expectations of most Victorian readers.

The early chapters of *The Irrational Knot* foreshadow such eventualities both by relating aspersions of the working class by the privileged and outlining the vicissitudes of marriage, particularly for the daughters of aristocrats. When Ned Conolly is introduced in the novel's opening chapter, for example, the Reverend George Lind responds to a question about his identity from Mrs Leith Fairfax with "Some young man who attracted the attention of the Countess by his singing. He is only a workman." An eagle-eyed observer of social niceties—she claims that Conolly's "manner of picking up [her] glass had his entire history in it"— Mrs Fairfax is nonetheless impressed by him, recommending that the "young man deserves to be encouraged" (*Knot*, 7). Lind is not so sure: "Injudicious encouragement might perhaps lead him to forget his real place in [society]" (8). When later assigning accompanists to the roster of singers for the concert, Conolly expresses his reluctance to accompany himself, to which Lind responds, hoping to induce him to play and thereby simplify his task, "Oh, they are not very critical: they are only workmen" (13). Because Conolly and his audience are "only" workmen, Marian Lind, his eventual wife, is "a little taken aback" by the richness of his voice and extent of his ability. Soon after his performance, the ever- curt Nelly McQuinch accuses Sholto Douglas of being "jealous of a plumber," and Marian is "still anxious to be affable to the workman" (15), an affability that leads to a longer conversation with Conolly in which he recounts his six-year apprenticeship in America to an electrical engineer. More references to Conolly as a workman follow, including Nelly's characterization of him as looking like a waiter, before she is moved to tears by his powerful singing of "Tom Bowling." The chapter concludes with Conolly's introduction to Marian's cousin Marmaduke Lind, whom everyone presumes will marry the sister of Lord Carbury, Conolly's patron and fellow experimenter with electrical energy. At least that is the rumor.

The second chapter opens with a brief summary of the unfortunate marital history of Marian's father Reginald Harrington Lind, the fourth son of a younger brother of the Earl of Carbury. As a young man, Lind had "no object in life except that of getting through it as easily as possible," an ambition which motivated his ill-advised marriage at 19 to the heiress of a wealthy Lancashire cotton spinner. After giving Lind three children, she abandoned him, "eloped" with a "spiritualist," and succumbed soon thereafter to scarlet fever after giving birth to a fourth child. Lind was "disgusted" by his wife's infidelity—after all, he had introduced her to many of his friends, "noblemen and gentlemen"—but eventually "consoled himself for her bad taste" by appropriating her jewels, among other items, and securing an income of "nearly seven thousand pounds a year." Soon thereafter, he "became so welcome in society" that there were "few marriageable gentlewomen of twenty-six and upward in London who had not been submitted to his inspection with a view to matrimony" (*Knot*, 31). Uninterested in nuptial opportunity, Lind decided that he had "nothing to gain" by remarriage and, passing his sons and daughter off to the care of schools and congenial relatives, he "pursued the usual routine of a gentleman-bachelor in London" (32).

This pursuit, however, in no way diminished his adherence to the unwritten social legislation concerning marriage and social class insofar as his daughter Marian is concerned, one codicil of which mandates an automatic rejection of any possible misalliance. After Marian agrees to marry Conolly, and not the long-admiring Sholto Douglas, Lind and Conolly meet, the latter attempting to gain the former's approbation of the marriage. Carefully mounting his argument, Conolly agrees with Lind that Marian should never wed a "foul-mouthed fellow, ignorant, dirty, besotted, and out of place in any company except at the bar of a public house," and asserts that her agreeing to marry him confirms the fact that he does not "answer to any such description." Responding to Lind's intimation that Conolly will accrue inestimable advantages by marriage to his daughter, the American inventor remarks that he would have no trouble "in purchasing that advantage," possessing appreciable financial means that he expects "to increase largely in the course of some years" (*Knot*, 154). Countering Lind's remark that Marian's marriage to him would be "imprudent," Conolly reminds him that "I possess actual competence, and a prospect of wealth"; he adds, with a modicum of self-aggrandizement, that his name is "beyond comparison, more widely known than yours" (154). The point is more modest than it might initially seem; as Marmaduke Lind and Sholto Douglas describe later, Conolly's rise in social stature has been almost meteoric. Besides, he is a "genius and a celebrity and all that," and "people don't expect him to be conventional" (233). Unpersuaded and adamantly opposed to the match, Lind finally throws down what he regards as the final gauntlet, the ultimate threat: "If my daughter marries you, she shall have neither my countenance in society nor one solitary farthing of the fortune I had destined for her. I recommend the latter point to your attention" (156). Conolly is undeterred, responding, "I should hardly have proposed to marry her but for her entire pecuniary independence of me" (157), and is convinced that the wealth she already possesses is sufficient for this purpose.

Money intrudes upon every intimate relationship and marital possibility in *The Irrational Knot*. Susanna Conolly and Marmaduke Lind, unmarried and "living in sin," survive on the income she earns through her work as an actress. Susanna, in fact, has no interest in marriage, regarding it as "all very fine for women who have no better way of supporting themselves" (*Knot*, 53), but in no way suitable for her. For the unfortunate Lady Constance Carbury, however, the more orthodox dispersal of a dowry, a tactic deployed in finding suitable matches for her two sisters, has created a strain on her brother's wealth and thus limited her possibilities:

> The illustrious matches made by her sisters had, in fact, been secured by extravagant dowering, which had left nothing for poor Lady Constance except a miserable three hundred pounds a year, at which paltry figure no man had as yet offered to take her. (56)

The Countess Carbury, like almost everyone else, had assumed Marmaduke Lind would marry Constance, a union she and Constance both endorsed. But Lind, tired of being a quarry "hunted" by these two women with the goal of "running me down at last in a church" (224), regards Constance as a "little fool" and has little interest in being so ensnared, especially after meeting Susanna. Marmaduke admires her courage as an "independent" woman possessive of a "sort of self-respect," even though he loathes her "dipsomania," a condition that eventually ruins their relationship and leads to her accepting an American theatrical producer's offer and moving to New York. The decision was disastrous, as I shall discuss in a moment, as it led to both the end of her professional career and her untimely death at 29 (and, finally, to Marmaduke's capitulation to social orthodoxy, as his impending marriage to Constance, a prospect he once could not abide, is announced in the novel's final book).

Constance's marital possibilities were, in fact, few, as her unmarried brother Lord Carbury—a tinkerer in all things mechanical whose fascination with electricity led him to meet Conolly—refused to increase his youngest sister's dowry, having already "*speculated quite heavily* enough in brothers-in-law" (my emphasis, *Knot*, 56). Besides, a more substantial investment in the marriage market might hinder his ability to accumulate "toys" of all sorts: 16 typewriters, though he wrote little; a collection of trumpets and trombones, though he had no ability to play brass instruments; rifles, though he was no sportsman; and warehouses more of things that had caught his fancy. (Like Grosvenor in *Immaturity*, he spends extravagantly, starts many projects, and finishes little.) However, given his Lordship's avocations, these were hardly investments. Dowries, by contrast, *were* and herein resides a crucial distinction. For typewriters, trombones, lathes (he bought the "most expensive" one he could find in an attempt to produce a perfect billiard ball), and the "really ingenious bicycle or tricycle" he purchased are material commodities (55). They may possess some element of futurity—someday a better billiard ball might lead to something—but the transactions to obtain such objects are subtended, as Shaw's narrator describes, by their use value in the present. Typewriters produce script on paper; lathes effect modifications in raw materials such as ivory. Conversely, the "figurative enterprise" of finance—speculation, investment, credit, and so on—operates imaginatively. In addition, Carbury, like bankers and poets in Anna Kornbluh's vivid analogy, attempts through his sisters' marriages and his manipulation of dowries to "'body forth the form of things unknown,'" effectuating "in present material form things heretofore unembodied and unknown."[42] Such is the fictive nature of capital, particularly in speculative investments like his Lordship's. More damagingly, the fact that not even a single suitor has been willing to "take" Constance begs the invidious question of her relative value as a young woman without a dowry. After the significant investment in two wedded sisters, her marginal utility is insufficient to warrant any further commitment of funds.

Shaw's introduction of Constance's dilemma by way of her wealthy brother's acquisition of equipment, particularly reproductive instruments—typewriters, lathes, trombones—and his narrator's use of the past participle "speculated" are hardly accidental in a novel that links marriage to money itself and, as in this instance, to the investment of capital. As sociologists understand all too well, money has played a formal part in marriages in a wide variety of societies, both primitive and advanced. Modern societies, however, typically distinguish between unions based on love and those, like prostitution, based on money. For Simmel, an inevitable "disparagement of personal dignity" arises "in every marriage that is not based on personal affection; in the modern moment, we might say, the choice of a partner in marriage is no longer determined by social motives," as love is "decidedly superior to money as a factor of selection." Further, and more damaging, in addition to the inherent degradation of the female in the dowry system, the male in the relationship customarily is granted "greater freedom" than his wife, who has been reduced to the status of a domestic object (*Philosophy of Money*, 412–13). Alternatively, as in the case of Marian's marriage, as Conolly readily admits, Marian has been reduced to a domestic *manager*, someone "capable of being mistress to her servants," thus sparing her husband "all the friction of housekeeping" (*Knot*, 277).

So many of the issues limned here—and many more outlined in earlier chapters—converge in Marian's abandonment of her marriage, a decision that ultimately and coincidentally brings her into the company of a dying Susanna in a New York City boarding house. Several of these issues equally inform Conolly's stoic response to her abdication. When he returns home from a business trip to Glasgow, Conolly discovers an upset Nelly McQuinch, who relates the news that her cousin has packed her bags and traveled to Euston Station with Douglas. No admirer of Sholto, who is, in her view, a "selfish, lying, conceited hound" (*Knot*, 275), Nelly presses Conolly to share with her his reaction to this news. A rational response, he submits, might be to divorce Marian, thereby allowing her the freedom to marry Sholto if she wishes. But this solution also confirms what Nelly has suspected all along: namely, that Marian left with Douglas because she desired "a human being to live with, not a calculating machine." How was Marian to know before her marriage, Nelly asks, that Conolly was "not made of flesh and blood" (276–77)? An exemplar of the metropolitan subjectivity that Simmel theorizes in which punctuality, calculability, and exactness predominate—and instinctive traits and impulses are subordinated—Conolly stands as a cold emblem of the modern Londoner, an accomplished and excessively rational older cousin of Robert Smith in *Immaturity*.

For Conolly, the marriage's failure signifies something more than his putative machinelike personality and possible unsuitability for marriage: namely, irrefutable evidence of the corruption and arrogance of the aristocratic class. He professes amazement that someone of Nelly's acuity never suspected his disdain for her class, one that smugly regards itself as "higher, more cultivated and refined" than anything he had ever experienced. It was only after his "*mésalliance*" with Marian, he claims, that he realized "how infinitely beneath me and my class was the one I had married into" (*Knot*, 281). Nelly's incredulity at this assertion elicits from Conolly the sharpest class critique in the novel:

> Now what am I, Miss McQuinch? A worker. I belonged and belong to the class that keeps up the world by its millions of serviceable hands and serviceable brains. All the pride of caste in me settles on that point. I admit no

loafer as my equal.... To me a man like your uncle, Marian's father, or like Marmaduke or Douglas, loafing idly round spending money that has been made by the sweat of men like myself, are little better than thieves. They get on with the queerest makeshifts for self-respect.... (282)

"Respectability" demands such queer makeshifts and perverted values. Further, the motif of the "workman" in *The Irrational Knot*—"he's *only* a workman"—is expanded and its ideological thrust redirected in these remarks. The difference between profectitious and adventitious money—money inherited as opposed to money earned, won, or even stumbled upon—also reemerges here, as does the Shavian indictment of loafers, those whom Vivie Warren in *Mrs Warren's Profession* contemptuously labels "wasters." The aristocracy that Reginald Lind is so desperate to protect, in short, is here characterized as a gathering of wasters with, as Vivie pronounces, "no purpose, and no character"—and "no grit" (*CPP* 3: 57). Conolly is overjoyed to be free of them.

Marian's motives for leaving him and their marriage are more complicated, tied both to the ideology of the ruling class and the suppression of desire inherent to it and "civilization," as Freud would later describe in *Civilization and Its Discontents* (1930). In the preceding chapter, she reveals to Nelly that her marriage to Conolly was never based on "obedience" to her "instincts"; rather, it was predicated on forging an alliance with a man "whom I felt I could respect as my superior." She recognizes too late the error of allowing "little wisdoms" to "stifle all our big instincts" and envies the happiness of those very people she and Nelly once despised "for always having done exactly what their hearts told them!" (*Knot*, 265). In making her case, Marian distinguishes between two kinds of love: that variety of which one's "good sense" approves and an "other sort" that has "nothing" whatsoever to do with good sense. "It is an overpowering impulse," she tells Nelly, "a craving—a faith that defies logic" (265). However much a "lazy good-for-nothing" Sholto has become, and however much he typifies a self-indulgent loafer who ought to be "put to work in some fashion" (267), he is probably right to accuse Marian of "committing a crime against nature" for living with a man she does not love (269). However, until this moment, the "drive" for respectability has overwhelmed this "instinct," this powerful "craving." Shortly thereafter, she takes a desperate step to reverse the current of this psychical circuit: she boards a ship bound for New York with Sholto, who very quickly behaves badly and totally destroys Marian's affection for him. He eventually abandons her there, in need of money, and—within a matter of hours of his departure—Marian finds herself in the company of a raving and dying Susanna Conolly at a shabby boarding house, which is all either woman at this point can afford.

After Susanna succumbs to the ravages of her disease, Marian is contemplating her limited options when she is startled by sounds coming from her sister-in-law's room. Maybe she isn't really dead, Marian imagines. Making a wary investigation, she discovers her estranged husband sitting by his sister's body. Conolly had traveled to New York because of his justifiable concern for Marian, having received indications of her financial dilemma. (For her part, much like Shaw's anxiety about Mrs Campbell's bank overdrafts discussed above, Marian reveals to her American friend Mrs Crawford that "the question of money" makes her "anxious" [*Knot*, 310]). Conolly initiates a somber retrospection of their lives and his sister's, placing the blame for her tragic death squarely on social hypocrisy and money. "Society," he alleges, "by the power of the purse, set her to nautch-girl's work, and forbade her the higher work that was equally within her power." She lies before them, he continues, "dead of a preventable disease, chiefly because most of the people she came in contact with had a direct pecuniary interest in depraving and poisoning her" (349). In the novel's final pages, Ned and Marian discuss the possibility of a reconciliation, with Conolly insisting that no one or nothing, not even London society, can make him feel disgrace. He also learns of Marian's pregnancy, promising to accept the unborn child as his own, but she won't allow it. The irrational knot of their marriage is thus undone, although as he leaves Conolly promises to see her the next day "and often afterward, I hope" (352). Perhaps his hope is realized, as the novel concludes leaving this question unanswered.

Conolly's diagnosis of the root cause, the pathology, of his sister's exploitation and alcoholism is hardly surprising, as Shaw establishes the relationship between money and the performance of social class throughout the novel. As the second book of *The Irrational Knot* opens, for example, Reginald Harrington Lind, Marmaduke's uncle and Marian Lind's father, visits Sholto Douglas's mother with the purpose of promoting a possible marriage between Sholto and Marian. Earlier, Sholto had expressed his ardor for her and perhaps he could be induced to press his case further. Shaw's narrator paints the scene:

> Sholto's mother was a widow lady older than Mr Lind, with a rather glassy eye and shaky hand, who would have looked weak and shiftless in an almshouse, but who, with plenty of money, unlimited domestic service, and

unhesitating deference from attendants ... made a fair shew of being a dignified and interesting old lady. (*Knot*, 107)

The Douglas's wealth, from Lind's perspective, outweighs Sholto's lack of a title. He is just a "plain gentleman," as his mother phrases it, but Lind quickly dismisses the importance of such societal accoutrements, noting that "we, who are familiar with titles, understand their true value" (108). As we eventually learn, however, Sholto is hardly a "gentleman," plain or otherwise, but no matter—money can transform him into one just as surely as it contributes to his mother's portrayal of an estimable dowager in the late-Victorian theatre of social opinion. In a different context, one defined by poverty and class affiliation, she might appear weak, even shiftless, but surrounded by attendants who were, in effect, "trained artists," the scene plays and reads differently. Aware of his own part in the spectacle, Lind, when offered a photograph to inspect, "pretended to admire it" so as not to mute in any way the tone of the "polished and skillful comedy" in which he was participating (107).

Meta-theatricality and performance give way later in the chapter to a more perverse intrusion of money into marriage when Lind and Mrs Douglas turn their attention to Susanna's illicit relationship with that "scamp," Marmaduke. In her own right, Susanna in her stage persona of Lalage Virtue is a well-known public figure, as her brother would soon be; in fact, Marian's father has seen her "photographic portraits" everywhere, as they are displayed prominently "in all the shop windows." Such public attention, however, in no way mitigates the scandal of her living with Marmaduke, whose father threatens to stop his allowance if the affair continues. Marmaduke, scamp though he may be, is also clever and counters with his promise to marry the actress, therefore broker an obvious and embarrassing *mésalliance*, if his income is in any way cut off by his father. Unaccustomed to any such evidence of Marmaduke's cleverness, Lind suspects that he is receiving "shrewd guidance" from his paramour (*Knot*, 113). He surely could not have arrived as such an extortive and effective counterstrategy on his own.

But first things first: namely, Conolly's intention to marry Marian. Hoping to persuade Susanna to intercede on his behalf and convince her brother to sell his interest in his company, perhaps return to America, or in any case forego a relationship with his daughter, Lind dispatches George to visit her and present the family's case. In a kind of distorted reprise of Lind's theatricalized meeting with Sholto's mother, he arrives at Susanna's and is received by a "remarkably plain" servant—as all of the house servants are instructed to be by their mistress—who ushers him to meet the famous actress. Led to a smaller back room, he enters a "luxuriously decorated," "sham Persian" scene "containing ornaments of all styles and periods," a miniature, less tasteful version of Grosvenor's Perspective in *Immaturity*. By far, the most expensive artifact in the room is the Parisian-designed dress that Susanna wears, worth some £200; and, like the room's decoration and her meticulously made-up face and coifed hair, the dress supplements her preparation for a role she is to assume as the wife of a Caliph. Before "laying out a heap of money" for a dress, she explains, she needs to experience it in the fictive context in which it will be worn (*Knot*, 176). After leaving Susanna having failed to accomplish his mission, George writes a sermon in which he describes the experience as a confrontation with Vice herself—a figure who "boasted to me that she bore upon her the value of two hundred pounds of money" (190). Only after the reflection necessary to compose his sermon did he realize the extent to which, more generally, "sin is committed in a great city for wages"—for money (191). The hypocrisy of his position is clear: such an expense was not a sin, it seems, in Mrs Douglas's performance of social class, but this sort of staging in the iniquitous home of an actress is a different matter. It is yet another instance of the "contamination of the theatre" (189).

In George's sermon, Susanna's performance, like so many in Shaw's early novels, is authorized by a vulgar materialism, much as marriage is in the social-class affiliation that Reginald Lind desperately hopes to preserve. Hardly a fool, Susanna quickly realizes that the Lind family hopes to "buy her off" as well as deter her brother from any relationship with Marian. Later in the novel and more desperate after Sholto Douglas abandons his daughter—and apparently indifferent to his behavior—Lind attempts to purchase Sholto's marriage to Marian and the respectability it will bring by guaranteeing him £10,000. In his appeal to Douglas, Lind alludes to the inextricable relationship between "society" and money:

> But I am urging you to make Marian your legal wife solely because it is the best course for both of you. That, I assure you, is the feeling of society in the matter.... I will give you ten thousand pounds down on her wedding-day. You will lose nothing. (*Knot*, 331)

By awarding the money to Marian "unconditionally," Lind explains, it will "become your property the moment you become her husband" (331–32).

Declining the offer, Sholto expresses his supreme confidence that Lind can "close" the deal for half that amount with other potential suitors, as numerous "poorer men" would be glad to cooperate "in consideration of so much cash" (332). Angering Lind, who vows to obtain "satisfaction," Sholto has a momentary regret and calculates—twice—just how significant £10,000 would be in compensation for the expenses he incurred on his ill-fated American trip. Better, he finally concludes, to leave London and society all together and travel to Brussels.

Like Constance Carbury and her paltry dowry in the early pages of *The Irrational Knot*, Marian is reduced by her father's negotiation to just another commodity in that commercial transaction known as marriage and the respectability it provides the Victorian aristocracy. In addition, if marriage is so irrevocably tied to money and commodity exchange—a unique bicycle here, another typewriter or trombone there—then it should come as little surprise that the performance of respectability is as well; that is, so long as the actors are of the appropriate class. Andrew Undershaft is unashamed of making or earning his money; so is Ned Conolly. Robert Smith feels similarly in *Immaturity*, so long as the cost of doing so does not transform him into a servile coward or one of a pack of hungry dogs. Money in Shaw's novels, as these examples testify, may indeed be the most important thing in the world.

Why *He* Would Not

As I mentioned in my introductory chapter, Shaw never really abandoned his analysis of the subjective effects of money in his later work, even if the feelings instantiated by money in plays such as *The Millionairess* and *Buoyant Billions* are not nearly so severe as those depicted in his early fiction. This grouping of later texts includes *Why She Would Not*, which is—incomplete though it may be—Shaw's last play. "She" in this instance is the wealthy Serafina White, granddaughter of industrial magnate Reginald White, who has been saved from robbery and possible assault by a brash young man, Henry Bossborn. Unemployed and apparently homeless, Bossborn is rewarded for his "plucky service" to Serafina with the offer of employment at White Sons and Bros., Ltd.; and in scene three of the playlet he negotiates with Old Reginald about the terms of his position. Bossborn flatly refuses to accept any position that requires him to "clock in," and it is difficult not to regard his decision as a commentary on Reginald's brief dissertation on "unpunctuality," a distasteful echo, perhaps, of Mr Figgis's upbraiding of Smith for arriving a few minutes late for work in *Immaturity*. Not wishing to become what in "End of a Clerk in Dublin" from *Sixteen Self Sketches* Shaw termed a "nobody on a stool" (*SSS*, 38), Bossborn cannot accept such terms, which is why he would not dream of working at White Sons and Brothers Ltd. unless his talents were given free rein. His insistence is rewarded, for a mere two years later, when Serafina and Bossborn meet again, he has risen to be director of the company and shareholder; and his "own business" includes land agency, private banking, real estate development, and more. Formerly a "tramp looking for a job," Bossborn has evolved into a successful entrepreneur and titan of business (*CPP* 5: 9); and this is precisely why Serafina, unlike Epifania in *The Millionairess*, cannot countenance the idea of marrying him, for to do so would be to "knuckle under" to his predominance (14).

Bossborn and Serafina are alike in this respect, because he would not accede to such subordination in his professional life either. He is, stated in another way, "impudent" or unashamed, the former of which aspersion is applied to Jack Tanner by Roebuck Ramsden in the opening act of *Man and Superman* (1905). In a brief dissertation to Ramsden, Jack lacerates the "atmosphere of shame" in which they live, one in which they are ashamed of "everything that is real about us," including both their considerable incomes and their "naked skins" (*CPP* 3: 528). Here, "shame" hardly functions as the autonomous or incipient affect created by an event or by contact with a thing that catalyzes an intense response impossible to control—think here of the sudden manifestation of Smith's blush when Mrs Froster praises him as surely having a mother proud of his gentlemanliness, or the "shadow" that comes over him without warning as he floats jobless and anxious down the Thames in *Immaturity*. The affective loop between the depths of his psyche and the surface of his reddening skin captured by his blush—in this instance, elicited by high praise—cannot be constrained. By contrast, shame in Jack Tanner's social philosophy relegates men such as Ramsden to being a "mere member of the British public," a thoroughly unremarkable fellow who, contrary to his asseverations to the contrary, cannot "advance" (*CPP* 3: 529). The inverse, one might say, of the younger Shaw shamed by his father's pretensions and the young Smith disgusted by a tawdry theatre and the potentially damaging impecuniosity which it might occasion, Ramsden wallows in his wealth, his mediocrity, and—from Jack's perspective—his all-encompassing shame.

Shaw's psychology of money seems similarly all-encompassing, as does his articulation and rearticulation of money's subjective effects. The topic dominates his novels and the prefaces that introduce *Immaturity* and *The Irrational Knot*; and insofar as it inflects his and his characters' self-perceptions, their perceptions of others, and the feelings of both author and character, we might conclude that Shaw's internal life is better understood not only by exploring its Freudian or Lacanian depths, but also by constructing a rival material psychology in which economics, drive, and affect or feeling are rendered more visible. By attending to surfaces, emotions, and feelings in his earliest novels—intensely positive feelings but, more often, both negative "filled" and "expectant" ones—we might access Shaw's psychology of money. As Simmel underscored, and the dreams of Freud's patients demonstrate, money exists not only as a measure of "objective value," but as a "psychological fact" of enormous determinative power. Few understand this fact better than Shaw, whose characters' sudden display of intense feeling and/or emotion is manifested in various ways, including the almost omnipresent blush to which he was so prone. How this topic functions as a trope in Shaw's fiction, especially in *Cashel Byron's Profession*, is the subject of a later chapter. Before then, and as a respite from lengthy exegeses such as this one, a short entr'acte and evening at the theatre in *Love Among the Artists* follows, allowing for a breather and, I hope, renewed energy to return to more sustained encounters with Shaw's material—and materialist—psychology.

Notes

1. In orthodox Marxian fashion, Shaw in various places defined capital as "spare money" or "surplus money." So in *The Intelligent Woman's Guide*, Shaw advises that, after living in the style "customary in her class," a woman who "still has some money to spare to use as capital" might do so to "increase her income" (225). *All* money, he emphasizes later, is not "spare money," as most people spend their scarce resources on necessary goods, not on investments in the Stock Exchange (251).
2. Susan Cannon Harris, *Irish Drama and the Other Revolutions: Playwrights, Sexual Politics and the International Left, 1892–1964* (Edinburgh: Edinburgh University Press, 2017), 92.
3. See Chap. 6, which briefly considers Jean Baudrillard's postulation of the signifying value of commodities as signs (of respectability, prestige, and so on), not as the satisfiers of "vital anthropological needs."
4. See Simmel, *The Philosophy of Money*, 407–11.

5. See Simmel, "The Metropolis and Mental Life" (1903), in *The Sociology of Georg Simmel*, ed. and trans. Kurt H. Wolff (New York: The Free Press, 1950), 409–24. Here, he argues that "Money is concerned only with what is common to all," reducing "all quality and individuality to the question: How much" (411). Although Wolff is cited as the translator on the book's title page, in a few instances he imported other translations. This essay was translated in 1936 by Edward A. Shils for a University of Chicago course book.
6. Eve Kosofsky Sedgwick, *Touching Feeling: Affect, Pedagogy, Performativity* (Durham and London: Duke University Press, 2003), 21. Here, Sedgwick is quoting from Tomkins' 1981 article "The Quest for Primary Motives: Biography and Autobiography of an Idea."
7. Sedgwick, 21.
8. See Simmel, "The Metropolis and Mental Life," 410.
9. See Simmel, *The Philosophy of Money*, 465–74; and "The Metropolis and Mental Life" where he describes the increasing "calculability" and "hardness" of the modern mind with its privileging of such matters as exactness and punctuality (411–13). Shaw explains the use of money as a means of exchange—and an improvement over the barter system—in *The Intelligent Woman's Guide*, 251–52. However, as Shaw very well knew, more than convenience is involved. Having studied economics in two separate reading groups with Wicksteed and others and announcing his familiarity with "General Walker's" work, he would also have been aware of the so-called "double coincidence" that impaired the exchange of goods before the use of currency as a general standard of value. See Walker, *Money*, 1–4, where he explains the concept and acknowledges Jevons's *Money and the Mechanism of Exchange* (1875) as the germ of this topic. For a brief discussion of Shaw's immersion in economic theory, see also Peter Gahan, *Bernard Shaw and Beatrice Webb on Poverty and Equality in the Modern World, 1905–1914* (London: Palgrave Macmillan, 2017), 3–6.
10. My characterization of Nelly as "acrid" stems from the depictions provided by Shaw's narrator. When a spurned Sholto Douglas takes Marian Lind to dinner, for example, he sat in an angry silence "heedless alike" to his host's "commonplaces" and Nelly's "acridities" (140). Later in the chapter, she "talked incessantly in her most acrid tones" (148).
11. Sedgwick, 18–19.
12. Sara Ahmed, *The Cultural Politics of Emotion* (New York: Routledge, 2004), 89.
13. Sianne Ngai, *Ugly Feelings* (Cambridge: Harvard University Press, 2005), 335–37.
14. Ngai, 210. Ngai is referencing Bloch's *The Principle of Hope, Volume 1*, trans. Neville Plaice, Stephen Plaice, and Paul Knight (Cambridge, Mass:

MIT Press, 1995), 74–75. In this discussion "feeling" and "emotion" tend to be used as synonyms, with my preference, after Altieri's distinction between the two, tending toward the latter term. "Respectability," "anxiety," and "fear" can indeed be described as feelings, but when the element of futurity is introduced the sense of larger narratives and histories also surfaces, as these feelings often imply a larger subjective context or emotion.

15. *Bernard Shaw and Mrs Patrick Campbell*, 66. Throughout this discussion of financial exigency, Shaw refers to Stella in the third person as "her."
16. Throughout *The Intelligent Woman's Guide*, Shaw alludes to "spare money" as the kind that is used in investment. He also notes that if an investor has every confidence that income earned will be subject "only to income tax," he or she will invest it (296). These topics—spare money and favorable taxation on investments—resurface in Act Three of *Buoyant Billions*. Sir Ferdinand assures Darkie that her father will remain "enormously rich" in part because by selling stocks and shares for a profit, the monies earned are "not taxed, as they are classed as capital, not as income" (*CPP* 1: 775). Later in the Act, she, also known as Clemmy, announces that with the money she could "spare" she has doubled her income (*CPP* 1: 788).
17. In this deprecation of the British pound as a "bit of paper," Shaw echoes the description Walker employs in *Money*.
18. Jevons, *The Theory of Political Economy*, 41.
19. In this regard, Richard Farr Dietrich's admonitions in *Bernard Shaw's Novels* are worth heeding. He argues that Shaw's biographers were frequently "misled" by his own commentary; in turn, they and other critics advanced "hasty readings of the novels" and were lured into "incautious acceptance of the critical clichés coined by Shaw himself" (29). See Dietrich, 28–35. Susan Harris makes a similar point in *Irish Drama and Other Revolutions*, 21–22.
20. Ahmed, 103.
21. I discuss this topic as it applies to tenement drama and fiction in *"Something Dreadful and Grand": American Literature and the Irish-Jewish Unconscious*, 138–42.
22. Peter Gahan, "Bernard Shaw: Dégringolade and Derision in Dublin City," *SHAW 32: Shaw and the City*, ed. Desmond Harding (University Park: The Pennsylvania State University Press, 2012), 44.
23. The resemblance of Robert Smith in *Immaturity* to his creator seems beyond dispute. St. John Ervine, for example, identifies passages in the novel that are "clearly a description" of Shaw's own discontent at the time, and Michael Holroyd proclaims "the character of Robert Smith" to be "Shaw himself at twenty." See Ervine, *Bernard Shaw: His Life, Work and*

    Friends (New York: William Morrow, 1956), 74–76; and Holroyd, 74. Holroyd calls Ned Conolly in *The Irrational Knot* "not a self-portrait in the sense that Smith had been," but nevertheless contends that Conolly "embodies much that Shaw had learnt to admire since coming to London" (81). Shavians have long recognized autobiographical elements in Shaw's plays as well. See, for example, Eric Bentley, *Bernard Shaw, 1856–1950*, amended ed. (New York: New Directions, 1957), where he describes Shaw's drama as a "series of self-portraits" (204).
24. Ervine, 5. Rather amazingly, Ervine infers from Irish "history" that people living outside of Ulster are "more class-conscious *than any other race*" with the result that they "possess in a high degree" a form of "inferiority complex"; thus, in a country where many were "deprived of their power and property," those few who did ascend to wealth were prone to evince a vicious strain of "snobbery" (my emphasis, 20–21).
25. Arnold Silver, *Bernard Shaw: The Darker Side* (Stanford: Stanford University Press, 1982), 17, 19.
26. Silver, 6, 9. Silver suggests that such readings will show that the Shavian play "often throws more light on the preface than the other way around precisely because Shaw reveals more of himself as playwright than as essayist" (10). My thesis here complements this assertion by trying to demonstrate that the early novels function in a similar way.
27. Jean Reynolds, "The Talking Cure," *SHAW 26: New Readings of Shaw at the Sesquicentennial*, eds. Heidi J. Holder and MaryAnn K. Crawford (University Park: The Pennsylvania State University Press, 2006), 30–31.
28. Kathleen Stewart, *Ordinary Affects* (Durham: Duke University Press, 2007), 2.
29. Brian Massumi, *Parables for the Virtual: Movement, Affect, Sensation* (Durham: Duke University, 2002), 25.
30. Nicholas Grene, "The Maturity of *Immaturity*: Shaw's First Novel," *Irish University Review* 20 (Autumn 1990): 238.
31. Dietrich, *Bernard Shaw's Novels*, 30–31.
32. Dietrich, *Bernard Shaw's Novels*, 35.
33. See Chap. 1 for this discussion of *On the Genealogy of Morals*.
34. Dietrich, *Bernard Shaw's Novels*, 36–37.
35. Both operas were indeed "enduringly popular," revived frequently in Dublin, for example, over a half century after they were composed, so it is hardly unusual that Smith would have seen them in the 1870s. See the "Dublin Theatrical Calendar" in my *Joyce, O'Casey and the Irish Popular Theatre* (Syracuse: Syracuse University Press, 1991), 201–39.
36. Niall Ferguson, *The Ascent of Money: A Financial History of the World* (New York: Penguin, 2008), 19.
37. Simmel, "The Metropolis and Mental Life," 410.

38. Simmel, "The Metropolis and Mental Life," 412.
39. Simmel, "The Metropolis and Mental Life," 418.
40. In one of the final scenes in Mrs Froster's house, she compares Fenwick unfavorably to Smith. After declaring Fenwick no "gentleman," Mrs Froster praises him as surely having a mother proud of his deportment, which contrasts markedly with Fenwick's ill behavior (93).
41. Simmel, "The Metropolis and Modern Life," 412.
42. Kornbluh, 26.

CHAPTER 4

Entr'acte at the Theatre: Marriage, Money, and Feeling in *Love Among the Artists*

At slightly past the midpoint of *Love Among the Artists*, the third "novel of his nonage," Shaw seems to redact the scene in *Immaturity* in which Robert Smith attends the theatre, becomes infatuated with the beautiful *prima ballerina* Signorina Pertoldi, and—in moments of sharp introspection—interrogates his newfound extravagances and their financial implications. Smith, as you will recall and as the narrator clarifies in the opening sentence of Chapter VIII, was in "easy circumstances"; his "material necessities were few" and, given his strong "aversion to debts of all description," he was blissfully "free from the demoralizing influence of pecuniary embarrassment" (*I*, 80). However, something was taking its course that not only threatened his ease, but also undermined the discipline he had imposed on both his financial affairs and his sense of self. "Before long," Shaw's narrator remarks, Smith felt "*compelled* to reflect that an expenditure of fifteen pounds and thirteen shillings per annum"—the amount he would pay if he continued to patronize the theatre at his present rate—would almost certainly precipitate his economic ruin. Equally important, this calculation was preceded by harsh self-recriminations, some of which are connected to his sense of shame: he "reproached himself with self-flattery" and felt "*ashamed*" of ever speculating about the dancer's "low origin," one of many potential defects that might detract from her allure (my emphasis, 81). From the perspective of London's privileged class, the greatest of these shortcomings, real or imagined, may very well have been

© The Author(s) 2018
S. Watt, *Bernard Shaw's Fiction, Material Psychology, and Affect*,
Bernard Shaw and His Contemporaries,
https://doi.org/10.1007/978-3-319-71513-1_4

Signora Pertoldi's decision to work as a theatrical artist in the first place, a prejudice also directed at Susanna Conolly in *The Irrational Knot* and, as I shall describe here, Madge Brailsford in *Love Among the Artists*.

One inference to be made from Smith's introspection, not unlike that derived from the dream of Freud's patient concerning Elise L.'s upcoming marriage and the half-empty auditorium, is that in Shaw's fiction the theatre frequently serves as a site not just for fantasy and emotional transport, but for searching self-interrogation on such topics as love, marriage, value, artistry—and, of course, money. For Gerald Bridges in "The Theatre of the Future," if the theatre can be emancipated from the corrupting influence of commercialism, it can convey the poetry and rhetoric of Shakespeare's history plays and, in doing so, realize his otherwise intangible sense of greatness, much as the blush—the topic of the chapter that follows—provides evidence of a person's feelings of embarrassment or shame instantiated in the present moment. In a very real sense, then, the theatre and the blush—or its opposite on the spectrum of facial expression, sudden pallor—make tangible what otherwise might remain mysteriously intangible, and in the process prise open human psychologies and allow us access to the desires, anxieties, and emotions that reside there.

In Chapter XII of *Love Among the Artists*, the brilliant but difficult Welsh composer Owen Jack is persuaded to share a box at the theatre with Mary Sutherland, Lady Geraldine Porter, and Mrs. Herbert, the mother of Mary's fiancé and friend Adrian. Although the chapter begins at a fashionable afternoon party, its inaugural sentence echoes that of Smith's trip to the Alhambra Theatre in *Immaturity* by alluding to the composer's financial health, thus contextualizing the action that follows within a distinctly materialist frame: "At this time, Jack was richer than he had ever been before. His works were performed at the principal concerts; he gave lessons at the moderate rate of fifteen guineas a dozen, and had more applications for lessons at that rate than he had time to accept" (*Love*, 174). Destitute and in need of employment in the opening scene of the novel, Jack—and certainly his fortunes—has improved dramatically. He now enjoys the attention of music publishers, who approach him with tempting offers; his compositions are performed by the most celebrated orchestras; and he has become a fashionable attraction as a pianist, frequently invited to perform at social functions like the gathering of wealthy Londoners at the home of Mr. Phipson, who had supported the performance of Jack's complicated fantasia by the Antient Orpheus Society. Prior to his playing, however, Jack pauses unceremoniously as Mrs. Herbert and Lady Geraldine Porter, heedless of the occasion's demand for a respectful silence, continue a conversation that earns the latter an icy stare of disapprobation from the mightily perturbed musician. Once aware of his disapproving glare, Lady Geraldine's color "rose slightly," a "phenomenon which no one present had ever witnessed before," and she begged the composer's pardon (175). Jack misreads the gesture as dignified and apologetic when in fact she intended to convey just the opposite message, but no matter, as later that day she prevails upon him and Mary to join her and Mrs. Herbert in her box at the theatre. The tendering of the invitation required a performance of *faux* embarrassment on her part, but it was an effective portrayal, as Jack, who initially appears uninterested in the offer, somewhat surprisingly appears later at the theatre, joining Lady Geraldine's party.

At this moment in the novel—in this veritable interval or "entr'acte" before a pair of marriages occur and the prospects of other romantic attachments are dashed—Shaw provides a kind of *précis* not just of *Love Among the Artists*, but of the larger material (and materialist) psychology that informs all his novels and much of his later work as well. Given the fact that this is the only one of Shaw's novels lacking any introductory commentary—for, although not preceded by a substantial preface written after the novels' publications, even *An Unsocial Socialist* has a brief "Foreword" and revealing "Appendix"—my reading of this scene at the theatre and one immediately following it might be considered, much as Shaw's prefaces are, as a distillation of its themes. Moreover, after the lengthy treatment of *Immaturity* and *The Irrational Knot* in the previous chapter and the sustained examination of blushing and feeling in *Cashel Byron's Profession* that follows, this brief essay might also serve, like an interval at the theatre, as a salutary respite from the lengthy interpretive action that surrounds it.

Before the play begins, Jack notices that "All the world and his wife are here tonight," including Madge Brailsford's irascible father and, in a box opposite theirs, Adrian Herbert and the difficult but brilliant pianist Aurélie Szczympliça, whose growing relationship signals the end of his and Mary's engagement (*Love*, 184). After Lady Geraldine, predictably enough, makes disparaging remarks about the lead actress's makeup and Madge Brailsford's obtuseness, a quality that in her estimation disqualifies Madge from assuming lead roles in plays such as the one they are enjoying, it quickly becomes clear that the woman in the starring role *is* indeed Madge; and her performance garners enthusiastic applause from the audience after the opening act curtain descends. During the interval, a pair of visitors makes its way to the box, beginning with a blustering Mr. Brailsford, who claims to be "disgraced" by Madge's performance, even as he praises her impersonation of a "Parisian drab" as "perfection" itself (186). Owing much to Jack's tutelage and her apprenticeship on provincial stages, Madge "walks the stage and gives out her lines in the true old style," talents that her father appreciates having studied himself with the mid-Victorian stage's leading lights. Still, he most certainly does not approve of his daughter's choice of profession, however praiseworthy her skills may be, because "No true lady would paint her face and make an exhibition of herself on a public stage *for money*" (my emphasis, 187). As we learn later in *Love Among the Artists*, Mademoiselle Szczmpliça, darling of London's musical world, insists upon being paid for her performances too, as she later clarifies to Adrian, who surprises her in the midst of her concert tour of European capitals: "You do not suppose that I play for nothing for people whom I do not know ... No, I play willingly for my friends, or for the poor; but if the great world wishes to hear me, it must pay" (277). However, given the strains on their marriage by this time, strains exacerbated by Adrian's misapprehension about what occurred the night before his arrival in Paris and his suspicion that she has lied about it, Aurélie fails to understand Adrian's protestations of love and explains her incredulity in terms that parallel Brailsford's criticism of his daughter's choice of careers: "It is because you love me that you are ashamed of me and reproach me with playing for hire" (287).

Money thus not only initiates this chapter, but also recalls the specific problematic of expecting or demanding to be paid for one's artistry—an issue raised so many pages ago in regard to Shaw's earning "lots" of money for his writing—and this issue forms but one flash point in the larger conflict between money, artistry, and class affiliation in *Love Among the Artists*. The issue devolves into an ethical and distinctly gendered quagmire as well. Adrian Herbert, in his mother's earlier and inaccurate reproach in a conversation with Mary, will "never add a penny to his income by painting" (*Love*, 24), clearly implying that this failing constitutes a reason for Mary *not* to marry him. Yet Madge and Aurélie feel the sting of social disapproval for just the opposite reason—for their ability to command significant sums for succeeding, respectively, as an actor and concert pianist. In Lady Geraldine's box at the theatre, Madge's father fumes that she is "the first Brailsford that ever *played for money* in a public theatre," a moral failing that proves she "is not a Brailsford at all" (my emphasis, 187). Brailsford's rage is mitigated by the arrival in the box of a second visitor—Madge herself, whom Jack had earlier informed of her father's presence. Her daughterly affection softens his position, and he readily agrees to see her the next day; she leaves contentedly soon thereafter to prepare herself for the next act of the play. For his part, as he exits the box Brailsford initiates a rapprochement with Jack, a nemesis from their first meeting much earlier in the novel, bowing to him "like an infirm old man, without any sign of his habitual jauntiness of bearing" (192).

Equally significant, and consistent, I think, with the notion that the theatre provides an analytical venue for investigating psychical realities—feelings, anxieties, perceptions—Mary, the first "to recover herself" from the enormous surprise of Madge's appearance in their box, observes, "You are a good deal more like yourself on the stage than off it" (*Love*, 191). All present agree that Madge has grown, becoming more independent and self-assured, traits to which Lady Geraldine feels an acute aversion. But when challenged by Jack for not having welcomed Madge with "good grace," an allegation she rebuts and one that causes her to redden slightly, Lady Geraldine makes an observation that, like Mary's intimation that Madge is more "real" on stage, troubles distinctions between reality and fiction when the actress reappears in character after the interval:

> The charm is considerably weakened," said Lady Geraldine, turning toward the stage. "She does not seem half so real as she did before. (193)

Is Madge truly "more like" herself on stage than off? Does her "real" appearance to playgoers in an intermission detract from her performed reality on stage? Is the process of surrogation—again, composed of substitution, performance, and memory—undermined by memory, in this instance Lady Geraldine's recollections of Madge as a young girl of limited ability? The chapter concludes with the revelation that the usually stoic Jack uncharacteristically betrayed "some emotion at the pathetic passages in the play" (194), with his and Mary's ready agreement that Adrian and Aurélie seemed happy together, and with Mary's note to Adrian that, in effect, releases him from their previous engagement so as to enable him to pursue a relationship with Aurélie that eventually leads to their marriage.

The conflicts raised in the entr'acte at the theatre grow more complicated in the next chapter, where Shaw's attention turns to Owen Jack. Set the day after Madge's triumphant performance, the chapter opens with Jack contemplating money, as the earning of it seems to him an impediment both to true artistry and marriage, suggested by a persistent and heretofore totally foreign swelling of feeling that troubles him. Crossing Hyde

Park after giving a round of music lessons, he meets Mary, who asks the gloomy-looking composer about his work and teaching. Alluding to his student lessons, he admits to having "put them off" in deference to his greater "work" as a composer and adds solemnly, "I cannot spend my life making money" (*Love*, 196). To this end, he has cancelled lessons for the day worth five guineas and is well aware that he can make twice that amount the next day. But, he asks, "are guineas wealth to a man who wants time and freedom from base people and base thoughts" (197)? Admitting that he has little regard for money, he predicts (accurately) that he will "live all the more quietly for being an old bachelor," turning the conversation to marriage and Mary's description of him as an "inspired hermit" (198). For this one brief moment, however, Jack entertains an antidote to his reclusiveness, telling her that he has, in fact, contemplated forming a relationship with a woman—Mary herself. Emboldened after she informs him that her engagement with Adrian is over, Jack declares himself possessed with a "heart and affections like other men," and that these affections all center on her. He then proposes marriage, promising that she will never have to complain "that [her] husband does not love her." Blanching at this revelation and somewhat terrified, Mary yields "to an extraordinary emotion" and bursts into tears, eliciting Jack's assurance that he will drop the matter and that his "mind is the clearer for it" (201). Some few moments later, and after clumsy small talk about the weather and the best vantage point for viewing the Duke of Wellington statue, Jack calls for a cab to take an obviously shaken Mary home, vowing that there will never be any reason in the future for her to fear his advance. She departs, and he resumes his trek, pausing to watch the sun set behind the steeple of the Bayswater Church.

It is at this solitary and reflective moment, I think, that Shaw's framing of highly emotive action within the context of money in both chapters of *Love Among the Artists*—and in the chapter from *Immaturity* detailing Smith's fantasies and monetary anxieties at the Alhambra Theatre—provides interpretive traction. For Jack's sense that Mary's rejection has rendered his mind all the clearer is immediately refined and made more psychically resonant. As he pauses on a bridge over the Serpentine of Hyde Park to admire the view of the steeple and gaze through the depths of hazel green water below, he reaches a startling epiphany:

> *I* hanker for a *wife*!" he said, as he stood bolt upright, with his knuckles resting lightly on the parapet, and the ruddy gold of the sun full in his eyes. "*I*

grovel after *money*! What dog's appetites have this worldly crew infected me with! No matter: I am free: I am myself again. (*Love*, 203)

This passage is remarkable for several reasons, one of which is Shaw's purposeful italicization of "I," "money," and "wife," the latter two serving as substitutions for each other in Jack's proclamation. That is to say, in this formulation his longing for a wife, like his contemptible groveling for money, is not only the product of his ascent in fashionable London society (his association with "this worldly crew"), but also a psycho-economic reality in which money serves as a metonym of marriage and viceversa. In late-Victorian aristocratic society, having a wife means possessing money; and acquiring money, whether from a dowry, bequest, or other source, is a prerequisite to finding a wife.

Equally important, for Jack, marriage and the earning of money necessarily denote an abandonment of art and an abdication of the values which comprise his sense of selfhood. In this regard, his use of the word "hanker" to describe his *drive* to find a wife—he doesn't say "I love Mary" or "I long to be with Mary" but rather only mentions an impulsion to wed absent a specific object of desire—is yet another significant aspect of Jack's revelation. In his articulation, *desire* for a specific woman is supplanted by a more generic *drive*, an almost perverse effect of money and social class subtly implied by Shaw's use of "hanker" which, as the *Oxford English Dictionary* (OED) confirms, frequently connotes more than mere "longing" or "craving." The *OED* lists several examples from later eighteenth-century and Victorian prose to demonstrate one connotation of "hanker" that implies a longing for something inaccessible, even illicit. From Abraham Tucker's *The Light of Nature Pursued* (1774), for example, the *OED* quotes the sentence "The mind always hankering after what she has not." In addition, from the first volume of Connop Thirlwall's eight-volume *History of Greece* (1835), the *OED* lists "The tendency of human nature to hanker after all that is forbidden." While attributing slightly different psychical realities or cathexes to, alternatively, the "mind" and "human nature," both of these passages imply the power of a similar subjective force that impels one toward entities well outside his or her ambit into, in the best cases, the rare or the exotic; in the worst, the prohibited or perverse. Money, acting as the currency necessary to purchase commodities in the marketplace and not primarily as investment or surplus capital, underlies this force. Standing in the waning sunlight of Hyde Park, the church steeple on the horizon, Jack understands the effect of both marriage and money in setting the sun on his own religion: music.

These issues reappear when, almost shockingly, Mary decides to marry Johnny Hoskyn, Philistine businessman and commercial traveler who, in his earliest conversation with her, urges her to visit America to "see what real life is" (*Love*, 210). Hoskyn himself has just come from New York, where Ned Conolly's electro-motor is gaining market share and will soon overtake steam as the most cost-effective source of power for industrial manufacturing. After meeting Mary, Hoskyn sets his sights on her and, in a brief and clumsy courtship, reintroduces her to fireworks, acrobats, conjurers, and other entertainments that she felt "ashamed of herself for enjoying" (218). Soon thereafter, Hoskyn authors a letter of proposal to Mary that adduces four points encouraging her acceptance, points that amount to little more than a product description: the first is his age and the other three concern his present and future income. Hoskyn stresses that the figures he provides "*far understate what I may reasonably expect my resources to be in the course of a few years*" (226). Aware of Hoskyn's intentions, Lady Geraldine lends her support for the match, basing her enthusiasm on the very rationale he employs in his letter:

> Altogether, [the Hoskyns] are a wonderful family: making money, marrying money, putting each other in the way of making and marrying more, and falling on their feet everywhere. (227)

Lady Geraldine's endorsement relies upon the same metonymic substitutions that Jack employs in his epiphany: in fashionable society, one does not marry a person but rather marries money—and then proceeds to make more. In the closing lines of the novel's Book I, however, and after feeling bound to respond to Hoskyns' proposal, Mary realizes that she "detests" him.

As the second book of the novel opens, however, Mary has relented and married Hoskyn, and from this point to the novel's conclusion this constellation of art, marriage, and money continues to inform its action. In the opening chapter of Book II, for example, Aurélie and Mary, among others, attend a performance of Jack's masterwork "Prometheus," and later express their disappointment at its uneven reception. Even though Hoskyn, who scarcely understands the nuances of and radical compositional strategies in Jack's masterwork, lends his voice of approbation to theirs, Aurélie undertakes a scathing critique of Londoners in which art and business predominate:

But it seems to me there is something unworthy—infamous, in the icy stupidity of these people here. Of what use is it to compose great works when one is but held in contempt because of them? It is necessary to be a trader here in order to have success. Commerce is the ruin of England. It renders the people quite anti-artistic. (247)

Oblivious to the irony of her own insistence that she be paid well for her performances—and later urging her husband to tidy up his studios so the affluent will be more eager to sit for portraits, which is the primary way that English painters "make great sums of money" (302)—Aurélie nonetheless seizes upon an issue central to Shaw's novel.

I cannot resist observing further that this passage from *Love Among the Artists* anticipates a similar criticism made two decades later in Georg Simmel's seminal essay "The Metropolis and Mental Life" and repeating it: "London has never acted as England's heart but often as England's intellect and always as her moneybag!"[1] A version of this critique appears again, albeit subtly expanded, in the novel's final pages, when Madge Brailsford professes her deep affection for Owen Jack. Here, too, recalling the observation in the interval at the theatre that Madge seemed "more real" on stage than off it, dialogue between Madge and Jack troubles distinctions between reality and romance; not surprisingly, money informs the parsing of these distinctions. Jack observes that men write plays of heightened romance to induce the audience to agree, "How wonderfully true to nature," even though, unlike in real life, heroes and heroines in such plays can be "depended on." In "real life," he continues, "it is just the other way. The incompatibility is not in the world, but in ourselves" (*Love*, 327). Madge remains unpersuaded by this thesis, recalling that the one and only "piece of romance" in her life occurred not in the theatre but on an occasion when a "perfect stranger"—Jack himself much earlier in the novel—"once gave me, at my mere request, all the money he had in the world" (328). Comprehending her expression of affection for him yet unmoved, Jack, without divulging the specifics of his former proposal to Mary, alludes to his languishing in solitude, his pining for a partner, and his suffering from the "symptoms" she describes of not finding art alone a sufficient consolation. As he did before, he connects these emotions to his rise from "poverty and neglect" to his present professional situation where he is earning "over a hundred a year" (328). However, with this economic success—with the entrance of significant sums of money into his life—come internal struggles he never endured in his poverty. These struggles, as was evident in his epiphany in Hyde Park earlier in *Love Among the Artists*, imperiled both his sense of self and his ability to devote himself entirely to his art. Moreover, as he advises Madge just before leaving her, only after she masters her art will she be able to "make true love." Bidding him "Adieu," she stands as a statue before sinking into an ottoman "in an attitude of despair" (330).

The interval or entr'acte at the theatre near the center of Shaw's novel conveys in rich and significant detail much of what the narrative of *Love Among the Artists* concerns. And, as I have endeavored to indicate, it also provides a kind of model of narrative and conflict in Shaw's fiction. As is the case with the West End house that Gerald Bridges establishes in "The Theatre of the Future," theatres in *Immaturity* and *Love Among the Artists* serve, at base, as sites of affirmation. What is affirmed in them, however, is not the greatness of Shakespearean rhetoric, man's humanity as reflected in the protagonists in Attic Tragedy, or the indomitability of the Beckettian character as construed by Alain Badiou. Rather, the theatre in these novels functions like the theatres, markets, dinner tables, and other public, communal, and thus performative sites in Freudian dream analysis: namely, as places where fiction meets the psychical realities of its audience, where conceptions of value are debated and either endorsed or toppled. Because material issues inform both staged fiction and audience reality, it seems inevitable that all of these would be informed by, or corrupted by, money's parasitical insinuation into both, leading finally to the destruction of borders separating the dyad.

Owen Jack's epiphany in Hyde Park and his reconsideration of his emotional life in the novel's final chapter make an even stronger statement about the complicated relationship between marriage, art, and money in *Love Among the Artists* than I have offered here. For in these two scenes Jack directly links his internal conflicts, his languor and pained "hankering" after a wife, to money's corrupting influence; money and wives—money and marriage—are metonyms of each other, as he seems to assert and Lady Geraldine reiterates in her praise of the Hoskyn family. Here, in short, we witness performances authorized by Shavian psychology in all of their socio-economic and econo-psychical connotations.

Notes

1. Georg Simmel, "The Metropolis and Mental Life," 412.

CHAPTER 5

Cashel Byron's Blush—And Others

Psychic economy or material(ist) psychology? Several chapters ago, I raised this question, outlining my reasons for replacing "psychic economy" with another phrase that might more effectively define a Shavian theory of psychology as exhibited by characters in his novels. Part of my intention in doing so, as I explained then and will say more about here as prefatory to a reading of Shaw's fourth novel *Cashel Byron's Profession*, is to address the defects that Anna Kornbluh identifies in what she regards as the "casual ubiquity" and uneven deployment of "psychic economy" in recent literary and cultural criticism. At base, the phrase both isolates Freud's borrowings from nineteenth-century economics and valorizes the premise that, for many Victorians, psychology was "fundamentally economic and the economic [was] fundamentally psychological."[1] But how does the concept enable or, alternatively, hobble our interpretive practice? At the end of the day, can it help us do more than merely identify the ways in which psychoanalytic thought at the *fin de siècle* of the nineteenth century and after was "steeped in economic language"?[2]

Initiating this critique in the introduction to *Reading Capital*, Kornbluh resumes it forcefully in the book's final chapter, focusing not on the writers she discussed earlier whose novels address the incipient financialization of Victorian society—Charles Dickens, George Eliot, Anthony Trollope—but on Freud's figurative use of "economy" and terms associated with it like "entrepreneur," "investment," and so on. Along with such other architectures as the so-called "topographic" (conscious, preconscious, and unconscious) and "structural" (id, ego, super ego) models, for instance, the economic amounts to one of Freud's three metapsychological hypotheses about the structures and operations of psychical life. In this instance, the "economic" metaphorizes the distribution of psychic resources as a system that regulates expenditures and balances them against other investments and obligations. Kornbluh's point is well taken, as there is no denying the prominence of the economic in the James Strachey translation of Freud in the *Standard Edition*, a translation with which she occasionally takes issue.[3] This is as true of Freud's earlier writing as it is of such later works as *Civilization and Its Discontents* (written 1929, published 1930). Explaining in the latter the myriad ways in which the social order produces discontent, Freud emphasizes civilization's reduction of the "yield" of pleasure individuals are able to accrue—a project aided by religion's depreciation of the "value" of life—returning frequently to the metaphor of investment yield in characterizing the drive to maximize libidinal and other satisfactions.[4] He even proffers analogies between balanced investment portfolios and diverse forms of gratification, between shrewd businessmen and desiring subjects:

> Just as a cautious business-man avoids tying up all his capital in one concern, so, perhaps, worldly wisdom will advise us not to look for the whole of our satisfaction from a single aspiration.[5] (*SE* 21: 84)

Kornbluh thus derives from Freud's writing a psychoanalysis in which the notion of economy is not so much a thing or "nominative" entity, but rather a "point of view" or "way of knowing." Yet, as such, "psychic economy" struggles to achieve much beyond its own figurative ingenuity:

> Inextricably bound up with obscurity and torment, all [psychic economy] can signify is denatured objects and inadequate figures. If this means that psychoanalysis offers no immediate insights into economics, no sanctification of the marginal utility revolution's desire theory of value, and no naturalization of capitalism, this is so much the better for the psychoanalytic contribution to the critique of political economy.[6]

If "psychic economy," this foundational concept of psychoanalysis, is "inextricably bound up with obscurity" and a "torment" that persists throughout Freud's career, before discarding it in favor of an alternative we might inquire further into the nature of both the term's turbidity and Freud's torment. What is wanted, it seems, what might serve as an analgesic to numb the discomfiture of the term's inadequacy, is a metric to quantify more accurately or make more tangible what are, finally, qualitative matters like pleasure, pain, and feeling. As a "tool, a makeshift of last resort," however, quantification at times seems too instrumental to represent psychical realities which, in the final analysis, we are destined not to know as fully as we might wish.[7] Paramount among these confounding realities are emotions and feelings, as Freud acknowledges in the early paragraphs of *Civilization and Its Discontents* when discussing the "oceanic feeling." In the opening pages, he recalls letters from a valued friend concerning his representation of religion's functioning in *The Future of an Illusion* (1927), an essay that might be regarded as a preface to *Civilization and Its Discontents*. The former begins with Freud's construal of "civilization" as an ensemble of practices that raise mankind above its "animal status," organize man's capacity to "control the forces of nature and extract its wealth," and authorize "the regulations necessary in order to adjust the relations of men to one another and especially the distribution of available wealth" (*SE* 21: 6). Not long after introducing this definition, however, Freud confesses to having "slipped unawares out of the economic field into the field of psychology," in part by asserting that civilization's functioning relies upon a measure of coercion because men must be compelled both to work and renounce some of their instincts (*SE* 21: 10), neither of which is easily achieved. As a result, and because men (and women) are also "profoundly influenced by the amount of instinctual satisfaction which the existing wealth makes possible," every "individual is virtually an enemy of civilization" insofar as it demands of its citizens a "heavy burden" of "sacrifices" to make "communal life possible" (*SE* 21: 6).

Two familiar tropes surface here: the gesture to quantity ("*amount* of instinctual satisfaction") and an emphasis on civilization's production of a suppressive pressure of considerable force ("heavy burden") on the individual to counter instinct or drive. (Freud is especially clear on this point later in *Civilization and Its Discontents*: "The liberty of the individual is no gift of civilization. It was greatest before there was any civilization" [*SE* 21: 95]). Abetting the latter enterprise, as Freud's friend insists, religion produces an "oceanic feeling," a "feeling as of something limitless, unbounded" and of "an indissoluble bond, of being one with the external world as a whole." The positing of this feeling, Freud responds, "sounds so strange and fits in so badly with the fabric of our psychology" and of a psychoanalysis that stresses a unitary and "autonomous" ego that learns in infancy to detach itself from the external world (*SE* 21: 65). After claiming never to have experienced such a sense of oneness himself, Freud offers what, for our purposes, is a more relevant admission: "It is not easy to deal scientifically with feelings," although "One can attempt to describe their physiological signs" (*SE* 21: 65). Just a few paragraphs later, he repeats his discomfiture working with or assessing feelings: "Let me admit once more that it is very difficult for me to work with these almost *intangible* qualities" (my emphasis, *SE* 21: 72).

In turn, this difficulty at least partially motivates Freud to appropriate metaphors from economics and to pose quantification as a palliative for a tormented analytical project. Yet, if "feelings" rival "strong needs" in terms of their cathexes, as he concludes in his response to his friend's extolments of the "oceanic feeling," then they might, as Eve Sedgwick suggests, also displace an "emphasis on Oedipality and repression."[8] This possibility accounts for Freud's view of the oceanic feeling as passing "strange," a "bad fit" with the catalogue of his case studies and the principles he derives from them. Sedgwick, engaging Sylvan Tomkins' work, had forecast in the early pages of *Touching Feeling: Affect, Pedagogy, Performativity* (2003) that the affect system responsible for feeling and emotion can be seen to inflect the drive system which Freud explored in his early work, complicated in *Beyond the Pleasure Principle* (1920), and returns to in *Civilization and Its Discontents*. The sense of oceanic oneness, in other words, compels Freud to concede "once more" the challenge that feelings pose for his psychoanalysis. That said, one affect in particular, shame—as scrutinized by thinkers as various as Charles Darwin in *The Expression of the Emotions in Man and Animals*, Tomkins, Sedgwick, and Sara Ahmed—not only occupies a privileged position in the catalogue of human feelings (including the young Shaw's), but also possesses an objective correlative, a physiological response that constitutes a material corroboration of its existence: the blush. Darwin devotes an entire chapter of his book to the blush, labelling it, as I mentioned in my introduction, the "most peculiar and most human of all expressions" and linking it directly to feelings of "self-attention": shyness, shame, and modesty.[9] Sedgwick, following Tomkins, refers to the "alchemy of the contingent" when discussing shame, observing that, contrary to any behaviorist-leaning sense of the etiology of the emotion, the "affect system includes internal as well as external events" and thus undoes or deconstructs the stimulus/response dyad.[10] Shame, for Ahmed, "conceals and reveals what is present in the present,"[11] and its primary means of revelation is the blush, although such other physiological signs as averted eyes and drooping shoulders provide evidence of its existence. Because it is both productive of an observable physiological change *and* the result of external and internal factors, a negative affect such as shame exemplifies a material psychology which Shaw's fictional characters exhibit with almost uncanny regularity.[12]

The confirmation of shame's existence through the blush, the stooped shoulder, or the averted gaze, in other words, is as *material* as the appearances of such explicitly *materialist* disagreements and anxieties over value, overpayment, and utility in Freud's dreams and those of his patients. Further, particularly where the prospect of marriage is concerned in Shaw's novels, the intrusion of social class and money—an obviously materialist concern linked to class consciousness—frequently catalyzes blushing and other physiological signs of badly strained feelings and deep emotion. For this reason, when discussing Shavian subjectivity the concepts of a "material" and "materialist" psychology—which above I have collapsed into one term, "material(ist)"—are in my view preferable to "psychic economy." For, as the preceding chapters outline, money, particularly in *Immaturity*, exerts more force on and catalyzes more feeling in Shaw's Robert Smith than libidinal cathexes do. Also, Smith, in this respect, is hardly unique, for the suite of emotions that typically radiate from monetary concerns—anxiety, fear, shame—play substantial roles in the interior lives of Shaw's characters in all of his novels, including Shaw's protagonist, a paragon of manly beauty and strength, in *Cashel Byron's Profession*. "Psychic economy" does not foreground these phenomena in the same way that "material" or "material(ist)" psychology does, however opaque the term may seem.

Such feelings as shame and anxiety, it is important to reiterate, are not *always* connected to money, debt, and financial uncertainty; nor are these feelings analogues of each other, as the former is "filled" in the present while the latter is "expectant" with a trajectory aimed at the future. That is to say, shame does not gesture toward a futurity in the same way that anxiety does (recall Shaw's alarm over the implications of Mrs. Campbell's overdrawn bank account in his December, 1912 letter to her and Niall Ferguson's description of indigenous tribes entirely ignorant of money and innocently free of concern about the future). Rather, shame is the product of contingent intrusions upon the present lives of characters, as Shaw's recurrent use of the blush attests. In fact, characters' blushing, "reddening," and "coloring" occur two *dozen* or more times in *Cashel Byron's Profession* and numerous times in all of his novels, offering material confirmation of the existence of the very feelings that tormented Freud's efforts to explain them and intimating, following Sedgwick, a determinative influence on subjects greater than that of Oedipal projects or primal herd instincts. Any tabulation of such moments in *Cashel Byron's Profession* is even higher when considering, as Darwin did, that the rose of a blush exists on a spectrum that includes, at the opposite pole, the sudden whitening of pallor.[13] Also, in some instances, this polarity collapses. In his chapter "Self-Attention—Shame—Shyness—Modesty: Blushing" from *The Expression of the Emotions in Man and Animals*, Darwin recalls "rare cases" when "paleness instead of redness is caused under conditions which would naturally induce a blush." In one instance, after a young woman at a party embarrassingly caught her hair on the button of a servant, she "imagined that she had blushed crimson; but was assured by a friend that she had turned extremely pale."[14] This is because, as Darwin hypothesizes, most of us feel "blame or disapprobation more acutely than approbation"; social deprecation and "ridicule" induce blushing more than praise does; and, as he adds and we shall see, young men and women are especially prone to performing their embarrassments in this way.[15]

Unlike Darwin, Shaw never conducted a scientific study of feelings, emotions, and their manifestation in physiological change, nor did he posit, as Darwin did, a much-debated thesis about the universality of facial expressions across societies both primitive and advanced.[16] But that did not keep him from implying that such expressions served as unfailing indicators of emotion and psychical reality more generally. His most strenuous articulation of this position emerges in his writing for *The Saturday Review* when juxtaposing the acting of two brilliant stars of the *fin de siècle* theatre: Sarah Bernhardt and Eleonora Duse. In June 1895, both actresses visited London and, in two instances, appeared in the same roles: Magda in Hermann Sudermann's *Heimat* (1893), translated as *Magda*, and Marguerite Gauthier in *La Dame aux Camélias*, first adapted in 1852 from the Alexandre Dumas novel. The latter play in particular proved a staple attraction in Bernhardt's repertory, but by the summer of 1895 Shaw was dubious about its merits and hers as well, beginning his comparison of the two *grandes dames* with the oft-heard complaint at the time that while the modern stage might present "'good acting plays,'" it does so without presenting any "*real* people in them" (my emphasis; *OT* 1: 148). As Sudermann's Magda, attired in "splendacious" costumes and elegant jewelry, with meticulously "painted" face ("strawberries and cream") including dimples (pink) and ears (crimson), Bernhardt may be "beautiful with the beauty of her school," but she is nonetheless "entirely inhuman and incredible" (*OT* 1: 149).[17] Worse from the point of view of modern acting, she "does not enter into the leading character; she substitutes herself for it"; and, as a result, her art fails to make audiences "think more highly or feel more deeply" *(OT* 1: 150). In sum, as Shaw had written a week earlier—in a review, interestingly enough, in which he lampoons dramatist William Ernest Henley for perpetrating a cult of athletics and hero-worship that assured his reading of a "puerile" novel of prizefighting such as *Cashel Byron's Profession*—Bernhardtian "explosions" on stage supplemented by her inventory of stale gestures were no match for the "reality" of Duse's impersonations (*OT* 1: 144, 147–48).

Like other discerning playgoers and theatre practitioners at this time and after—from Georg Simmel in 1901 to the accomplished actress-producer Eva Le Gallienne, who played Mrs. Dudgeon in the 1959 film version of *The Devil's Disciple*—Shaw was entirely taken with Eleonora Duse and the realism of her performances. Hailing her work in *La Femme de Claude* as "the best modern acting I have seen," Shaw praised Duse's "most unstudied and 'natural' way," a "rare consummation" untainted by studied "points" and executed in "simple strokes" (*OT* 1: 147). While the "Divine Sarah," as Bernhardt was frequently called, relied upon a "stock of attitudes and facial effects," her Italian counterpart could make audiences "feel rather than see" with a mere "tremor of the lip" as supplemented by a line in her face or "gray shadow" hanging over it. "Ambidextrous and supple," Duse's movements on stage, rather like overdetermined images in dreams, were for Shaw the "physical expression" of a "multitude of ideas" (*OT* 1: 150–51), a capacity about which Georg Simmel rhapsodized six years later: "… in her movement, she is the most perfect, complete expression of the soul and its flows."[18] Unlike members of most "foreign audiences" who, as Guido Noccioli observed, reacted to Duse's performance with "more bewilderment than understanding," Simmel immediately detected the intangible—in this case, the spiritual meeting of body and soul—as expressed in the actor's simple movements, gestures, and presence on stage.[19] For Le Gallienne, summarizing the art of this incomparable "mystic" decades later in her book on Duse, the Italian actress harbored the "dream" of a theatre that was about as far removed from Bernhardt's school of acting—and from the lavish pictorial stage of London's leading actor at the time, Henry Irving—as one can imagine: "Quite small, quite simple, with plain white-washed walls—no ornaments. Very little scenery."[20]

The climactic point of the actorly "consummation" that Shaw experienced—the most thrilling element of the Italian actress's "annihilation" of Bernhardt's portrayal of Sudermann's Magda (*OT* 1: 152)—was Duse's blush. A widely celebrated opera star returning to her provincial home with her illegitimate son, Magda discovers soon after arriving at her father's house that "one of the most intimate friends of the family" is the father of her child, and a tense inquisition by her father ensues (*OT* 1: 153). That this issue of paternity is decided so belatedly is only partially explained by Magda's admission to her apoplectic father in the play's final moments that she had several lovers at the time, but a scrupulously mean interrogation of this plot element will have to wait for another occasion. Shaw's commendation of the "stroke of acting" that emerges in this climactic scene as one "which will never be forgotten" is far more important:

> Then a terrible thing happened to her. She began to blush; and in another moment she was conscious of it, and the blush was slowly spreading and deepening until, after a few vain efforts to avert her face or to obstruct its view of it without seeming to do so, she gave up and hid the blush in her hands.[21]

Amazed, Shaw could detect "no trick" in the performance, which struck him as "perfectly natural" and dissimilar even from Duse's flushed face after weeping in a moment in the third act of *La Dame aux Camélias* (*OT* 1: 154). This moment admitted to a physiological explanation, a stooping posture that directed blood downward to her face, but Magda's blush—this highlight of an "unforgettable" evening in the theatre—was a different matter altogether.

Shaw's lionization of Duse conveys a great deal about his larger endorsement of an emergent, less exclamatory acting style; as such, here he implicitly welcomes a modern drama and theatre that might replace the predictable plots, histrionics, and extravagant pictorialism of a late Victorian stage he despised. His withering critique of Henry Irving's excesses, for example, defects on stark display earlier in 1895 in the star-actor's production of J. Comyns Carr's *King Arthur*, describes a residual theatre in which a play's dialogue is written by a "jobber" such as Carr, yet designed beautifully by such master-artists as Sir Edward Burne-Jones and Hawes Craven. Even the acting of Shaw's friend Ellen Terry and Irving in one moment—the only really "great" acting in the entire play—could not mitigate Shaw's revulsion that his own art, "the art of literature," was left "shabby and ashamed amid the triumph of the arts of the painter and actor." Shaw's phrasing in his backhanded compliments of Irving is, I think, telling. Irving, whose popular revivals, in Shaw's view, "mutilated" Shakespeare and "travestied" Goethe (*OT* 1: 14–15), mercifully concluded one odious scene by employing an "old Richard the Third effect"; and the vulgarity of a Guinevere (Ellen Terry) splayed on the floor beneath her "nobly wronged" husband recalled for Shaw the tastes of the later 1850s when Lord Tennyson wrote *Idylls of the King*. Duse's new theatre, by contrast to this musty one, was marked by restraint, subtlety, and thoughtful language, as no character, no matter how "splendacious" her attire, should mouth the talk of a "costermonger," which was all that Carr's dialogue afforded Irving.

As Victorian theatrical conventions yielded to modern revisions, ideals of men and women changed as well. Bernhartdian "explosions" gave way to the quieter acting style associated with the emergent realistic drama of Henrik Ibsen and the stage practices of Duse, Mrs. Patrick Campbell, and Elizabeth Robins, among other impersonators of Ibsen's characters. Equally important, and Cashel Byron provides a formidable, if complicated, example of this notion, the Foucauldian "repressive" hypotheses associated with the Victorian age and inscribed in Freud's suppressive "civilization" undergo a meaningful redaction. Joseph Valente explains this revision as it pertains to ideals of Irish manhood at the end of the century:

> The ideal of manhood, in sum, consisted in the simultaneous necessity for and achievement of a vigilant, rational self-control—in *strong passions strongly checked*.

In other words, manly *behavior* alone—and, in many ways, Cashel's victories as a prizefighter and his quick dispatch of young toughs who accost women epitomize this behavior—does not, given this criterion, constitute manliness. Rather, the ideal of manliness operative at the time was comprised not by "a set of sublime properties but a logic of sublimation, a dialectical organization of contents that was located 'in men,' yes, but *as* men's proper beyond, a fully immanent mode of self-overcoming."[22]

From this definition, masculinity required a kind of subjective "torment"—not the kind that plagued Freud because of the unavailability of a quantifiable inventory of feelings, or his more general uneasiness with affect, but a kind of economy of checks and balances on emotion as registered by the body. "*Strong passions strongly checked*" combine with other potent feelings, emotions, and inhibitions in Shaw's protagonist to allow for a reexamination of Cashel Byron that not only revises our understanding of the novel, but also adds defining texture to both Byron's masculinity and Shaw's material(ist) psychology.

Feeling, Materiality, Manliness: Cashel Byron

> Two days later, Mary was finishing the sketch which Mrs Henderson had interrupted. Something was wrong with her: at every sound in the house she changed color ...
> —Bernard Shaw, *Love Among the Artists*

At this early point in the *Love Among the Artists*, Mary Sutherland is on edge. She is "afraid to stir" lest the at times obstreperous music professor Owen Jack, who has just received a letter dismissing him from service at the family home in Windsor as her brother's tutor, engage her in conversation. Indeed, she "had never been so unreasonably nervous in her life before" (*Love*, 39). She cannot avoid a confrontation with Jack, however, nor be spared his accusation that his successor will be "at the mercy of [her] ignorant caprice" as the mistress of the house (40), even though her father, not Mary, authored his letter of dismissal. Jack is unaware of the pressure earlier brought to bear on Mary by the predictable spokespersons of a rigid Victorian social orthodoxy—older women, in this case Mrs. Herbert, her fiancé Adrian's mother, and Mary's overbearing aunt Jane Beatty. (In fairness, Marian Lind's father Reginald assumes the same role in *The Irrational Knot*, thus providing a male version of the brittle and vigilant protector of the status quo so common to late Victorian social comedy.) Enduring a tense interchange with both in the preceding chapter, Mary had experienced a gamut of emotions, many of which were registered on her face. She "blushed" shyly when Mrs. Herbert recommends that she should get married and return to London society (*Love*, 23); she "reddened" with anger but said "nothing" in rejoinder to Mrs. Herbert's disparagement of her own son as a "duffer" with fatuous aspirations to earn a living as an artist and insufficient enterprise "to marry a woman with money" (24); and she laughed when the elder woman predicted that if she marries her son, Mary will "live to see all [her] own money spent" (25).[23] The addition to the conversation of the "fat and imperious" Mrs. Beatty does little to reduce its tensions. Jack, she charges, has been seen carousing with drunken soldiers who play in her husband the Colonel's military band, one of whom, an exceptional clarinetist, is the "lowest of the low" (26–27). No servant of her brother's, she fumes, has the "right" to speak to a "profligate soldier" in broad daylight and therefore must be dismissed. Undeterred and annoyed, Mary counters by recalling her aunt's relentless criticism of the way she walks and her "bold appearance" (29). Angered by this counteroffensive, Aunt Jane "reddened," as Mary does several more times in the chapter while navigating this unpleasant interlocution.

In several respects, this episode from *Love Among the Artists* is typical of the ways in which facial expression confirms feelings evoked by contingent events in Shaw's fiction. As people anger, for instance, they turn scarlet or crimson, some as frequently as the feisty Aunt Jane does. On other occasions, many of these incidents confirm Darwin's observation that young people blush more than older people—a hypothesis that Shaw's novels tend to corroborate—and that women blush more often than men. The latter assertion, as we shall see, is revised in *Cashel Byron's Profession*, but describes most facial coloring in *Love Among the Artists* and, to cite another example, Marian Lind's frequent blushing in *The Irrational Knot*. Mary's blush at Mrs. Herbert's recommendation that she marry is but one instance of many in Shaw's novels where facial coloring attends the awkwardness inherent to this topic and the early moments of courtship.[24] The progression of Harriet Russell and Cyril Scott's relationship in *Immaturity* exhibits this tendency, for example. When Scott, after discovering Harriet's shop in Richmond, asks her whether she dislikes him, the attractive dressmaker responds, "Not at all," which is accompanied by a "faint blush" (*I*, 199). Scott is falling in love with her, and as they walk—and quarrel lightly—their conversation veers toward the misunderstanding conventional to the plots of romantic comedy which, in turn, leads to Harriet's second blush, one she "could no longer restrain."[25] Immediately charmed by her complexion and the grace of her bow, Scott finds both entirely different from the manner of Isabella Woodward, who had induced his own facial coloring in the preceding chapter. Primed by her sister Clytie to "cut" Scott socially, Isabella approaches him at a gathering at Perspective, the lavish scene of aristocratic socializing in Book Two of *Immaturity*.

Catching a glimpse of herself in a mirror, Isabella "saw her state of mind so faithfully reflected in her face" that she was moved to apply makeup, then remove it. Spotting Isabella approaching, Scott, "whose complexion deepened to brick red as he turned hastily aside into the music room," pretended not to see her (193). More blushing accompanies his profession of love to Harriet, with the blush itself becoming a topic of conversation (as it does in one scene in *The Irrational Knot*).[26] When Harriet tells him that she prefers solitude to the soirées and other gatherings of the upper class, he flatteringly replies, "Such attractions were not meant to blush unseen in out-of-the-way places." Harriet rejoins his gallantry by quickening her walking pace and gazing downward while her color was "notably deepening" (216).

A taxonomy of facial coloring in Shaw's fiction would organize dozens of instances such as these, many of which are far more overdetermined in origin than the deep red of anger or the faint rose of mild embarrassment or modesty. Many of these support Darwin's assertion that we feel "blame or disapprobation" more acutely than praise, particularly when one's appearance or social conduct is in question. Other manifestations of the blush venture more closely to contemporary readings of shame, confirming Darwin's notion that "It is not the simple act of reflecting on our own appearance but the thinking what others think of us, which excites a blush."[27] When Sara Ahmed defines shame as both an emotion "that requires a witness" *and* a feeling not only of being bad, "but to have been 'found' or 'found out' as bad by others," she both echoes Darwin and adds dimension to his findings:

> To be witnessed in one's failure is to be ashamed: to have one's shame witnessed is even more shaming. The bind of shame is that it is intensified by being seen by others *as* shame.[28]

More than loosely connected, then, to what others think of us, some blushes originate not only in the *feeling* of being discovered, but also in an *emotion* attached to a personal history or a cultural consensus about what is shameful, disgusting, or just generally "bad." Unlike desire for a specific object or the drive to satisfy an instinct such as hunger or thirst that, even though it is indifferent to objects, nonetheless narrows the range of those able to appease it—bread will not satisfy thirst, water will not satisfy hunger even if it temporarily blunts its pangs—"any affect," shame included, may "have any 'object.'" This, Tomkins posits, is the "basic source of complexity of human motivation and behavior."[29]

Most of these definitions of shame and blushing inform *Cashel Byron's Profession*, an analysis of which, I hope, will extend Richard Farr Dietrich's insights into the novel in *Bernard Shaw's Novels: Portraits of the Artist as Man and Superman*. Paramount among these, albeit couched in different language, is the way in which the novel's principal characters—Cashel Byron and the wealthy and well-schooled Lydia Carew, who later becomes his wife—are emblematic of Freud's assertion in *Civilization and Discontents* that "the motive force of all human activities is a striving towards the two confluent goals of utility and a yield of pleasure" (*SE* 21: 740). In Dietrich's reading, Lydia and Cashel convey not merely a body/mind duality, but an unusually gendered dyad with Cashel's chiseled muscles representing the body—and corporal "pleasure" and "delight"—and Lydia representing both the mind and a utilitarian ideology modeled on the intellection of John Stuart Mill. Her upbringing, Dietrich notes, is "suspiciously like" Mill's. Her late father was a polymathic intellectual and author; their wealth afforded them opportunities for world travel, sightseeing, and studious reflection; and, as Shaw's narrator underscores, by the time Lydia was 25 she enjoyed a "reputation for vast learning and exquisite culture."[30] While the narrator alludes to the social inequity represented by Lydia's inordinate wealth—"she was now, in her twenty-fifth year, the independent possessor of an annual income equal to the year's earnings of five hundred workmen, and under no external compulsion to do anything in return for it" (*Cashel*, 24)—she nonetheless values work as "one of the necessaries of life" (72). This value distinguishes her from several feckless aristocrats who populate Shaw's fiction: Marmaduke Lind, Sholto Douglas, Lydia's uxorious cousin Lucian, and others. "Readily interested by facts of any sort" (112) and described by Alice Goff as "purely intellectual" (181), Lydia spends all afternoon reading in the British Museum conducting the diligent work of a scholar. Of equal importance, her father made use of her abilities in overseeing his "money affairs," enabling her to acquire a "knowledge of business" necessary to manage her very considerable fortune (29–30).

Does this accomplishment, this Mill-like utilitarianism, scholarship, and financial acumen intimate Lydia's mannishness and contribute to a radical reimagining of gender in the novel? Perhaps it does, as I shall discuss in relation to Cashel. Yet Lydia's accomplishment comprises only one aspect of her uncommon character, for none of these same qualities are in evidence when she first spies Cashel exercising in an opening in the forest on her estate grounds:

> At last she saw an opening. Hastening towards it, she came again into the sunlight, and stopped, dazzled by an apparition which she at first took to be a beautiful statue, but presently recognized, with a strange glow of delight, as a living man. (*Cashel*, 37)

This "glow of delight" or unexpected *frisson* was in no way undone by her closer inspection of what might be mistaken for an "antique god in his sylvan haunt": his "bare arms shone like those of a gladiator"; his "broad pectoral muscles, in their white covering, were like slabs of marble"; and even his hair "short, crisp, and curly, seemed like burnished bronze in the evening light" (37). If not an apparition or statue, Cashel might also have been a dream image, something suggested by the narrator's reference to "daydream" and the possibility that his groom "must have been one of those incongruities characteristic of dreams." (In yet another instance of Shaw's early writing anticipating Freud, here the narrator seizes on the notion well described in *The Interpretation of Dreams* that while a dream element may be perceived in the light of waking reflection to be unreal, the affect it generates in the dream is nonetheless genuine.)

When Cashel's "groom-like man," Mellish, glowers forbiddingly at this lovely intruder, a potential distraction to his charge's regimen of physical exercise, Lydia exits quietly and apologetically. Still, as she hurried toward her castle, for her home Wiltstoken Castle was precisely that, it was impossible for her to forget this "glorious vision of manly strength and beauty" (38). More specifically, her incredulity at what she saw—this "god-like figure was only the Hermes of Praxiteles, suggested to her by Goethe's classical Sabat" and thus a daydream—was transformed. That is to say, this response, mediated by her superb knowledge of art, yielded to a prolonged "pleasure she would not have ventured to indulge had it concerned a creature of flesh and blood" (38). This unexpected moment of sensation that elicited immediate delight and prolonged pleasure foreshadows the attraction between Lydia and Cashel that leads to their marriage, children, and happy life together (made happier, it seems, by Lydia's viewing Cashel as yet another child). Even as the chapter turns to Lydia's introduction to Alice Goff who, coming from a very poor family, has traveled to Wiltstoken Castle with the aim of becoming Lydia's companion, it concludes that evening at an awkwardly quiet dinner with Lydia still thinking of the epitome of masculine beauty she had stumbled upon: "I had a vision of the Hermes of Praxiteles in a sylvan haunt today; and I am thinking of that" (45).

However, if this unexpected meeting provokes pleasure, delight, and finally desire in Lydia, Cashel's physical response materializes another feeling, as it also proves that he is, in fact, not a daydream, statue, or vision but a "creature of flesh and blood":

> The statue-man, following [Mellish's] sinister look, saw [Lydia] too, but with different feelings; for his lips parted; his color rose; and he stared at her with undisguised admiration and wonder. (*Cashel*, 37)

Often in Shaw's fiction a character's rising "color" indicates irritation, anger, or exasperation, but clearly this is not the case in this moment as Cashel's blush is connected to something(s) else. Nor are the downcast eyes of slight shame or awkward embarrassment—one of Harriet Russell's responses to Cyril Scott's flattery in *Immaturity*—in evidence here. Even more significant, while Darwin and numerous commentators reiterate that "an ashamed person can hardly endure to meet the gaze of those present,"[31] Cashel automatically returns Lydia's gaze by staring directly at her. There is no concealment in his response, no revelation of inadequacy, but only the embarrassment of instant attraction, "admiration," and "wonder." This moment, in the terms of a critical metaphor that Sedgwick cultivates, might serve as an example of digital-like reflexivity and automatic stimulation; something in Cashel, in other words, is simply turned "on" by Lydia's appearance. But of "greater conceptual value," Sedgwick argues and I very much agree, is a method that "layers" this digital approach with another more analog-like reading practice that both privileges the gradual evolution of feeling into Altieri's more complicated, narratively rich emotion and is able to discern the finer grains of affectual differentiation.[32]

Such a conceptual layering is especially useful in approaching Cashel Byron's emotional life, precisely because no male character in the entirety of Shaw's oeuvre blushes as frequently as he does and in such various circumstances. Indeed, this motif in the novel, rather like his being the *object* of Lydia's female gaze and thus inverting the gender dynamic inherent to contemporary understandings of spectation,[33] puts pressure on various consensuses about the relationship of blushing and gender. For if young women blush more than young men do, as Darwin asserts, and if Cashel serves as a kind of paragon of masculinity, then his prodigious blushing marks a singular revision of late-Victorian ideas about masculinity and approaches the gender ideal Valente describes as a complicated figure with "strong passions strongly checked." I do not mean to imply that men do not blush—recall Shaw and his inadvertently rolled-up sleeves—and certainly it is the case that male characters blush in Shaw's novels. I have already mentioned Cyril Scott's doing so in *Immaturity*, his complexion deepening to "brick red" at the approach of Isabella Woodward. Ned Conolly in *The Irrational Knot* also blushes when, in the early stages of his relationship with Marian Lind, she offers to raise £500 in support of the experimentation needed to refine and market one of his inventions. His reaction, however—"Conolly blushed. 'Thank you, Miss Lind,' said he" (*Knot* 62)—is complicated by several factors. Earlier in his conversation, he had explained to Marian that "Invention is the most expensive thing in the world" and that it "costs a fortune to make experiments enough to lead to an invention," £500 or more. He is slightly nonplussed when Marian remarks that his "fortune" is a "mere nothing" and advises, "make up your mind to spend the money. Banish all scruples about the largeness of the sum" (60). Complicating any analysis of the psychical origins of his blush, Conolly quickly admits that he isn't quite so ready to begin experimentation as his comments might have led her to believe, thus eliminating any immediate need for her venture capital. Whether his blush, then, is attributable to their socio-financial and class differences, their growing personal attachment (though this is barely intimated in the text at this point), Conolly's mildly embarrassing revelation that his invention is not so advanced in development as it seemed, or a combination of these and other factors isn't clear. And it shouldn't be, as blushing is not always reducible to an off/on switch automatically being triggered. On the contrary, Conolly's blush may be the product of a number of both internal and external factors and extend beyond the "analog-like" possibilities listed here.

Much the same is true of incidents of blushing in *Cashel Byron's Profession*, especially where the novel's protagonist is concerned. In fact, and not unimportantly, our introduction to the young Cashel in the novel is accompanied—even marked—by blushing. When, in the novel's Prologue, Cashel's mother visits Moncrief House, "scholastic establishment for the sons of gentlemen, etc." (*Cashel*, 1) and meets Dr. Moncrief, she hears an exceptionally unflattering report about her son's academic performance: he is making "no progress whatever," shows "little inclination for study" and "little ambition to excel in any particular branch," and exhibits "no special aptitude" (2–3). Worse, he manifests a "tendency to violence" that, in young men, "sometimes results" from the "possession of unusual strength and dexterity" (3). Concluding that her son's lack of progress "must be his own fault" (2), Mrs. Byron is not in a cheerful mood when her son, nearly 17 years old, greets her:

> Master Cashel Byron entered blushing; made his way awkwardly to his mother; and kissed the critical expression which was on her upturned face.... (5)

When his actress-mother, "elegantly dressed, of attractive manner, and beautiful at all points except her complexion, which was deficient in freshness" (2), seems to criticize his "very awkward" manner, Cashel again "colored and looked gloomy" (5). She summarizes for him Moncrief's report of his idleness and roughness, the latter allegation Cashel refutes as the result of his and a friend's innocent watching of two men fighting before a large crowd on the village common. Unpersuaded by this excuse, Mrs. Byron sternly reminds him of the significant expense of £120 per year that she incurs to send him to Moncrief House and the work that this sum represents. The inquisition ends with her admonition, his vexation and ruffled feelings, and his resolve to escape the school at the earliest opportunity, which he does soon thereafter.

A number of issues surface in the Prologue that both drive the narrative and reveal elements of Cashel's interior life. Perhaps most obvious, his unsuitability for further education and keen interest in fighting, combined with his prodigious strength and nimbleness at such a young age, presage his storied career as a prizefighter and his almost unavoidable involvement with sporting gentlemen, whose assistance in finding him a secluded place to train eventually leads to his meeting Lydia. His quickness to anger, evidenced by his loud slamming of the door after his interview with his mother, surfaces in the Prologue, but this impulse is strongly suppressed by the time Cashel, after traveling to Australia and learning to box, returns to England to train. However, most important, this uncommonly strong boy, possessed of physical gifts and dexterity that will later contribute to his godlike status as an epitome of masculinity, is also uncommonly susceptible to feelings of awkwardness, embarrassment, and even shame when he is the epicenter of female attention. His easily colored face, in contrast to his mother's heavily made-up complexion (a mask guarding her comparatively inaccessible feeling), reveals his emotion quickly, as it does throughout the rest of Shaw's novel. Albeit a small detail in this scene, money—its amount and relative value, topics that partially cause Conolly's blush in *The Irrational Knot*—also informs Cashel's strained conversation with his mother. Typically figured as a sign of class difference, and seemingly *always* a problematic consideration in marriage, money in this scene further erodes Cashel's powers of self-determination and is exploited by his mother to exacerbate his feelings of failure and trigger his feeling of shame. His inadequacy has been exposed, and Cashel's reaction resembles not merely the shame that Darwin and, after him, affect theorists today describe, but that exhibited by young women such as Alice Goff, who was "ashamed" even to remember her late father's inebriety at public events (*Cashel*, 47).

The day after their first, extraordinary encounter in the forest, Lydia and Cashel meet again quite by accident on a train platform and—given the pugilist's propensity for awkwardness around women—it is hardly surprising that he finds their conversation more emotionally draining than fighting the enormous William Paradise later in the novel. Spying the dandyish Lord Worthington, Cashel's financial backer and "investor" in his fights, with the "Hermes of the day before," Lydia and Alice approach the pair. Overhearing Cashel's reassurance to Worthington that his wagered money is as "safe as the Mint, my boy," Lydia detects a certain "rough quality" and loudness in Cashel's voice that distinguish him from an "English gentleman" (*Cashel*, 52). Nonetheless, she is attracted to this "handsome, powerful" young man (52) and is formally introduced to Cashel, who immediately blushes:

> Mr Cashel Byron reddened a little as he raised his straw hat, but, on the whole, bore himself like an eminent man who was not proud. As, however, he seemed to have nothing to say for himself, Lydia set Lord Worthington talking about Ascot.... (53)

For her part, Lydia experienced an "*unaccountable* thrill of pleasure" at meeting him, although the "latent danger" she sensed was far less agreeable to her cousin Lucian Webber (my emphasis; 53), who along with Worthington and others boarded the train and departed. In these early meetings between Cashel and Lydia, the terms with which Shaw's narrator describes Lydia's feelings are as revealing as the prizefighter's blushes: her thrill is "unaccountable," literally not able to be quantified or calculated; and her earlier "glow of delight" at seeing him in the forest was "strange," residing somewhere outside the ken of her considerable cultural expertise. Only analogies to art works could mediate her response to what she had witnessed and communicate the resulting tumult in her subjective life.

Worthington's and the others' departures leave Cashel alone with Lydia and Alice, and the trio walk back to Wiltstoken with Alice initially separating herself somewhat from them. Cashel explains to Lydia that when he saw her in the forest clearing the day before he mistook her for a ghost, and Lydia admits to the same uncanny misperception, amazing Cashel and causing him to be "unmindful" of his steps. As a result, he loses his finely calibrated sense of balance, stumbles, and becomes "very red." After Lydia explains that Lord Worthington has told her about him, Cashel is "deeply mortified" at the possibility that his background and profession may have been revealed to her (*Cashel*, 54). When Alice reenters the conversation, smiling at him in a transparently false show of courtesy, Cashel "turned away from her, hurt by her manner, and so ill able to conceal his feelings that Miss Carew, always watching him, saw what he felt and knew with delight that he was turning to her for consolation" (55). As they prepare to part ways a little later, Cashel extends his hand to meet, first, Lydia's, and then Alice's gloved hand, which she had extended "stiffly," revealing in the process his enormous paw "discolored almost to blackness." Once inside her gate, Lydia turns to thank Cashel for helping her close it and two subtle, but key things occur: "…in that moment he plucked up courage to look at her. The sensation of being so looked at was quite novel, and very curious." Shaw's narrator notes that Lydia was "even a little out of countenance, but not so much so as Cashel, who nevertheless could not take his eyes away" (57).

One might infer from this otherwise unremarkable parting that two psychical events have occurred, both reflected materially in the facial expressions and demeanors of the novel's two principal characters. Cashel, who blushed when first seeing his mother earlier in the novel and again when formally meeting Lydia on the train platform, is clearly awkward, even shy in this first conversation with Lydia; and, in both of these encounters, a blush was summoned by the exposure of his failings—poor academic performance, on the one hand, feelings of inadequacy and clumsiness on the other. We can reasonably infer that downcast eyes accompanied these feelings, because in the latter scene Cashel gradually "plucked up" the courage to look at Lydia, and from this scene onward his comportment around her is generally more confident. At the same time, Lydia experienced the entirely new "sensation" of "so being looked at"—as a woman, a figure of elegance and desire, and not as a wealthy intellectual. Gender, as culturally constructed as it is, is represented more conventionally in this moment, anticipating the couple's later wedding and happy marriage. Yet this idyllic conclusion is troubled moments earlier by Cashel's turning to Lydia for "consolation" from Alice's icy manner, an implicit criticism that "hurt him" but oddly provided Lydia with "delight." Posture and facial expression thus both clarify feeling in this scene and prefigure future events, particularly Lydia's later view of Cashel as one of her children, beloved to be sure but also emotionally vulnerable.

Feeling, then, particularly negative feeling such as shame and embarrassment, finds its material expression in blushing, pallor, averted eyes, posture, and even nervous laughter in Shaw's fiction and especially in *Cashel Byron's Profession*. Although Cashel's ease around Lydia increases as their relationship flowers, he remains anxious about it for the bulk of the novel. When, for example, he receives a letter from her requesting that he come to her home in Regents Park to meet a "friend," a "deep red color mounted to his temples," the result of his recognition of Lydia's handwriting (*Cashel*, 214). However, as is also the case in all of Shaw's novels, more overtly materialist concerns represented by both wealth and poverty also inform his representation of emotion and feeling. One fecund instance of this occurs in an extraordinary chapter that frames the relationship between money and feeling within the broader context of late-Victorian economic inequity. In chapter VII, an African king, visiting London for the first time, is being shown the "wonders of English civilization" and, in Undershaftian fashion, these wonders include cannon firings and the detonation of "high explosives." However, the potentate proved challenging to entertain, in part because the opacity of social and economic inequality that defined British class privilege were mystifying to him:

> A stranger to the idea that a handful of private persons could own a country and make others pay them for permission to live and work there, he was unable to understand why such a prodigiously rich nation should be composed chiefly of poor and uncomfortable persons toiling incessantly to create riches.... (107–08)

Afflicted also by a variety of fears about his health and general well-being produced by London's filthy streets and polluted air—fears heightened by stories of the assassinations of monarchs and other public figures in European streets—the Colonial Office finally decides to present a military show or "assault-at-arms" and prizefight as entertainment for him. At this exhibition, Cashel spars with the barbarous William Paradise, and Lydia witnesses for the first time the rebarbative elements of her future husband's profession.

Within this context of the massively unequal distribution of income, the predominance of poverty, and urban blight—themes Shaw returned to repeatedly in his future work, perhaps most concertedly in his "*de facto* leadership" with Sidney Webb of the Fabian Society from 1884 to 1911[34]—Lucian Webber appears at Lydia's home in Regent's Park where, while enjoying a leisurely stroll, they discuss wealth and Lydia's marriage prospects. Lydia admits to setting "great store" by the "esteem" her "riches command," which serves as a compensation for the envy they also inspire (*Cashel*, 112). They also discuss her adamant refusal to marry an adventurer with no profession or money, and later Lucian proposes marriage, an offer she declines flatly and decisively. Terming the matter one of "feeling," Lucian soon departs, leaving Lydia to navigate the streets by herself in a neighborhood that once boasted "fashionable dwellings" and later "small shops" and tenements, but now had succumbed to a "slow but steady invasion of large business houses" (117). Lydia notices a small boy gazing longingly through the window of a sweetshop and obviously lacking the funds necessary to purchase a treat, and she asks him to guide her back to Bond Street, giving him a shilling for his trouble. The payment led to his affective "transport at possessing what was to him a fortune" and, overly excited by his stroke of luck, he ran to show his treasure to a group of young men, hurting himself as the result of a collision with one of them. Crying over the modest pain he suffered, the boy stood whimpering until Lydia "reminded him of all the money he had to spend. He seemed comforted" (117). While other significant events occur in this episode—Cashel's dispatching of a young tough who was bothering Lydia and obstructing her path, for instance—this chapter reintroduces the relationship between money and feeling so apparent in *Immaturity* and *Love Among the Artists*. Not surprisingly, a blush or two also surfaces in the chapter—most notably, by a young butcher who befriends Lydia and is tongue-tied when she offers her thanks. However, more important, this at times chaotic scene in the streets serves both as a microcosm of the larger socio-economic reality that so befuddled the visiting African monarch *and* another example of the material(ist) representation of feeling in

Cashel Byron's Profession. In this chapter, rather than catalyzing anxiety or unease, money transforms a poor boy's keen "want"; it "transports" his feelings and "consoles" in a way that no other balm could.

Blushing and money reemerge conspicuously when Cashel makes his first of two proposals of marriage to Lydia. Confidently assuring her that if she agrees to marry him they will have at least "a thousand a year" and live "like fighting cocks on that much," she deflates his confidence by informing him that she possesses an annual income of some £40,000. Immediately comprehending both the enormity of this amount and the insipidity of his previous boast, he "became very red" and responds in a voice "broken by mortification": "I see I have been making a fool of myself" (*Cashel*, 148). Turning to leave, Cashel pauses after Lydia requests that he stay and gently reminds him that she has enjoyed the attention of male friends who are also "much poorer" than she; moreover, "Most of them, I fear, are poorer—much, *much* poorer" than he is as well (149). At this preliminary point in their advancing relationship, however, Lydia is unwilling to accept his offer of marriage.

Later, after Cashel is sought by the authorities for participating in an illegal fight, her unwillingness calcifies into antipathy, or disdain, leading Mrs. Skene, whose husband took Cashel in as a boy and trained him to fight, to Wiltstoken to intercede on his behalf. "Whatever you said to him, it has gone to his heart," she reports ominously to Lydia; "and he is dying" (*Cashel*, 202). What Lydia said to him earlier, after intentionally misleading policemen intending to arrest him for participating in the prizefight, is this: "Let me never see you again," and "I have told a lie. I have made my servant—an honorable man—my accomplice in a lie. We are worse than you; for even your wild-beast's handiwork is less evil...." Her deprecation of him and self-censure are punctuated by flared nostrils, dilated pupils, and "wreaths of rosy color ... chasing each other through her cheeks" (196). Shrinking like a child and emotionally devastated, Cashel stood in silent desperation as she left him. Mrs. Skene entreats Lydia to understand the true dimension of Cashel's emotional life and the extent to which her stance has injured him:

> You cant believe he has any *feelings* because he fights. Ah, miss, if you only knew them as I do! More tender-hearted men dont breathe. Cashel is like a young child; his *feelings* are that easily touched.... Just think what a high-spirited young man must *feel* when a lady calls him a wild beast. (my emphasis; 202)

In the end, Mrs. Skene's appeal to Lydia's sympathy is successful, a conclusion foreshadowed by Lydia's response to the news that Cashel has honorably surrendered to the police in search of him: "'What will they do with him?' she asked, turning quite pale" (197). Later reconciled, and after learning of his class affiliation and substantially larger income from a reunion with his mother, when Cashel again asks her to marry him, Lydia becomes "very pale" again and accepts (224).

Material expression and materialism thus both manifest themselves in Cashel and Lydia's burgeoning relationship, the former serving to communicate endearing character traits and, more often, uncomfortable psychical realities; the latter, predictably, acting as an obstruction to what Peter Gahan in *Bernard Shaw and Beatrice Webb on Poverty and Equality in the Modern World, 1905–1914* labels as "intermarriageability." In this light, "materialism" is irreducible to "wealth" or "money," but rather pertains to both its pervasive effect on marital possibilities *and* its unequal distribution, as the visiting African king recognizes soon after arriving in London. Hence, for Gahan, ventriloquizing Shaw and echoing political theorist Bernard Crick, the "elimination of income inequality would ensure 'intermarriageability' by removing social barriers that complicate two individuals' hopes of marrying." Equally important from a socialist perspective, the destruction of income inequality would lead to the instauration of a "classless society."[35] Although such a socially ameliorative project is not directly addressed in *Cashel Byron's Profession*, its opposite—the mindless defense of social orthodoxy and class boundaries—is frequently made to look ridiculous. After Lydia discovers Cashel's familial background, his bona fides as a "gentleman," for example, she visits her cousin Lucian, who declares her plan to marry a prizefighter "a greater tragedy than I have ever witnessed on the stage" (*Cashel*, 228). After informing him of the class from which Cashel hails, however, Lucian's objections dissipate: "If he is a gentleman, that of course alters the case completely" (230). But Lydia will not allow his flimsy logic and class bias to pass without remark:

> The discovery of his rank does not alter the weight of one blow he has ever struck.... It was not prizefighting that you objected to: that was only a pretence [sic]: your true repugnance was to the class to which prizefighters belong. (230)

She goes on to disparage the concept of "gentlemen," categorizing those she has met as either "amateurs of the arts, having the egotism of professional artists without their ability," or "men of pleasure, which means they are dancers, tennis players, butchers, and gamblers." Such inferior specimens prove that the "arena" of the fighter is a "better school of character than the drawing-room" and that the prizefighter is a "hero" by comparison to them (231).

Materialism, marriage, and class are thus intertwined in *Cashel Byron's Profession*, as they are in all of Shaw's novels. But so, too, is a profusion of affectual responses, which in turn serve as indices of a character's psychical life. Also, although much of the blushing and pallor in *Cashel Byron's Profession* is the predictable result of the awkwardness and embarrassment that attend the evolution—or devolution—of romantic relationships, more serious feelings and the emotional narratives to which they are tethered also play prominent roles. In *Cashel Byron's Profession*, then, Shaw accomplishes an important reconstruction of late-Victorian masculinity, in effect feminizing his handsome prizefighter and refining further dimensions of a material(ist) psychology.

On Blushing and Shame: A Postscript

> Not so long ago, in the East End of London, a Pakistani father murdered his only child, a daughter, because by making love to a white boy she had brought such dishonor upon her family that only her blood could wash away the stain…. The news did not seem alien to me. We who have grown up on a diet of honour and shame grasp what must seem unthinkable to people living in the aftermath of the death of God and of Tragedy….
> —Salman Rushdie, *Shame* (1983)

A century after Shaw wrote *Cashel Byron's Profession*, Salman Rushdie published his postmodern novel *Shame*, and this excerpt is taken from a chapter entitled "Blushing," which describes the twentieth-century ghost who haunts Rushdie's historical phantasmagoria. Anna Muhammad, a young girl sacrificed in an honor killing by a father who professed to love her, immigrated with her family to the East End of London—long a home for immigrants—and Rushdie's narrator cannot escape her influence. Anna, it seems, had found a white boyfriend and her father, believing erroneously that she had been intimate with him, "butchered" her for an offense she had never committed. When pressed by the media to condemn this "honor killing," the man's neighbors and family manifested a "beleaguered reluctance" to do so, professing to understand his "point of view."[36] Anna lingers in the narrator's imagination and reappears in various guises before settling into the role of ghost, a specter that embodies a particularly Eastern variant of shame that leads him almost inevitably to Sufiya Zenobia and the fifteenth century (and modern Pakistan as well in what is a sprawling and enormously engaging narrative).

Sufiya, like Anna, embodies shame; she was born blushing, or so the legend goes, and her parents were "perplexed by these reddenings, these blushes like petrol fires," that continued unabated during her childhood. "Anyone puts eyes on her," the narrator relates, "or tells her two words and she goes red, red like a chilli!" Rushdie's narrator even quotes from a physiological description of blushing: the "arterio-venous anastomoses of the face" suddenly constrict and flood the capillaries with blood, thereby demonstrating that the phenomenon is as "'clear an example of mind over matter as one could wish for.'"[37] Consistent with both Darwin's observation and those of contemporary affect theorists, Sufiya Zenobia "blushed uncontrollably whenever her presence in the world was noticed by others"—to the point that she may even have "blushed for the world—because of shame." Shame, in Rushdie's inventive metaphorization, is figured as a "sweet and fizzy tooth-rotting" soda pouring from a vending machine into a cup. Accessing greater portions of shame is thus as simple as pushing a button: "Tell a lie, sleep with a white boy, get born the wrong sex. Out flows the bubbling emotion and you drink your fill." This button is connected to an even longer litany of "shameful things" both men and women do: getting caught cheating at cards, blowing a wicket at a crucial moment in a Test Match, extramarital sex, and more, most of which are done, the narrator emphasizes, *shamelessly*.[38]

Although these shameful and shameless things include many gender-neutral and obviously masculine failings, it seems clear enough that Rushdie—or, rather, his narrator—yokes shame more specifically to women: sleeping with white boys and being born the "wrong sex," for example. As I mentioned in the opening chapter, shame was also gendered female in the tenement literature of the 1920s and 1930s, linked with a daughter's unwanted pregnancy and the distrainment of a family's property that could no longer afford to pay the rent (and its humiliating exhibition on the street so that all can witness the spectacle of a family's failure). Yet, perhaps the most conspicuous embodiment of shame in Bernard Shaw's *oeuvre* is Cashel Byron, the epitome of manly beauty and paragon of prizefighters. To be sure, and consistent with Jack Tanner's dissertation on shame in *Man and Superman*, moments in *Cashel Byron's Profession* seem to indict British society which, like fifteenth-century

Pakistan in Rushdie's novel, serves as an incubator of shame. Perhaps the strongest articulation of this indictment comes from Alice Goff, who had known poverty in her life and desired both money and social position in any future marriage. After sharing a waltz with Lucian, she meditated upon "the way in which society regulated marriages"; in the process, Shaw's narrator inserts the possibility that while Alice was "quite unconscious of the privation caused by living with meanly-minded people," she was nonetheless "acutely conscious of that caused by want of money" (*Cashel*, 182–83). Determined to remedy this in marriage, Alice was also sensitive to the deficiencies of the commercial middle class from which she emerged:

> She found it all a huge caricature of herself—a society ashamed of itself, afraid to be itself, suspecting other people of being itself and pretending to despise them for it.... (178)

Eventually, Alice marries Lucian, keeping his house and dominating "his select social circle with complete success." Her "empire" over her husband and household was "never shaken" (242), and her co-optation by the society she despised was complete.

As we learn in the final chapter of *Cashel Byron's Profession*, Lydia and Cashel marry and live as happily ever after as any couple in all of Shaw's fiction. But that doesn't mean the pathway to this happiness was easily navigated, as Cashel's experience of shame, especially around his wife, persists until the novel's conclusion. When, for example, a bloodied Paradise bites him at the boxing exhibition, Cashel ferociously shouts out his intention to seek reprisal. However, when Lord Worthington whispers to him that Lydia is in the audience, he "suddenly subsided, pale and ashamed, and sat down on a chair in his corner as if to hide himself." Shaking hands with Paradise some minutes later and preparing to exit the arena, Cashel "did not raise his eyes to the balcony" and seemed "in a hurry to retire" (*Cashel*, 174). When Mrs. Skene later visits Lydia in an attempt to impress upon her the devastating impact her reproach has had on him, she alludes to his boxing exhibition and shame as well: "Cashel heard that you were looking on; and then he read the shameful way the newspapers wrote of him; and he thought youd believe it all" (203). It is in this context, this larger circuit of shame and blushing, that Cashel's later proclamation to his mother just prior to asking Lydia to marry him (again) accrues meaning. When explaining to her his great success, his victories and gold champion's belt, he exclaims with an Undershaftian confidence, "I am not ashamed of it" (219).

Such a moment has been a long time in gestation. From the several blushes that accompany our first glimpses of Cashel with his mother; from his repeated coloring in his first conversation with Lydia and after stumbling foolishly while walking her home; from his foolish assumption in his initial proposal to her that she would be impressed by an income of £1000 a year; from his averted eyes and effort to hide in a corner at the military exhibition—all of these displays of shame and anxiety as materially registered in his blush, pallor, and posture appear to be vanquished by the novel's conclusion. "I am not ashamed" serves as a kind of epiphany that distinguishes Cashel from a society of ashamed Londoners, as Shaw's use of the materiality of affect demonstrates.

This deployment of emotion continues in his last and most successful novel, *An Unsocial Socialist*, but also at times plays a role secondary to Shaw's vigorous examination of industrial practices and the deployment of capital, the unequal distribution of wealth, and questions of value in commodity exchange. In these ways, Shaw's "material(ist) psychology" vitally informs his fiction, dominating the subjective lives of such characters as Robert Smith, Owen Jack, and Cashel Byron. Moreover, given the critique of late Victorian class society delineated in all of Shaw's novels, the *tangibility* of blushes, averted eyes, stooped posture, and anxious laughter complements the materiality of money in all of its forms—capital, currency, dowries, investments, sports wagering, and shillings for little boys to buy candy—in at least partially addressing the "torment" that Freud experienced in engaging the problem of feeling and emotion. Like Freud, Shaw could not quantify or measure feeling with absolute mathematical precision, but his novels nevertheless demonstrate the pervasive effects that materialism exerts on psychical reality as evidenced by a myriad of material expressions of emotion. The most conspicuous of these is shame as evinced by the blush.

Notes

1. Kornbluh, 3.
2. Kornbluh, 11.
3. Kornbluh refers to a "naturalization of capitalism" in critical exegeses of Freudian thought that originates, in part, in Strachey's translation of a term such as "cathexis" as "investment." "Investment," she charges,

"occludes the diversity of processes at work; characterizing the Freudian subject as an 'investor' and thus a typical bourgeois agent of finance dangerously reduces the intricacy of Freud's ideas." See Kornbluh, 144–45.
4. In *Civilization and Its Discontents*, for example, Freud suggests that "one gains the most if one can sufficiently heighten the yield of pleasure" from such "sources of psychical and intellectual work" as scientific problem-solving or artistic creation. He describes the "capacity of the psychical constitution to adapt its function to the environment and then to exploit that environment for a yield of pleasure"; and he alludes to the diminished pursuit of happiness in a man's "later years" that may lead him to "find consolation in the yield of pleasure of chronic intoxication" (*SE* 21: 84).
5. Analogies to economics, both overt and more subtle, abound in *Civilization and Its Discontents*. Adverting later to the same issue of the diversification of libidinal aims, Freud, like a prudent businessman and "wise men of every age," advises against making "genital eroticism the central point" of one's life, even though it might afford "the strongest experiences of satisfaction," because of the "extreme suffering" that results from rejection or loss of the love-object (*SE* 21: 101). Besides, man does not have "unlimited quantities of psychical energy at his disposal" (*SE* 21: 103), scarcity being a feature of both the psychical and ascendant money economies.
6. Kornbluh, 142. The previous quotations from Kornbluh are taken from *Realizing Capital*, 137–41.
7. Kornbluh, 146.
8. Sedgwick, 98.
9. Darwin, 310, 324.
10. Sedgwick, 98, 104.
11. Ahmed, *The Cultural Politics of Emotion*, 104.
12. Freud was well aware that some feelings are elicited from both external and internal stimuli. Guilt or remorse and some varieties of fear provide examples in the later pages of *Civilization and Its Discontents*. Describing the relationship between "conscience" and the operations of the super ego, he alludes to "two strata" of guilt—"one coming from fear of the *external* authority, the other from fear of the *internal* authority" (*SE* 21: 137)—and concedes that the existence of a remorse "older" than conscience has "perplexed" him. Here, again, the intangibility of feeling surfaces in the essay as a kind of intellectual "torment," albeit one not so acute as Freud's earlier complaint about the problems inherent to assessing feeling more generally.
13. Two examples night be adduced to delineate the range of uses to which Shaw puts paleness in *Cashel Byron's Profession*. In an early conversation with Lydia, Cashel becomes self-aware of the inelegance of his language and his reference to himself as a "professional pug." Shaw's narrator

describes his reaction: "He recollected himself, and turned quite pale" (69). Later in the novel, when Cashel asks her to marry him, Lydia "became very pale," pointing out to him that although her wealth will allow him to be exceptionally "idle," she will always be a "busy woman" who is "preoccupied with work" (224). Cashel responds by saying that he would not be idle and, in fact, after their marriage he undertakes a variety of productive activities.

14. Darwin, 312.
15. Darwin, 324.
16. See Paul Ekman, "Cross-Cultural Studies of Facial Expression," especially 169–86. Here Ekman addresses directly Darwin's view of the universality of expression, finally agreeing with Sylvan Tomkins that "the number of feelings which have a distinct facial appearance is probably small" (182). Here, Ekman also offers useful observations about both gesture as it pertains to expression and so-called "emblematic expressions" (which are used when one is located physically at a distance from another and attempts to convey a message nonverbally).
17. Shaw's comparison of the two star-actresses is, in this respect, not entirely unique. When Duse first appeared in Paris two years later and the pair reprised their performances of Marguerite Gauthier, the "sumptuously gowned" and more demonstrative Bernhardt contrasted sharply with the "more subdued and poignant" Duse. See *Duse on Tour: Guido Noccioli's Diaries, 1906–07*, trans. Giovanni Pontiero (Amherst: University of Massachusetts Press, 1982), 30.
18. Simmel, "La Duse" (May 8, 1901), trans. Thomas M. Kemple, in *Theory, Culture & Society* 29 (7/8) (2012): 277. Simmel wrote considerably more about the theatre than this, including a 1912 essay "The Dramatic Actor and Reality," trans. K. Peter Etzkorn, in *Georg Simmel: The Conflict in Modern Culture and Other Essays* (New York: Teachers College Press, 1968), 91–97. Here, Simmel argues that "the genuine and incomparable dramatic art ... lives in the realm between the written play and reality" (95), an assertion that would render irrelevant the search for "real" people on stage. Simmel also completed a book manuscript, believed to be lost, near the time of his death in 1918 on the sociology of the stage actor. For details, see Henry Schermer and David Jary, *Form and Dialectic in Georg Simmel's Sociology: A New Interpretation*, 54–55.
19. Noccioli, 20.
20. Eva Le Gallienne, *The Mystic in the Theatre: Eleonora Duse* (Carbondale: Southern Illinois University Press, 1965), 81.
21. Here Shaw's description echoes Darwin's dissection of the blush and physical gestures that typically accompany it and shame. "Under a keen sense of shame," Darwin notes in *The Expression of the Emotions in Man and*

Animals, "there is a strong desire for concealment. We turn away the whole body, more especially the face, which we endeavour in some manner to hide. An ashamed person can hardly endure to meet the gaze of those present..." (319). In this way, Duse's blush is emblematic of what is, *perhaps*, a universal and involuntary reaction.

22. Joseph Valente, *The Myth of Manliness in Irish National Culture, 1880–1922* (Urbana: University of Illinois Press, 2011), 3.
23. It is important to note that laughter is construed by many anthropologists as a facial expression potentially conveying a range of emotions, some of which have little to do with amusement or pleasure. Paul Ekman discusses this phenomenon along with cultural "emblems" in relation to the argument about universal facial expressions in "Cross-Cultural Studies of Facial Expression," 179–85.
24. Blushes may be transformed into facial signs of more turbulent emotion in the later, failing moments of intimate relationships as well. In *Love Among the Artists* Adrian Herbert, falling hopelessly in love with the enchanting Polish pianist Aurélie Szczympliça, visits Mary Sutherland to discuss ending their nearly three-year engagement. Mary turns "red" when Herbert implies that she is eager to break off their relationship, and Herbert, "also reddening," rejoins the insinuation by pleading his innocence in the matter (162–63).
25. Marian Lind's tendency to blush manifests itself in the early moments of her relationship with Ned Conolly in *The Irrational Knot*. When she happens across Conolly in his laboratory and interrupts his work, for example, she blushes "vigorously" after discovering who it is (58).
26. In *The Irrational Knot*, Marmaduke Lind confronts his cousin Marian about sending Conolly to him to discuss his growing disfavor over his relationship with Susanna Conolly and his indifference toward Constance Carbury. Marmaduke notes her strange look and Marian admits that she had "only blushed." His response: "Blushed! Why don't you blush red, like other people, and not green!" (*Knot*, 91).
27. Darwin, 324.
28. Ahmed, *The Cultural Politics of Emotion*, 103.
29. Tomkins, qtd. in Sedgwick, 99. Sedgwick adds yet another dimension to this conversation by suggesting both the "digital" and "analogue" connotations of affects and the affect system. An example of the latter, the affect system encompasses more and "qualitatively different" possibilities than the off/on switching of the sexual or instinctual drive (101).
30. Dietrich, *Bernard Shaw's Novels*, 131.
31. Darwin, 319.
32. Sedgwick discusses through the metaphoric opposition digital/analog approaches to affect that privilege the on/off effect of stimulus over the analog model of multiple differentiation and gradual reaction (101).

33. See, among many others, Laura Mulvey, "Visual Pleasure and the Narrative Cinema," *Screen* 16 (Autumn 1975): 6–18. For a generation or more now, the premise that the dynamics of spectation include a male viewer and a female object of his gaze has animated innumerable scholarly projects.
34. Peter Gahan, *Bernard Shaw and Beatrice Webb on Poverty and Equality in the Modern World, 1905–1914*, x.
35. Gahan, x. Here Gahan refers to Crick's article "Shaw as Political Thinker, or the Dogs That Did Not Bark," *SHAW 11: Shaw and Politics*, ed. T.F. Evans (University Park: Penn State Press, 1991), 21–36.
36. Salman Rushdie, *Shame* (1983; New York: Random House, 2008), 117–18.
37. Rushdie, 124, 126.
38. Rushdie, 125.

CHAPTER 6

The Antinomies of *An Unsocial Socialist*

Most readers of Bernard Shaw's *An Unsocial Socialist* (written in 1883, serialized in 1884, and published by Swan Sonnenschein and Company in 1887) tend to agree on two things. The first is conveyed, I hope, by "antinomies" in the title of this chapter: namely, that paradoxes, contradictions, and even mysteries abound in the novel's narrative. For Stanley Weintraub, quoting Shaw, *An Unsocial Socialist*, which was intended as a "gigantic grapple with the whole social problem," inevitably "[breaks] down under the weight of its incongruities."[1] One of these incongruities, for Richard Dietrich, emerges in the "satirical contrast" that Shaw draws between "the gay irresponsible world of English society and the dark crime of social mismanagement of which it is guilty": "In short, the critical confusion has been caused by another Shavian paradox: the relevance of Marx is most substantial where the life of England is most insubstantial."[2] The second point of critical consensus, related to Weintraub's observation, pertains to Shaw's note in the novel's abbreviated "Foreword," written in 1930, that his "original design" was to use the book as the "first chapter of a vast work depicting capitalist society in dissolution, with its downfall as the final grand catastrophe." This ambition, both author and critics agree, was unrealized, but not necessarily because of contradictions or incongruities—or because, as Shaw suggests, after writing *An Unsocial Socialist* he had nothing more to say about the inequities perpetrated by capitalism or that the economic doctrines of his protagonist Sidney Trefusis

© The Author(s) 2018
S. Watt, *Bernard Shaw's Fiction, Material Psychology, and Affect*,
Bernard Shaw and His Contemporaries,
https://doi.org/10.1007/978-3-319-71513-1_6

merely anticipated those of the "real" V.I. Lenin (*US*, v). However intriguing in intimating Shaw's evolving education in economics, especially on matters related to markets, commodities, and value, and however inexhaustible Shaw proved to be in scrutinizing the vicissitudes of capitalism, this rationale finally provides little purchase on the most perplexing elements of the novel. Also, uncharacteristically for Shaw, in the remainder of his "Foreword"—a veritable footnote compared to the lengthy prefaces of *Immaturity* and *The Irrational Knot*—Shaw drops such subjects entirely.

As a primer of authorial intentionality, then, the three slim paragraphs that constitute the "Foreword" to *An Unsocial Socialist* are mostly irrelevant or simply unhelpful, as they deflect attention from the very issues in which the fit, though few, readers who have labored over Shaw's last completed novel are most interested. These include not only the devastating societal effects of capitalism to which Shaw alludes in his introduction—the enslavement of factory workers, their replacement by more efficient and profitable machines, the squalor in which they are forced to live, and so on—but also the formation or, rather, deformation of the human subject, the warp and the woof of the material stitched into Shaw's representation of the psychological. The last two paragraphs of Shaw's "Foreword" are particularly remote from this or any interpretive endeavor, for instead of addressing the novel's emplotment or illuminating the motivations of its principal characters, they outline his decision to abandon the novel form and follow in the professional footsteps of Shakespeare and Molière. For these reasons, *An Unsocial Socialist* may be said to be preceded by a largely ineffectual instance of the strategy that Susan Cannon Harris identifies as typically deployed in Shaw's Prefaces, Afterwords, and Epilogues: "Protecting his own authority by striving to eliminate lack, subtext or ambiguity, Shaw foreclosed the kinds of reading that the past half-century has shown to be most generative." As a consequence, at least in part, we have witnessed—and, at the risk of succumbing to melodramatic handwringing, some of us have even bemoaned—the "depreciation of his stock since the theory revolution."[3]

As Harris's use of queer theory to map the borders of Shaw's utopian desire in *John Bull's Other Island* amply demonstrates,[4] the time has come to reverse this overcorrection in the market of ideas and rebalance our intellectual portfolios accordingly, for subtext, ambiguity, and complex, even contradictory, representations of class, gender, and human subjectivity are just as central as economic theory to *An Unsocial Socialist*, as the adjective in Shaw's vaguely oxymoronic title implies. That is to say, while the opening of Shaw's prefatory note gestures exclusively to the "socialist" side of his title, it remains silent about the "unsocial" aspects of his central character, about their etiology in Victorian culture (including economics and psychology), and about how these two terms might inform each other. Equally obvious, the title focuses reader attention on Sidney Trefusis, as if he were the sole repository of critical interest. In what follows, I hope to engage the complexities and antinomies of both the subjective and the material in the novel, unpacking elements of both the "unsocial" and the "socialist."

Shaw's Foreword is also silent about the range of disciplinary pursuits he undertook through his fiction—his "reverse anthropology" of late Victorian society, for example, as Declan Kiberd terms it—or the ways in which *An Unsocial Socialist*, as Arnold Silver describes, illuminates Shaw's own "psychological processes" in responding to his "most intimate problems" while writing the novel.[5] I shall have more to say about both of these topics in the discussion that follows. But, apropos of Susan Harris's point about the freighting of the Shavian text with opening and closing essays designed to delimit our reading, because it lacks such apparatus *An Unsocial Socialist*, like *Love Among the Artists*, provides an opportunity to examine Shaw's critique of capitalism *and* its distortive effect on human subjectivity unimpeded by his efforts to mute contradiction or marshal explication. By seizing this opportunity, we might recognize Shaw's novel as more than an illustration of a sociopolitical or economic thesis adumbrated in a preface and reprised in an afterword and, instead, see it as a culmination of political themes *and* refinements of the material psychology outlined in his earlier fiction, including the prominence of such affects as shame and anxiety in everyday life, and their relationship to both the commodification of women transacting the "business" of marriage, and— surprisingly—the motives of highly successful capitalists.[6]

This relatively unfettered reading, I hasten to add, is not *entirely* free of the influence of the Shavian apparatuses with which we are familiar. For in addition to a title that directs readers' attention to Trefusis, the novel concludes with an "Appendix" in the form of a "letter to the author" from Shaw's protagonist, a device added to the text after sales lagged and Shaw's publisher requested the addition of an accompanying essay.[7] Yet, in part because it is presented as communicating the observations of a character rather than the wisdom of his creator, this otherwise typical Shavian tactic thickens the novel's contradictions rather than minimizing them. Ostensibly written to appease Trefusis's "friends," who are "not quite satisfied with the account" Shaw provided in his "clever novel," the letter both extends the novel's plot and attempts to refute censure of Trefusis for his heartless abandonment of his beautiful first wife, Henrietta Jansenius (*US*, 254). In a narrative replete with letters and telegrams—some of which, like documents in nineteenth-century melodrama, motivate action and in one case form the proximate cause of Henrietta's death near the middle of the novel—Trefusis's letter, like the final chapter of *Cashel Byron's Profession* and Shaw's concluding note to *Pygmalion*, advances the novel's narrative by conveying soothing news about the unlikely marriages between Trefusis and Agatha Wylie, and the poet Chichester Erskine and Gertrude Lindsay, the latter actually very much in love with the unsocial socialist himself. Trefusis reports, for example, that Gertrude, far from being "dead from a broken heart," has flourished in her marriage to Erskine; further, it has allowed her to escape the "vile caste" of her family who complained about the money she required as a single woman, and in turn she has become "relatively rich, as well as pleasant, active, and in sound health." Addressing "foolish questions" about his second marriage, Trefusis similarly proclaims it a "success," albeit one attained on his terms, which remain as opaque after reading the letter as they were throughout the novel. For her part, Agatha's views of their marriage "vary with the circumstances under which they are expressed" (256).

However, also like the endnote to *Pygmalion*, in which Shaw announces his larger iconoclastic project to dismantle the "ragshop in which Romance keeps its stock of 'happy endings' to misfit all stories" (*CPP* 1: 281), Trefusis's "Appendix" has ambitions greater than mere reportage about domestic matters. Chief among these include a consideration of the connotations of "unsocial" in the novel's title to counter negative responses to his abandonment of Henrietta and his callous treatment of her thereafter, and a recognition of, if not a respect for, his father's rise to affluence as a powerful industrialist. In the letter's early paragraphs Trefusis initiates the former ambition, attempting to refute the aspersion grounded in the "fictitious and feminine standard of morality" inherent to late-Victorian "noveldom" that he is one of the "heartless brutes" who routinely populate such fictions. In describing him as "unsocial," Trefusis alleges, Shaw has branded him with "the last adjective" he expected to find "in the neighborhood of [his] name," thereby creating contradictions in the text and "misapprehensions" among readers that require firm correction (*US*, 255).

The matter of his father Jesse Trefusis's rise to power and his accumulation of massive wealth is equally productive of confusion, some of which originates in Trefusis's couching his defense of his father as friendly advice to Shaw, the fledgling novelist:

> Industrial kingship, the only real kingship of our century, was his by divine right of his turn for business; and I, his son, bid you respect the crown whose revenues I inherit. If you dont, my friend, your book wont pay. (*US*, 257)

More than concern for the success of Shaw's novel seems to motivate this passage. Through the metaphor of "industrial kingship," Trefusis argues that like royalty—and like such characters as the aptly named Bossborn in the "comedietta" *Why She Would Not* that Shaw began nearly 70 years after writing the novel—his father possessed from birth a pedigree that accounted for his ascent: not the traditional familial privilege or "divine right" of a monarch, but an inherent acumen for business. Yet, at the same time, his father was not merely "shrewd, energetic, and ambitious," as Trefusis explains to Henrietta when she appeared at Alton College to confront him about abandoning her, but something more sinister and socially deleterious. In his socioeconomic analysis, Trefusis's father Jesse stands as a kind of econo-intellectual despot who, through "the tyranny of brain force," creates the factory as a site of labor exploitation, thereby refining the brutality of the larger "machinery of the system" of which it is a part (74). Bluntly put, this system starves and enslaves workers as it enriches industrialists and bankers such as Henrietta's father. As a result, his father didn't actually "make a fortune"; rather, "He took a fortune that others made" (71). When he could increase his wealth by ruthlessly clearing peasants off his land and replacing them with cows and sheep—or by firing men from his factories and hiring women and children, who were "cheaper and more docile" (70)– he didn't hesitate to act.

Yet, as Trefusis appears to advise Shaw, "industrial kingship," however abhorrent its consequences, like the notion of "divine right," commands a certain respect. Such an insistence, as Oscar Wilde would later observe in "The Soul of Man under Socialism" (1891), is itself a subtle indictment of the very capitalism Trefusis preaches against: "The true perfection of man lies, not in what man has, but in what man is."[8] Trefusis's effort to illuminate the "extraordinary destiny" of his father, the "true hero of a nineteenth-century romance," then, creates yet another of the many confusions and incongruities in *An Unsocial Socialist* which, precisely because it is the very antithesis of the nineteenth-century romance novel, undermines the commendation.

One task of this chapter is to disentangle the antinomies inherent to the title and narrative of *An Unsocial Socialist*. In at least one respect, such a labor parallels that of Trefusis's "Appendix," which, as I have mentioned, attempts to refute any insinuation of his "unsocial" demeanor and inclination. Stanley Weintraub would appear to concur about the problematic nature of "unsocial" by arguing that Trefusis's "lack of effectiveness as a socialist missionary is not due to his being unsocial but rather to his being an excessively social socialist, particularly towards females of no use to his cause."[9] This sense of Trefusis's hyper-sociability to women far removed from his political agenda also requires further investigation. So, too, does Kiberd's observation that, as a playwright, Shaw is "routinely" accused of "creating unreal, over-schematic characters without a credible basis in human psychology," deflating them into comic types and thereby achieving a "reconciliation between socialism and comedy."[10] While *An Unsocial Socialist*, like several of Shakespeare's later plays, might be described as a "dark comedy"—its narrative, while admitting a death, concludes with two marriages and is populated by character types conventional to social comedy like the effete gentleman-poet Chichester Erskine and lavishly "comfortable" Lady Jane Brandon—it is hardly the case that Trefusis's psyche (or that of his first wife, Henrietta or "Hetty") is schematized for comic purposes. Moreover, where Kiberd in *Irish Classics* reverts productively to anthropology in reading *Arms and the Man*, I want to rely, as in earlier chapters, upon psychoanalysis, affect theory, and theories of value in addressing, first, the "unsocial" in *An Unsocial Socialist* and, second, the "socialist" connotations of Shaw's title, particularly as these pertain to theories of value. Not surprisingly, in what follows these two intersect; similarly unsurprising, given the Shavian strategies Susan Harris identifies to constrain critical reading, this discussion will focus on two issues foregrounded in the novel's "Appendix": first, the overdetermined nature of Trefusis's unsocial "heartlessness" and, second, the broadly subjective dimensions of "industrial kingship," particularly its mechanizing and fracturing of the human subject.

THE "UNSOCIAL": NARCISSISM, INTERTEXTS, AND "SECRET DOUBLES"

> My Dearest—I am off—surfeited with endearment—to live my own life and do my own work. I could only have prepared you for this by coldness or neglect, which are wholly impossible to me when the spell of your presence is upon me. I find that I must fly if I am to save myself.

> I am afraid that I cannot give you satisfactory and intelligible reasons for this step. You are a beautiful and luxurious creature: life is to you full and complete only when it is a carnival of love. My case is just the reverse. Before three soft speeches have escaped me I rebuke myself for folly and insincerity. Before a caress has had time to cool, a strenuous revulsion seizes me: I long to return to my old lonely ascetic hermit life; to my dry books; my Socialist propagandism.... Love cannot keep possession of me: all my strongest powers rise up against it and will not endure it. (*US*, 10–11)

These sentences initiate Sidney Trefusis's letter to his 19-year-old wife Henrietta who, after slightly more than five weeks of marriage, finds herself abandoned.[11] Receiving the letter before the action of the second chapter of *An Unsocial Socialist* begins, she rushes to her parents' mansion in St. John's Wood to seek the counsel and sympathy of her mother, Ruth. Gaining access to her mother's drawing room, she blurts out that Sidney is "Gone! Gone! Deserted me! I—" before "utterance failed" and she hurled herself on an ottoman, "sobbing with passionate spite" and "stamping" on the carpet (9). Speculating that her dilemma is only the temporary result of the predictable quarrels newly-weds experience, Henrietta's mother is quickly disabused of her hypothesis; Trefusis's desertion is more than the temporary result of a spat. In the same conversation, Henrietta also pleads her innocence to a charge that her mother never actually levies, "solemnly" swearing that she has not "lost" her "temper" and, convinced that she must be cursed, vowing to kill herself as "there is no other way" (10). Both of these issues—her hyper-emotionalism and the hint of an untimely death—recur until the middle of the novel when she succumbs to a fatal illness after visiting her estranged husband in Lyvern.

In a novel intended as either the inaugural installment of a multivolume chronicle of the "dissolution" of capitalism or as a social comedy aimed at eviscerating the arrogance, enervation, and greed of the privileged class, such emotional excess and ominous possibility seem wildly out of place, as does the opening chapter centering around the juvenile antics and resultant discipline of teenage girls at the Alton College in Lyvern, one of whom is Mr. Jansenius's ward, Agatha Wylie. However, the *excess* in the novel's second chapter presaging Hetty's tragic death is conveyed not only by her unconstrained behavior, about which there will be much more to say, but also more subtly by the diction of her estranged husband's letter. In it, Trefusis claims to be both "surfeited" with "endearment" for his wife, a "beautiful and luxurious" creature, while also being ensnared by "the spell" of her "presence." It is difficult to ignore the sexual overtones of a word like "luxurious," which, as the *Oxford English Dictionary* relates, for several centuries connoted lasciviousness and designated someone "prone to the rage of venery." Connected to Trefusis's description of Hetty's intimate project to create a "carnival of love," then, "luxurious" bristles with a hint of sexuality that catalyzes his equally "strenuous revulsion," all of which recall Eve Sedgwick's thesis referenced in an earlier chapter that a powerful "affect system"—and in this case the production of "revulsion"—coexists with libidinal cathexes and the pleasure principal. Revulsion, the kernel of the disgust that Sara Ahmed theorizes, is felt on the skin and involves a body recoiling from proximity to another. As an "intense bodily feeling of being sickened," disgust is "dependent upon contact" and compels a necessary distancing from the object, event, or situation which instantiates the feeling.[12] As such, our introduction to Trefusis is hardly one of reduction to a familiar and shallow comic type; on the contrary, if Shaw's protagonist effects a narcissistic retreat to a world of one—or, as Richard Dietrich phrases it, if he attempts to "withdraw from the world of vain flesh"[13]—it is an "escape" *prompted by an affect* that, in the end, trumps sexual desire. It is also a retreat steeped in the complexity of several intertexts, each of which informs our understanding of what might otherwise be regarded as Trefusis's selfishness. In characterizing the irreducible oneness of this world away from Henrietta, Trefusis requires three adjectives—"old, lonely, ascetic"—to portray the "hermit life" that acts as a counter to his wife's powerful and enthralling "carnival of love." Perhaps most important, he concludes the letter's opening paragraph with a hint of desperation: "I feel that I must fly if I am to save myself" (10).

One hardly needs to remark that Trefusis's letter and Hetty's response to it resonate with both complication and context, but I will say it anyway. For Arnold Silver, who underscores Trefusis's narcissism and, again, privileges the value of *An Unsocial Socialist* in "illuminating the psychological processes of its author," Trefusis's dilemma parallels Shaw's own struggles in negotiating his relationship with Alice Lockett, with whom he "instantly fell in love."[14] In Silver's reading, Shaw sought to "console himself for Alice's rejection by discrediting marital happiness" and thereby renounce the "real world of womankind as variously embodied in those pain-producing creatures Hetty, Jane, and above all Gertrude Lindsay," the latter two classmates of Agatha with whom years later in the novel's later chapters Trefusis socializes.[15] Silver even goes so far as to postulate the existence of Shaw's and Trefusis's "murderous impulses" directed at the objects of their desire, impulses accompanying the latter's "withdrawal into the ego" and a less conflicted state of "primary narcissism."[16] A more benign way of expressing this withdrawal and an echo of Trefusis's letter, as James Strachey's translation of Freud's lecture "The Libido Theory and Narcissism" (1917) indicates, is that a narcissistic retreat has as much to do with "self-preservation" as it does with introversion or cruelty directed at the love-object. As Freud notes, sexuality, "in return for an unusually high degree of pleasure, brings dangers which threaten the individual's life and often enough destroy it." Consequently, sexual instincts coincide and at times clash with "self-preservation instincts," however impractical or difficult it may be to separate this pair (*SE* 16: 413).

While considerable evidence suggests that Trefusis's desertion of his wife constitutes this kind of narcissistic retreat, I want to observe, as Matthew Yde does when alluding to Silver's understanding of Shaw's psychical conflicts as displaced onto Trefusis, that the matter is more overdetermined than this. And, again, not because of any intimation of "murderous impulses" or sadistic tendency in Trefusis (and Shaw).[17] Indeed, the language of Trefusis's letter to Hetty and that of his subsequent encounters with her motivate alternative readings of his "escape," several of which trouble understandings of Trefusis's "unsocial" sensibility as rooted in "heartlessness" or "brutality." One counter reading begins with his fear of being overwhelmed subjectively by Hetty. Uncannily, his reference to the "lonely" hermitage of his dry scholarship and propagandism anticipates Freud's rejection in "On Narcissism: An Introduction" (1914) of Carl Jung's use of an "ascetic anchorite" as an example of sexual introversion:

> ...an anchorite of this kind, who 'tries to eradicate every trace of sexual interest' (but only in the popular sense of the of the word 'sexual'), does not even necessarily display any pathogenic allocation of the libido. He may have diverted his sexual interest from human beings entirely, and yet may have sublimated it into a heightened interest in the divine, in nature, or in the animal kingdom, without his libido having undergone an introversion ... or a return to his ego. (*SE* 14: 80–81)

Whether Trefusis's flight from Hetty signals a "return to his ego" or not, his experience also demonstrates what Shaw later regarded as the internal conflict between "two tyrannous physical passions: concupiscence and chastity."[18] Yet, more significant for my purpose, Trefusis's *fear* of loss of self—"I find that I must fly if I am to save myself" (*US* 10)—and his "strenuous" *revulsion* at the prospect of his wife's caress confirm not only the proximity of desire and self-preservation, but also the copresence of a powerful affect system.[19] Stated more pointedly, the pressures of negative affects—one (fear) marked by futurity, the other (revulsion) "full" or completed in the present—overwhelm Trefusis's sexual desire and, in turn, trigger his "heightened interest" in the secular religion in which he is an acolyte: political economy.

Beyond the specific contexts of narcissism, self-preservation, and introversion within which Trefusis enacts his "unsocial" retreat, three additional *intertexts* might deepen understanding of him and his wife, the latter of whose actions and pathos inevitably influence our views of Shaw's unsocial socialist. The first, as Silver emphasizes, originates in Shaw's emotional distress at the time of the novel's composition caused by his troubled relationship with Alice Lockett. It is hardly a revelation on Silver's part or my own to detect autobiographical traces in such protagonists in Shaw's novels as Robert Smith in *Immaturity*, Owen Jack in *Love Among the Artists*, and Trefusis; nor is it surprising that both Smith and Jack are unmarried at the end of the novels in which they appear, and that Trefusis is married to Agatha, who in no way harbors the affection for him that Gertrude Lindsay does. As Silver notes, strong parallels exist between intimations in *An Unsocial Socialist* of Trefusis's emotional aridity—one connotation of "unsocial"—and Shaw's strategic coolness in letters exchanged between him and Alice.[20] As Dan H. Laurence observes in introducing Shaw's letter to her on September 11, 1883, Alice had written him a letter that morning which questioned points in an earlier correspondence, asserting that "All people are not machines: some are capable of genuine feelings" (*CL* 1: 65). (In an earlier letter on September 9, Shaw referred to his own heart as a machine, a topic to be addressed more fully in the next section of this chapter, and in some ways she merely echoes his prior use of this metaphor.) At the same time, his September 11 letter advances a diagnosis of its own that Alice is actually two people: one repressive and judgmental whom Shaw names "Miss Lockett"; the other, Alice, "the sweetest of companions" whom he vows to champion. In his indictment (and psychological analysis), Miss Lockett is "ashamed" of the "natural, simple, humble, and truthful" Alice. As a consequence, an ashamed Miss Lockett attempts to suppress her other half—shame never being far from the internal calculus that Shaw and his characters negotiate—and he pledges to strive for

Alice's emancipation from her absolutism. At the same time, he admits to a similar psychical splitting: "Have I not also a dual self—an enemy within my gates—an egotistical George Shaw upon whose neck I have to keep a grinding foot—a first cousin of Miss Lockett?" (*CL* 1: 66). In these and other ways, *An Unsocial Socialist* is, for Silver, an "obliquely autobiographical" novel authored by a "young writer variously responding to the frustrations of unrequited love, as well as a still unprofitable career and some burdensome traits of character."[21]

A second intertext emerges from both Trefusis's sense of being *enthralled* by Hetty and her emotional collapse caused by his desertion of her, and this intertext is cultural, not personal or biographical. More specifically, Shaw's depiction of Hetty as both an ill-fated young Jewess *and* a figure of sexual exoticism is hardly unique, as *An Unsocial Socialist* is preceded by a significant corpus of texts—plays and novels—that cultivate such characters, including Sir Walter Scott's *Ivanhoe* (1819) and its many stage adaptations, the French opera *La Juive* (1835), Augustin Daly's adaptation of *Deborah* by S.H. Mosenthal (*Leah, the Forsaken*, first published in 1863), and others.[22] For theatre historian Harley Erdman, Rebecca in *Ivanhoe* and Rachel in *La Juive*, two "products of European Romanticism," largely "shaped the century's performance of the Jewess" as a stunningly beautiful woman with "an unhappy destiny."[23] Although, unlike her predecessors, Hetty lives in London and not a rural Eastern European village, her introduction in chapter 2 leaves little doubt about her uncommon attractiveness, her role as an object of both temptation and desire, her wild swings of emotion, and the pathos that inevitably awaits. In introducing her, Shaw's narrator describes Henrietta's appearance in ways that complement the delicate balance of her psychical life and imply her assumption of this role:

> She was of olive complexion, with a sharp profile: dark eyes with long lashes; narrow mouth with delicately sensuous lips; small head, feet, and hands, with long taper fingers; lithe and very slender figure moving with serpent-like grace. Oriental taste was displayed in the colors of her costume.... Without making any inquiry, she darted upstairs into a drawing room, where a matron of good presence with features of the finest Jewish type, sat reading. (*US*, 9)

Hetty's dark eyes, long lashes, sensuous lips, and "serpent-like grace" communicate her exotic Orientalism and role as an object of male desire, while her emotive displays in this introductory scene precede similar outbursts later in the narrative: her "sobbing with passionate spite," for example, and—in the second chapter's closing moments—her "throwing herself upon her father's bosom," lapsing into "hysterics," and "startling the household by her screams" (15).

This representation of the tempting, highly emotive, and tragic Jewess enjoyed a long history on the London, New York, and world stages—and in fiction—well before Shaw wrote *An Unsocial Socialist*, and a brief comparison of Hetty with one of her predecessors, Augustin Daly's Leah, may help clarify this genealogy. This is not to suggest that Shaw knew *Leah, the Forsaken* intimately, although in the 1890s he reviewed—and disparaged—several of Daly's London productions of social comedy and revivals of Shakespeare.[24] Daly's *Leah*, an enormous success in the United States after premiering in Boston in late 1862 and moving to New York, was produced in London at the Adelphi Theatre later in 1863 and revived throughout the nineteenth century; it was adapted as a silent film in 1908; and it even received a rare New York revival in 2017.[25] Famously, Leopold Bloom in James Joyce's *Ulysses* (1922) remembers his father seeing American star Kate Bateman in the title role at the Adelphi and quoting lines from the play, and it was produced numerous times by celebrated actresses touring Dublin through the turn of the century. (For her part, Kate Bateman first appeared as a child star in Dublin in the early 1850s.)

The action of Daly's play centers around a beautiful and "wild" young woman leading a small band of Jews driven from their homes in Hungary, arriving at a Christian village, and falling in love with a local man, Rudolf. The village, however, harbors anti-Semitic sentiment and superstition, including the fears of so-called "blood libel" and of unethical business practices should Jews be allowed permanent sanctuary. A calumny contrived by a local resident, who is actually a Jew in hiding, and echoed by his anti-Semitic convinces Rudolf, in love with the "strange woman," that Leah has accepted a bribe to leave him; after all, as the local priest advises, "My son, she is a Jewess. Her tribe have been noted always for their avarice and greed."[26] Rudolf confronts Leah about her supposed betrayal, calls his father and his longtime friend Madelena to his side "lest [Leah's] looks, her words exercise the old spell" upon him (28), and—as a final, cruel gesture to refute her protestations of innocence—throws a bag of money at her feet, demeaning her as a "huckster" with "maddening charms" (29). The scene and third act of the play conclude with the poignant tableau of her sinking abjectly to the ground in distress; like Hetty, she has been forsaken by the man she loves.

This scene prepares the audience for what reviewers agreed was the emotional climax of the play: Leah's return to the village at the precise moment of Rudolf's later marriage to Madelena and her curse of him for so ruthlessly deserting her. The curse's ferocity intimates the frighteningly unrepressed and vindictive tendencies of its author: "May you wander as I wander, suffer shame as I now suffer it. Cursed be the land you till.... Cursed be the unborn fruit of the marriage! May it wither as my young heart has withered" (35). As I have noted elsewhere, while Leah's imprecation stems from her being, as one reviewer noted, a "much-wronged, deeply loving" woman, the intensity and speed with which she delivers it also reveal a powerful and heretofore hidden dimension of her psyche; some internal process is at work that cannot be contained.[27] The last act, set years later, features a physically weakened Leah's return to the village and both her rescue of Rudolf and Madelena's young daughter and her return of the child to her grateful parents. At one point in the play's final scene, Leah faints and is believed to have died. Once revived, she identifies the villain among their midst who caused her ruination and declares her intention "to wander into the far-off—the promised land!" (44). However, she is grievously ill and will clearly not survive; indeed, in some productions, she didn't, as the play's final curtain descended upon the stage tableau of her death. The ominous overtones of Leah's curse, in short, are replaced in the play's conclusion by the pathos of a gravely ill woman dying before our eyes, a woman who, innocent of wrongdoing and having been forsaken by the man she loved, can never find happiness in the community she has helped restore.

Hetty exhibits many of these emotional characteristics and, of course, suffers Leah's fate of a lonely physical decline preceded by moments of intense distress. She is, one the one hand, and as Sidney's letter underscores, beguilingly sensual, as is Daly's melodramatic heroine. Much as Rudolf describes Leah as "wildly beautiful, so full of feeling"—in fact, his father Lorenz believes that his son has been "dazzled by her beauty" (19)—and possessive of seductive power akin to a "spell," Trefusis, when later meeting Hetty in Lyvern, claims, "When you are with me, I can do nothing but make love to you. You bewitch me" (*US*, 77). Yet, on the other, if he is unable to resist her charms, Hetty seems equally helpless to rein in her own feeling. Although perhaps not rising to the highly charged vehemence of Leah's curse—an effect heightened onstage by extravagant gesture and the breathless cadence of the speech's delivery—Hetty's reaction to Agatha's letter which seems to confirm her husband's transgression is shocking:

> Henrietta looked round for something sharp. She grasped a pair of scissors greedily and stabbed the air with them. Then she became conscious of her murderous impulse, and she shuddered at it; but in a moment more her jealousy swept back upon her. She cried, as if suffocating: "I don't care; I should like to kill her!" But she did not take up the scissors again. (110)

Much as she had responded to her husband's letter of abandonment, Hetty uttered a "scream of rage," tore Agatha's letter, and stamped upon it in a "paroxysm" of anger (110). As these reactions indicate, references to Henrietta's hyper-sensuality and bewitching effect on her husband are connected to disturbing evidence of her excessive volatility, even "hysteria" (as the last sentence of chapter two specifies). Such traits confirm her kinship with both the stereotype of the Jewess in nineteenth-century culture *and* the divided Alice/Miss Lockett. Trefusis's desertion thus marks not merely his narcissistic retreat or libidinal inversion, but also an accession on Shaw's part—however unintended—to a familiar conflict between desire and repression in Victorian culture and the larger social drama eventuated by Jewish "Otherness." In this intertext, if Henrietta exemplifies what Zygmunt Bauman terms "allo-Semitism"—a figure not of hatred or love, but of radical ambivalence—Trefusis reprises Rudolf's role, forsaking an innocent woman and relying upon a stereotypes of Jewish exoticism, at least in part, to rationalize his actions.[28]

Henrietta's "hysterics" and her "startling" her father's household by her screams imply the presence of a third intertext: the discourse of hysteria emerging as Shaw wrote *An Unsocial Socialist*. As Elaine Showalter demonstrates in *The Female Malady: Women, Madness and English Culture, 1830–1980* (1985), while hysteria has long been regarded as the "quintessential female malady," the period between 1870 and World War I qualifies as the "golden age" of hysteria as "it assumed a peculiarly central role in psychiatric discourse and in definitions of femininity and female sexuality." The term evolved to signify all "extremes of emotionality" and to encompass a "vast repertoire of emotional and physical symptoms—fits, fainting, vomiting, sobbing, laughing paralysis—and the rapid passing from one to another suggested the lability and capriciousness traditionally associated with the feminine nature."[29] Although focusing on British culture, Showalter summarizes the work of Jean-Martin Charcot (1825–93), with whom Freud once studied, and Freud and Josef Breuer's landmark publication *Studies on Hysteria* (1895), particularly the case history of 21-year-old Bertha Pappenheim, renamed Anna O., whom Breuer treated between 1880 and 1882. Working with female patients, Charcot found hysterical symptoms to be "genuine" and "not under the conscious control" of the sufferer, and he employed photography to illustrate his findings (not unlike Trefusis's use of photography to persuade Erskine and Sir Charles Brandon of the horrors of sweatshop labor later in *An Unsocial Socialist*).[30] Showalter's emphases of the relationship between hysterical symptoms and excessive sexuality, and of hysteria as a rebellion against patriarchy, are also relevant to Shaw's novel (even as Anna O. revered her deceased father). Trefusis's letter to Hetty implies the former and more important similarity, and the latter is intimated in her travails in finding a suitable residence after her separation. Returning from her first visit to Lyvern to see Trefusis, she finds it impossible to reside with, in turn, her "unsympathetic" parents; a "hospitable" friend whose criticism of Sidney she could not "bear"; a relative, a "discreet lady," who refused to discuss the subject at all; and her uncle Daniel, whose derision she could not "endure" (*US*, 108). Within this cadre of potentially sympathetic, yet finally unsuitable, friends and relatives, Hetty deems her parents and uncle particularly unendurable and, if not providing a compelling instance of a feminist rebellion against patriarchy, her exodus from the homes of her father and uncle is nonetheless noteworthy.

Breuer and Freud refined Charcot's earlier findings, perhaps most famously by cataloguing the behaviors and considerable abilities of Anna O. Of course, some of her attributes do not find correspondences in Henrietta, Anna's effusive generosity in caring for her gravely ill father, for example, and her "astonishingly undeveloped" sexuality (*SE* 2: 21). She also displayed a penchant for daydreaming, a regular immersion in her own "private theatre" (*SE* 2:22), and manifested a repertory of physiological symptoms from which Hetty did not suffer including ophthalmic maladies such as a severe squint, a persistent cough, intermittent paralysis, and so on. In his later adaptation *Jitta's Atonement* (1921), set in Freud's Vienna and centrally concerning the issue of women's psychologies, Shaw creates a protagonist who, as with Anna's response to her father's death, becomes bedridden after the traumatic and fatal heart attack of her lover.[31] In addition, like Hetty, who in certain fits of pique is unable to complete sentences, Anna experienced verbal "absences," albeit more severely debilitating ones that worsened as evening fell; like Hetty, Anna "bubbled over with vitality," in her case "intellectual vitality" that, when juxtaposed to the "monotonous existence" in her parents' house, made residence there difficult (*SE* 2: 22). Perhaps most important, like Hetty, Leah, and a divided Alice Lockett, Anna manifested two "very distinct states of consciousness" which "alternated very frequently and without warning." (Does a perhaps subtle analogy exist here as reflected in these women's dual naming: Alice/Miss Lockett, Bertha/Anna O., Henrietta/Hetty?) In one state, she was "melancholy and anxious," yet "relatively normal"; in the other, she was "naughty" and abusive, throwing cushions and tearing buttons (*SE* 2: 24). Henrietta's uncontrollable screaming in her first scene in *An Unsocial Socialist* and later wielding of scissors to attack a nonexistent Agatha Wylie, when juxtaposed to her sobbing and "unintelligible expression of wretchedness and rage" when seeing her husband for the last time (*US* 112), resemble this internal division and sudden alternation between the abject and the volatile. And, as her husband's desertion triggered Hetty's descent into an intense and debilitating state—a decline manifested in numerous behaviors including her determination to confront her estranged husband at his Lyvern cottage on the coldest night of the year—Anna's hysteria was likewise precipitated by a significant, even traumatic, event in the death of her father.

Does *An Unsocial Socialist*, as a product and, in some cases, prescient antecedent of these cultural and scientific discourses, thus advance an analysis of "unsocial" that rivals the complexity and range of Trefusis's several dissertations on socialism: the disastrous consequences of the ownership of the means of production by a privileged few, the origins of value, and the deprivations suffered by the working class? Might such an analysis, given its parallels with emergent psychoanalytic insight, qualify as "scientific"? If so, what are its methods and procedures in analyzing the "unsocial"? The latter two questions constitute a veritable motif in Declan Kiberd's cogent reading of *Arms and the Man* in which Shaw's artistic "challenge" prominently included the convincing of his audience to "free themselves of their unexamined preconceptions and adopt a scientific attitude." For Kiberd, like Oscar Wilde, Shaw "welcomed science but warned against the danger of making it a new religion," yet he endorsed the "scientific method" even as he recognized that it was "incomplete" and would eventually be co-opted by the Life Force.[32] More important for my purposes, and however inadvertently, Kiberd identifies one Shavian tactic that routinely confuses, even mystifies, readers of *An Unsocial Socialist*: namely, his deployment of a "secret double" or "doubles" to extend his mapping of subjectivity, a tactic which is not delimited by gender. So, for example, while discussing Raina and Louka's preference in *Arms and the Man* for men "to be utterly different from women," Kiberd detects a "shrewder instinct" that "tells them that is not so." Given the premise that "androgyny was part of Shaw's programme for transcending mere sexuality," he concludes that what "seems to be an opposite" in his plays and novels "might on inspection be revealed as a secret double."[33]

More so than most of Shaw's plays and novels, *An Unsocial Socialist* teases readers with this possibility. That is to say, nearly every scrupulous reader of Shaw's last novel has recognized textual details that are the products of more than mere coincidence and contribute to the novel's confusions or antinomies. Several pertain to what Freud identified as "splitting" or the fragmentation and displacement of dream thoughts, including the appearance of figures in dreams who represent some aspect of the dreamer or someone the dreamer knows. Indeed, one of the exemplary entries for the term "antinomy" in the *Oxford English Dictionary*, taken from a mid-Victorian study of John Locke, expands the denotation of antinomy from a contradiction in the law or a paradox between equally reasonable conclusions to include the phenomenon of psychical division: "the mind was divided against itself; antinomy was its very law." One commonly discussed detail in *An Unsocial Socialist*, for instance, is the inscriptions on Hetty's gravestone. Her birthdate identified as "the 26th July, 1856," as many Shavians note, is Shaw's birthday as well. In *Bernard Shaw: The Ascent of the Superman* (1996), Sally Peters extends this curious parallel by noting not just the coincidence of both Shaw and Hetty's birth dates, but the specification of the latter's death as occurring on December 21, 1875. Peters speculates that this date, the shortest day of the year and the date on which the narrative of *Immaturity* begins, may also have been the date when Shaw left Dublin; and Trefusis's protracted negotiations to acquire the tombstone call "exaggerated attention" to the dates.[34] Could it be that not only such characters as Robert Smith and Trefusis serve as surrogates for Shaw, but also the beautiful and sensual Hetty Jansenius does too? Can she be a "secret double" of the "unsocial socialist" and his creator? For what other reason would the parallel dating of Hetty's life and Shaw's exist, and of what interpretive value beyond Kiberd's nod to "androgyny" are they? Does the antinomy suggest that Trefusis, who "curses himself for being unable 'to act like a rational creature for five consecutive minutes'" in Hetty's presence, must kill off this passionate part of himself if he is ever to be fully the intellectual he aspires to be? If so, then such a process is related to that by which Trefusis and his impersonation as Jeff Smilash function as the "penultimate stage" in the rebirth of Shaw into "G.B.S."[35]

The positing of "secret doubles" sparks further questions about other kinds of doubling in *An Unsocial Socialist*, their connection to Shaw, and our recasting of the novel as a psychodrama in which several characters function as counterparts of their creator. In so doing, these also thicken connotations of the "unsocial." Silver's reading of the novel, for example, emphasizes that Shaw "divided himself into Erskine and Trefusis, each one possessing some of his own present traits, but the former representing the self he would like to disown...."[36] There is little question about this purposeful splitting, as in *An Unsocial Socialist* the poet-gentleman Erskine reprises the role of the effete aristocrat-artist of modest talent who frequently populates Shaw's fiction. Such a persona, marked by economic naïveté and limited ability, is one that Shaw would quickly want to disown. However, Silver also postulates Agatha's similarity to both Trefusis and Shaw himself, recalling that Shaw was not only "aware of the resemblance between Agatha and himself," but also that by resolving the novel's relationships in the way he did, he was, in effect, turning away from the "tormenting Alice figure" and marrying "his own self again in the person of Agatha."[37] In this way, Shavian doubles extend well beyond the conventional appearance of physically identical characters—the two mirror images in Edgar Allan Poe's "William Wilson" (1839) or the twin Golyadkins in Dostoyevsky's *The Double* (1846)—or nightmarish opposites like Dr. Jekyll and Mr. Hyde in Robert Louis Stevenson's 1886 novella, to include, in these examples, women like Hetty and Agatha as avatars of both Trefusis and Shaw.[38]

Yet another pair of "secret doubles" in *An Unsocial Socialist* are the novel's two lions of business, Hetty's father and successful banker John Jansenius, and Trefusis's father Jesse, the "Great Employer" and industrial "monarch." What connects this pair is not just their wealth and social power, but their similar relationship to such negative affects as shame, as Shaw's narrator specifies in his introduction of Jansenius:

> Mr Jansenius was a man of imposing presence, not yet in his fiftieth year, but not far from it. He moved with dignity, bearing himself as if the contents of his massive brow were precious. His handsome aquiline nose and keen dark eyes proclaimed his Jewish origin, *of which he was ashamed*. Those who did

not know this naturally believed that he was proud of it.... Well instructed in business, and subject to no emotion outside the love of family, respectability, comfort, and money, he had maintained the capital inherited from his father, and made it breed new capital in the usual way.[39] (my emphasis, *US*, 12–13)

Like Jesse Trefusis, Jansenius was a wealthy man who loved money and respectability—Jesse rose to become a Member of Parliament—and like Jesse he strove to "intercept" the immense wealth he might generate, while leaving "the rest of the world working just as hard as before banking was introduced" (13). Still, as Shaw's narrator indicates, because no one would involve themselves in the transactions of a bank unless there were some benefit from doing so, Jansenius's depositors prospered as well, which is more than can be said of the factory workers that Sidney's father exploited.

Jansenius's love of money and respectability is also a marker of class in Shaw's fiction; after all, Mrs. Douglas in *The Irrational Knot* and the vivacious Lady Brandon, the former Jane Carpenter, in *An Unsocial Socialist* revel in their wealth. Aided by her significant resources and the show of respectability they can buy, the former performs social standing much as Jansenius enacts dignity while concealing his shame; the latter, like Jansenius, felt little responsibility for the world outside the borders of her own realm of consumption, one marked by "plenty of money, plenty of servants, plenty of visitors" (*US*, 142). Similarly, when Jesse Trefusis drove peasants from their cottages, he demonstrated that he simply "didn't care" about their final destinations at the workhouse or in crowded factory towns (73). However, most striking, the elder Trefusis shares Jansenius's sense of shame originating in his heredity, as Sidney relates to Hetty:

> My father was a shrewd, energetic, and ambitious Manchester man, who understood an exchange of any sort as a transaction by which one man should lose and the other gain.... I do not know exactly what he was, for *he was ashamed* both of his antecedents and of his relatives, from which I can only infer that they were honest, and, therefore, unsuccessful people. (my emphasis, *US*, 68)

Although Trefusis does not stress his father's love of money and respectability, he tells Hetty that he saved money and "borrowed some more on the security of his reputation for getting the better of other people in business," which is not quite respectability but is nonetheless an ability that allowed him to garner a certain kind of esteem (68). However, unlike Jansenius, the elder Trefusis also is said to have experienced anxiety. He "claimed his fortune as the reward of his risks, his calculations, his anxieties," and had he lived a century earlier he would have likely made his money as a highwayman, pursuing a similar life of "activity and anxiety" (72).

Perhaps this last speculation is correct, but the analogy between a reputable industrialist whose mere name can secure needed financing and a daring highwayman ignores the kind of sociology he limns in this and similar characterizations of his father. Here Shaw's "science" is not so much an instance of Kiberd's "negative anthropology," but rather resembles a Simmelian sociology in which the authority wielded by such an individual leads to the myriad prerogatives of superordination and its effects imposed on those subordinate to him. Through a process of concretization, this individual's significance ("the security of his reputation") both grows superior to that of his fellows and "assumes for his environment the physical state—metaphorically speaking—of objectivity."[40] In such a process, as Simmel argues, such super-individual authority may be attained by the reputation or dignity which institutions (state, church, school) can confer or by the less concrete means of prestige, which is "determined entirely by the strength of the individual."[41] Jesse Trefusis possessed both authority *and* prestige, the former related to his eventual position in Parliament, whereas the latter was gained largely by the strength of his own personality, ability, and resultant financial success. Through his father, Trefusis describes a modernizing society in which both authority and prestige, as in Simmel's sociology, can be manipulated to subordinate—even enslave—an entire class of people.

Somewhat ironically, however, neither John Jansenius nor Jesse Trefusis can escape the clutches of shame and, in Trefusis's case, anxiety as well. These twin affects permeate Shaw's fiction, and shame in particular is much in evidence in the interactions of Agatha Wylie, Gertrude Lindsay, and Jane Carpenter at Alton College in the early chapters of *An Unsocial Socialist*. Indeed, one might argue that the practice of students there writing entries, many of which detail their faults or personal failings, in a log named the "Recording Angel" is, in effect, a mode of public embarrassment or shaming. Shame and the blush that frequently reveals it are much in evidence in these chapters by both female students and administrators; for example, Miss Wilson, the College principal, was "ashamed to find herself growing nervous at the prospect of an encounter with Agatha" (*US*, 18), and students "redden" frequently from both indignation and shame. Two young clergymen walking near the school helplessly blush when noticing the girls, something Agatha recognizes and, finding it enormously entertaining, exploits, causing one of the pair to color "all the deeper because he was enraged with himself for doing so" (27). But he couldn't help himself, as such is the power of the affect system.

The combination of shame and anxiety suffered by Jesse Trefusis may also correspond to the similar combination of affects with which Shaw contended. His propensity to feel shame acutely and its relationship to his "chromic impecuniosity" have been discussed in earlier chapters, but just a bit more might be said about anxiety. Sally Peters diagnoses the impact of both affects on the young Shaw, attributing his boldness as a child to his conscious strategy to "divert attention from his self-incriminating blush" as he learned that "aggression veiled vulnerabilities." At the same time, Peters speculates that his shame was accompanied by both "rage and self-hate," which at times gave away to a very specific anxiety: the likelihood of his father George Carr Shaw coming home drunk. This prospect led to Shaw's perception of experience as essentially dramatic and "anchored in expectancy,"[42] just as anxiety is linked to an uneasy futurity and, in the worst cases, fear. If Peters' understanding of Shaw's subjectivity possesses any interpretive potential, then the list of his secret doubles in the psychodrama that is *An Unsocial Socialist* can be seen to include Trefusis, Erskine, Henrietta, Agatha, Jansenius, and Trefusis' father, Jesse. Moreover, the intertexts from which Henrietta/Hetty emerge magnify the pressures of both sexuality and human sympathy with which Shaw and Trefusis struggled. In one of these, Trefusis plays the role of Gentile suitor bewitched by the Oriental exoticism of the Jewess; in the other, he performs as a surrogate scientist, advising his hysterical patient while he lectures on political economy and a Simmelian sociology of authority and prestige. The presence of a banker and an industrialist in this roster of secret doubles also hints at the role that shame and materialism—manifested as the desire for both money and capital to increase its supply—inflects the operations of Shavian subjectivity. In *this* context Kiberd's observation, quoted in an earlier chapter, that Shaw wrote for money and "earned lots" accrues meaning, as its accumulation finds its provenance not in avarice, but in shame and anxiety. The "unsocial" in *An Unsocial Socialist* emerges from all of these registers—biographical, cultural, and scientific—as materialism in Shaw's fiction is rooted in the subjective, and human subjectivity is equally tethered to the material. As we shall see, Shaw's transpositions of the psychical and amatory with the material and the economic in *An Unsocial Socialist*—and Trefusis' several lectures on commodity exchange, value, and capitalism—amplify this very point.

SHAW'S SOCIALIST AND THE CONNOTATIONS OF VALUE

[Factory workers] were to work long and hard, early and late, to add fresh *value* to his raw cotton by manufacturing. Out of the *value* thus created by them, they were to recoup him for what he supplied them with: rent, shelter, gas, water, machinery, raw cotton—everything, and to pay him for his own services as superintendent, manager, and salesman. (my emphasis; *US*, 69)
 —Trefusis to Hetty explaining value as created by production

"What do you know of the feelings of a respectable man?" persisted Jansenius, breaking out again in spite of his wife. "Nothing is sacred to you. This shows what Socialists are!" (*US*, 130)
 —John Jansenius to Trefusis standing over Hetty's deathbed

These excerpts are two of many such instances in *An Unsocial Socialist* that, as in the first epigraph above, either attempt to theorize the origin and nature of value or, as in the second, articulate affect, human feeling and emotion, with the material, economics in particular. Consistent with the Marxist theory that Shaw read, in the first passage Trefusis emphasizes that the value of commodities is created by labor in *production*. As Shaw engaged economics more deeply and was exposed to the tenets of marginalism in the 1880s, however, his understanding of value grew more nuanced and was informed by the myriad considerations inherent to *consumption*.[43] But even before undertaking his study of Jevonian theory with Philip Wicksteed and others, Shaw was developing a more capacious sense of this issue, as meditations on value, especially those of his protagonist, indicate. A prominent concern throughout the novel, the complications of value in commodity exchange occupy Trefusis's thoughts. This centrality is perhaps made most apparent in his conversation with Sir Charles Brandon and the gentleman-poet Chichester Erskine at Sallust's House, Trefusis's eccentric country estate. After listening to his host expatiate on the social consequences of capitalism, Sir Brandon concedes, "I must study this question of value" and asks him, "Can you recommend me a good book on the subject?" (213). One answer to this question may very well be *An Unsocial Socialist*.

Following conventional scientific practice at the time, Trefusis's exposition of socioeconomic theory to Brandon and Erskine, much like Charcot's lectures on hysteria and Darwin's taxonomy of human facial expressions in *The Expression of the Emotions in Man and Animals*, is supplemented by an album of carefully selected illustrations, particularly photographs, that neither gentleman exhibits any enthusiasm for viewing. For in it, scenes of exploited workers and filthy sweatshops, albeit occasionally relieved by an image of a comfortable monarch or wealthy businessman, exercise the unsettling effect on his audience that Trefusis had intended. In a novel replete with antinomies, paradoxes, and contradictions, it is almost predictable that Erskine would label the collection "A Portfolio of Paradoxes," with a picture of 20 terrorized girls laboring in a "lace school" for a brutal overseer eliciting Brandon's most vocal disapprobation (*US*, 206). One prominent exception to their disdain for Trefusis' exhibitions emerges, however, when shortly after arriving at his estate they become aware of a portrait of a strikingly beautiful woman draped in ruby velvet and displayed on a miniature easel. "What an exquisite face!" Erskine exclaims, a sentiment echoed by Sir Charles: "Charming," he observes, "It certainly is an extraordinarily attractive face" (200). Trefusis informs the pair that the portrait is of his wife Henrietta, whom neither of them had ever met, and Erskine in particular appears both self-conscious and anxious, as his color "deepened" after Trefusis tells them that she has died. His explanation of the portrait's meaning for him is particularly noteworthy:

> I keep her portrait constantly before me *to correct my natural amativeness*. I fell in love with her and married her. I have fallen in love once or twice since; but a glance at my lost Hetty has cured me of the slightest inclination to marry. (my emphasis, 201)

For Trefusis, Hetty thus not only represents the epitome of beauty, but also embodies a desire related specifically to connubial feeling. Equally important, her portrait, not unlike the forged portrait of Shakespeare's boy-actor in Oscar Wilde's *The Portrait of Mr W. H.* (1889), performs with special psychical resonance (in Trefusis's case, it exerts a repressive effect).[44]

At the same time that Hetty paradoxically represents both an object of desire and a means of repression, she is also connected, however indirectly, to Trefusis's conception of *value*, as he outlines when relating to Erskine and Brandon his frustrations when attempting to purchase her gravestone:

> How can you justly reward the laborer when you cannot ascertain the value of what he makes, owing to the prevalent custom of stealing it? I know this by experience. I wanted to pay a just price for my wife's tomb, but I could not find out its value, and never shall. (213)

Through the multiple connotations of her portrait and memorial headstone, her overdetermined iconicity, we might say, Hetty symbolizes the analytical puzzle that is value; and, insofar as the latter image of her is purchased, she also functions as a commodity like other young women of marriageable age from the privileged class, including Trefusis's future wife, Agatha Wylie. In fact, Agatha's mother feared that her daughter had been too dilatory in her pursuit of a "lady's business in society": namely, to land a partner in marriage (139). By foolishly throwing away "capital bargains in their first season" in society, many young women in the "marriage market" are later "compelled to offer themselves at greatly reduced prices, when their attractions begin to stale" (139, 140). Value, as calculated in this market, is not created by production, as Trefusis suggests in his first lecture to Hetty about his father's "industrial monarchy" and the practices that sustained it. In addition, although value cannot be permanently decoupled from production in other markets,[45] Trefusis's understanding of value encompasses more than production as the novel progresses—much as Shaw's does in the decade of the 1880s and later—to include not only consumption and the desiring subject, but also the immaterial or *signifying* value of objects circulating as signs of reputation, status, or prestige in exchange.

Trefusis's psychical conflation of Hetty as both love-object and object of value also evokes the larger issue of the deformation of man's "soul" or subjectivity by capital, recalling statements like Michael Hardt's that "Humanity and its soul are produced by the very processes of economic production. The processes of becoming human and the nature of the human itself were fundamentally transformed in the qualitative shift of modernization." In this shift, one to which Trefusis alludes several times in the novel, the movement from an agrarian economy to a ruthless and highly urbanized industrialism transforms not only human relations, but "human nature" itself.[46] Evidence of such a transformation is both various and abundant in *An Unsocialist Socialist*, and perhaps its most graphic expression is the metaphor of human feeling and emotion as mechanical. This same metaphor informs Shaw's correspondence with Alice Lockett in November of 1883, Alice even connecting it to conceptions of gender:

"Some genuineness and manliness would find a responsive chord in my heart, but mechanical sentiment is only a bore" (*CL* 1: 71).

Given Alice's figure of speech and accusation, it is hardly a coincidence that one of the most striking photographs in Trefusis's album is not of suffering laborers or urban hovels, but rather the image of an "elaborate machine," the acquisition of which enabled his father to fire some 300 men and replace them with a mere handful of women and children. His photograph gallery also features a portrait of his father, the "portly, pushing, egotistical tradesman" (*US*, 203), and even he is not totally immune from the psychical cost levied by the ruthless machinery of industrial progress. That is, inherent to this image of commercial success resides a conflict wrought from the contradictory affectual consequences of capitalism.[47] For such a man, Trefusis urges, is riven internally when his need for "self-approbation" clashes with his "instinctive sense of baseness in the money-hunter"; he is irreparably fractured by his role as the "seller of his own mind and manhood for luxuries and delicacies he was too low-lived to enjoy" (204). In this subjective calculus, while money provides self-affirmation, as it did for Gerald Bridges in "The Theatre of the Future," at the same time it also papers over a deeper internal fissure. It is within this historical moment of the changing of the "soul of man under capitalism" that Trefusis undertakes his analysis of value, industrial practice, and the human damage it wreaks. In this and other ways, Shaw's voice joins those of Oscar Wilde and such socialists as William Morris and Edward Carpenter who, during the 1880s and 1990s, argued that a detached art produced by effete dilettantes—poets completely divorced from the realities of labor such as Erskine and the other "gentlemen-artists" who frequent Shaw's novels—was a "sham" and "unmanly."[48]

Negotiations over the headstone and arrangements for Hetty's funeral—and its circuitry between feeling and performance, its traversing of both emotional and material ground—importantly expand conceptions of value in the second half of *An Unsocial Socialist*, as they also demonstrate money's intrusion into the expression of personal sorrow and the construction of cultural memory. At the same time, such arrangements reveal the manner in which late-Victorian polite society purchased and choreographed performances of mourning at such moments. That is to say, recalling Joseph Roach's definition, the process of surrogation involves three elements—memory, performance, and substitution—and events such as Hetty's carefully staged funeral illuminate the operations of this process, in part because memories of the deceased and responses to her departure are inevitably foregrounded in funereal performance. Moreover, like Henrietta's velvet-bordered portrait, her gravestone enacts a kind of performance insofar as, through its substitution for an original, it fills a void or vacancy caused by absence. In so doing, statues, headstones, and even effigies function both as a "quotation," delimiting what recollections of the original might be retained, and as an "invention," generating future meaning by shaping, in some instances even falsifying, the legacy of the person represented.[49]

In this light, Trefusis's objections to the arrangements for Hetty's funeral are partially rooted in his disdain for the conventions of social performance, as Chapter X of *An Unsocial Socialist* opens with an adumbration of the elaborate choreography and cost of the event. To begin, the bier was "covered with a profusion of costly flowers," one of several manifestations of Jansenius' directive to "spare no expense" in staging the procession. Long-tailed black horses crowned with black plumes and impeccably dressed coachmen carry the decedent's casket, while "many hired mourners" walk beside it, aware that if they "presumed to betray emotion, or in any way overstep their function" they would be "instantly discharged." Shaw juxtaposes the emotional reserve of this hired parade to a more florid display of emotion later at the cemetery, where Jansenius "burst into tears at the ceremony of casting earth on the coffin," and a cousin who had once asked Henrietta to marry him "was enjoying his despair intensely" (*US*, 132). Repulsed at the prospect of this spectacle, Trefusis had earlier refused to attend, and his conspicuous absence becomes fodder for wildly inaccurate gossip during and after the funeral. However, his refusal is hardly surprising, as he had intimated to Henrietta's mother earlier: "Do you suppose my feelings are a trumpery set of social observances, to be harrowed to order and exhibited at funerals?" (126–27). His impatience with this frippery is preceded by a tense interchange with Mrs. Jansenius about the expense of Hetty's medical treatment—"Do you think I will wrangle over her body about the amount of money spent on her illness?" (126)—and Hetty's father expresses his love for his daughter publicly by spending considerably more on her funeral procession. Money, feeling, and social performance, in short, define this sad episode.

So, too, does value. Some days after the funeral and its "trumpery set" of performances, Jansenius, with the help of a "literary friend," composed an epitaph complete with "a couple of pretty and touching stanzas" extolling his daughter's "sweetness and virtue." He also obtained the services of a "monumental mason" with whose assistance he selected a "highly ornamental" tombstone. Much as he had found the funeral arrangements distasteful, Trefusis objected to the stanzas proposed for Hetty's headstone as perpetrating falsehoods, inventions as it were, about her; and he demurred further to the hiring of this particular monumental tradesman, infamous "as an 'exploiter' of labor," employing instead a young mason whom he intended to compensate fairly (133). This is the origin of Trefusis' complaint about the difficulty of ascertaining a "value" for the monument, as the memorial business, like most others, was run by capitalists who, in their control of the means of production, withheld needed materials. By constraining the supply of necessary materials, capitalists effectively also manipulated the market and complicated the assessment of value, as the expertise of Royal Academicians did when consulted about such design issues. Indeed, while the artist Trefusis consulted about Hetty's gravestone initially seemed sympathetic to socialist views, he eventually deemed them "odious and dangerous" when he realized that "artistic genius" was not part of the widower's calculation of value (134–35). Trefusis's intervention into these performances of mourning leads to his purchase of a simpler headstone and the revision of its inscription to record only basic facts about Hetty's life: her date of birth, her marriage, and the date of her death. Yet another result of this transaction is the young tradesman's parlaying of the money that Trefusis paid him to start his own business, from which he "soon began to grow rich, as he knew by experience exactly how much his workmen could be forced to do, and how little they could be forced to take" (136).

Money and capital are thus heavily implicated in the expression of feeling in this scene in *An Unsocial Socialist*. So, too, are conceptions of value (with production again privileged in this instance), including the supply of and demand for objects; and these emerge as metaphors both in analyses of the failings of Victorian society and in more innocent observations about love, desire, and emotion. The most obvious example, referenced above, concerns the marriage "market" and the notion that, something like day-old bread, a young woman grows "stale" if she waits too long to land a husband—or, as is the case with Constance Carbury in *The Irrational Knot*, her value is reduced if her family cannot provide a handsome dowry because it has already "speculated quite heavily enough" in the market to secure "illustrious matches" for older sisters (*Knot*, 56). In this regard, Shaw's unsocial socialist unwittingly accedes to late-Victorian convention for, like the polite society he loathes, he is prone to mix metaphors of emotion with those of business when parsing his own relationships. When

Hetty, for example, upset by the letter she received from Agatha, arrives at his cottage with an "unintelligible expression of wretchedness and rage" (*US*, 112), he admonishes her with, "You are angry because Agatha has infringed your monopoly. Always monopoly!" (115). Later in the novel, attempting to persuade Gertrude to marry Erskine, Trefusis similarly rationalizes his decision to marry Agatha:

> I wanted a genial partner for domestic business, and Agatha struck me quite suddenly as being the nearest approach to *what I desired* that I was likely to find in the *marriage market*, where it is extremely hard to suit oneself, *and where the likeliest bargains* are apt to be snapped up by others if one hesitates too long in the hope of finding *something* better. (my emphasis, 248)

In this formulation, delay on either side of the exchange—seller or buyer, as it were—can prove detrimental, a temporal dimension that reduces marriage not merely to a market, but to an impulsive shopping expedition. Still, desire *is* involved, and a consumer/husband seeks satisfaction at a bargain price in a commodity/wife, always aware that the ideal product/object of desire—some thing, not someone—may have already been "snapped up" like a fashionable suit or pair of stylish shoes.

Value is typically implicated in such discourse in *An Unsocial Socialist*; and Trefusis's decision to marry Agatha provides added dimensions to his earlier emphasis of the relationship between labor, production, and value: namely, the consumer's desire, the quality of a commodity to satisfy this desire, the consumer's inventory of the commodity or others complementary to it, the availability of opposing or competitive commodities, and so on. Such considerations are central to the marginal economics Shaw studied under Philip Wicksteed's tutelage. Wicksteed's chapter "Margins. Diminishing Psychic Returns" in *The Common Sense of Political Economy* (1910), for example, his *magnum opus* of the subject, references several of these matters:

> *The significance of any given addition to our supply of a commodity or other object of desire declines as the supply increases.... This marginal significance therefore rises or falls as the supply itself is contracted or expanded, and the margin drawn back or advanced.* (emphasis in original)

One result is that "*all the early increments of supply have a higher value than at the margin*"; another, following from this, is that "*the satisfactions we secure are worth more than the price we pay for them.*"[50] Wicksteed uses the example of a family's copious supply of potatoes, observing that "when we say of anything that we 'would not take any more at a gift,' it means that its marginal value to us has been reduced to zero." Conversely, and assuming no alternatives providing greater satisfaction are easily obtainable, a hungry family totally lacking in this basic foodstuff would be eager to accept the gift of a pound of new potatoes or, if they had the means to do so, exchange money for it, as its value would be at its highest.[51]

Wives and potatoes are, of course, very different things; the totality of the economy in which they exist and the possibility of alternatives are among the many unique factors that distinguish the marriage "market" from others in which commodities are situated. My point here is a simple one: the supposition that value inheres in a realm outside of production represents an alternative view to the one that Trefusis initially posited to Hetty. That is to say, and at the risk of over-schematization, one might divide Trefusis's most substantial ruminations on value in *An Unsocial Socialist* into three sections: his initial exposition to Hetty of his father's industrial practices and labor's creation of value (65–80), his efforts to purchase at a fair price an appropriate memorial for Henrietta's grave (132–37), and his tendentious lecture to Brandon and Erskine at Sallust's House (196–219). Such topics as a miserably poor working class, the social ravages of capitalism, and related matters surface throughout the novel, but these three "sections" trace his increasingly sophisticated conception of value most fully. This is not to suggest that these sections serve as discrete units or points of argumentation, or that even in the earlier pages of *An Unsocial Socialist* Trefusis does not possess a nuanced understanding of value as more than the exertions of laborers. In his screed to Hetty in her first appearance at Lyvern about "Modern English polite society," Trefusis both exhibits deeper insights and introduces fecund contradictions into how an exploitative and "wealth-hunting" class also chases such immaterial matters as "celebrity" and prestige:

> A canting, lie-loving, fact-hating, scribbling, chattering, wealth-hunting, pleasure-hunting, celebrity-hunting mob, that, having lost the fear of hell, and not replaced it by the love of justice, cares for nothing but the lion's share of the wealth wrung by threat of starvation from the hands of the classes that create it. (*US*, 67)

In this contradictory formulation—yet another in a novel replete with them—polite society pursues "celebrity" with the same avidity that it seeks wealth, yet Trefusis claims that it "cares for *nothing* but the lion's share of wealth." Perhaps he might be forgiven this slight confusion because, as he confesses to Hetty, "I feel my heart and brain wither in your smile" (66).

But the contradiction is a productive one. Phrases such as "celebrity-hunting" intimate social and semiotic provenances of desire, and the value of entities satisfying them that, at this point in the novel, Trefusis has not fully considered. One step preliminary to such an assessment is the positing of a commodity's *use value* as compared to its *exchange value*. By 1910, when Wicksteed published *The Common Sense of Political Economy*, such a distinction was already much discussed; in fact, he alludes to "older economists" who considered this distinction, announcing his preference for the alternative formulations "total significance" (value in use) and "marginal significance" (value in exchange). The former represents the amount of money that one would require for "entirely surrendering" a commodity "we consume," while the latter represents the money one would demand for surrendering "one unit" of this commodity, always the "least valued" part of the supply.[52]

Three "older" economists as intrigued by such distinctions as Wicksteed are Adam Smith, to whom Trefusis alludes in outlining differences between "value in use" and "value in exchange" (*US*, 215), Karl Marx in several texts, and William Stanley Jevons who, in *The Theory of Political Economy* makes even more finely grained discriminations based on his reading of Smith's *The Wealth of Nations*. Jevons finds one paradox identified by Smith in the discourse of value of particular interest:

> The things which have the greatest value in use have frequently little or no value in exchange; and, on the contrary, those which have the greatest value in exchange have frequently little or no value in use. Nothing is more useful than water: but it will purchase scarce anything.... A diamond, on the contrary, has scarce any value in use; but a very great quantity of other goods may frequently be had in exchange for it.[53]

Jevons quickly revises this insight by suggesting that Smith's contrast is premised upon abundance or "total utility": water has no exchange value until its supply is extremely scarce or nearly eliminated; then, it "acquires exceedingly great purchasing power." This precious water might then be exchanged for large amounts of some lesser valued items—bushels of corn, pounds of iron, or paving stones—or smaller amounts of rubies, sapphires, or other highly coveted commodities. His conclusion from this exercise is relevant to our purposes here: "Thus I am led to think that word value is often used in reality to mean *intensity of desire or esteem for a thing*" (emphasis in original).[54]

Trefusis introduces the distinction to Erskine and Sir Charles through a convoluted, but highly resonant, story of his struggle to estimate the value of a painting his mother had once purchased from a then unknown artist for £30. After the painter, Donovan Brown, became famous, Trefusis was offered £800 for the same painting, which he declined as an "unearned increment to which [he] had no righteous claim" (*US*, 214). While his solicitor recommended that he accept the offer, Trefusis refused it, although he conceded that neither his mother nor he had "received any return in the shape of pleasure in contemplating the work," now marred and diminished even further by fading. Instead, he returned the painting to Brown, received the £30 his mother originally paid for it, and related this news to the wealthy collector who had offered him £800. The man then approached Brown raising his offer to £1500, but the painter refused it as he considered the work "unworthy of his reputation" (214).

Terms like "reputation," the same word that Trefusis employed in describing his father's ability to borrow money, hint at what is finally the constellation of immaterial cultural codes inscribed in the concept of exchange value. Trefusis goes on to explain that, after he learned that Brown had refused to sell the painting and having no initial desire to take £30 from the artist, he attempted to return the sum to Brown, who would not accept it. Somewhat perversely and to prove his murky point, Trefusis then demanded the £1500, explaining that since the painting had no use value because he "disliked" it, he should not be forced to keep the lower amount that he tried to return, but rather was entitled to its much higher exchange value. A board of arbitrators, after consulting Adam Smith on such distinctions, decided rather absurdly that Brown must take the £30 back—the painting's use value, the arbiters believed—and he and Shaw's unsocial socialist became "very good friends" after that (*US*, 215).

This anecdote, at base, indicates the evolving and at times complicated adumbration of value in Trefusis's (and Shaw's) thoughts: from its genesis in production, to markets and consumption, and finally to failings in theories of consumption more recent theoreticians—the very same intellectuals who, we might recall in Susan Harris's observation, have neglected Shaw—dissect in painstaking detail. This is as much to ask, does a painting actually have a *use value* and by what calculus could it be specified as precisely £30? Certainly one could argue that it does have use value insofar as, say, interior designers deploy color and shape in their creations of corporate offices, bank lobbies, and the décors of restaurants. However, as Shaw's example indicates, the exorbitant *exchange value* of Brown's painting has nothing whatsoever to do with its *use value*; a painting, in other words, is not a potato a hungry family craves or, for that matter, a wife located in the odious late-Victorian marriage market. This realization that less tangible factors inflect an object's value—indeed, that an object may possess *no* use value at all and still be exchanged for money—leads to postmodernist critiques of consumption's relationship to value such as Jean Baudrillard's. His chapter "The Ideological Genesis of Needs" in *For a Critique of the Political Economy of the Sign* (1981) begins this attack on the metaphysic of consumption as if it were no more significant than day-residue in the manifest content of a dream:

> The rapturous satisfactions of consumption surround us, clinging to objects as if to the sensory residues of the previous day in the delirious excursion of a dream. As to the logic that regulates this strange discourse—surely it compares to what Freud uncovered in *The Interpretation of Dreams*.... We believe in "Consumption": we believe in a real subject, motivated by needs and confronted by real objects as sources of satisfaction. It is a thoroughly vulgar metaphysic.[55]

Baudrillard argues that consumption is grounded in the "myth" of primary needs, the "alleged existence of a vital anthropological minimum," which, in turn, acts as an "alibi" for use value. Arguing that this minimum does not exist in any meaningful way, he regards "consummativity" as a mode of "productivity"; systems of power *need* a citizen-consumer's *needs* which, in the end, as partially the product of the systems themselves, are only chimeras or congeries of status, class affiliation, prestige, and reputation.[56] In other words, the wealthy collector who offers £1500 for Trefusis's painting isn't ascribing this exchange value to the work because of use value or some "vital anthropological minimum." The painting's value originates in less material, socially symbolic, phenomena, some of which have been effectuated by capitalism itself and are misrecognized by the consumer as needs.

Even as it underscores the immaterial basis of exchange value—the "vulgar metaphysic" of need that Baudrillard's cultural semiosis challenges—the discussion of Brown's painting also provokes one of the more unfortunate exchanges in *An Unsocial Socialist* from the perspective of gender. Erskine admits to having his "head spin" after hearing Trefusis's story, and attributes his condition to the latter's at times dizzying calculations: "Everything is a question of figures to you." Trefusis concedes the point, arguing that this tendency originates in his lack of poetic sensibility. And he observes further—and somewhat damagingly—that "Socialists need to study the romantic side of our movement to interest women in it." For, "if you want to make a cause grow, instruct every woman you meet in it"; she "is or will one day be a wife, and will contradict her husband with scraps of your arguments." The inevitable "squabble will follow" with the effect that differences will be "leavened," socialism will no longer seem such a fearful corpus of theory, and, perhaps, progress will be made (*US*, 215).

However, this observation is unfortunate for two reasons. First, Trefusis's representation of women in this exchange, consistent with his accusation in his "letter" to Shaw or "Appendix" that his reputation has suffered at the hands of readers who misjudged him by way of a "fictitious and feminine standard of morality" (*US*, 255), communicates a narrow, essentially avuncular perspective of women as disinterested in "figures" and requiring romance to grapple with the complexities of socialism. Second, this aspersion implicitly disavows the very immaterial connotations of exchange value that his anecdote about Brown's painting confirms. Again, the painting is hardly an "object" of exchange—it has no use value, as Trefusis acknowledges—and in making the point he thus calls into question the privilege of "need," the totality of a consumer's supply of a commodity, and the nature of a desiring subject in marginal theory. Baudrillard's more radical deconstruction of consumption emphasizes its illusory nature:

> To reduce the conceptual entity "object" is, by the same token, to deconstruct the conceptual entity "need." We could explode that of the subject as well.
>
> Subject, object, need: the mythological structure of these three ideas is identical, triply elaborated in terms of the naïve factuality and the schema of a primary level psychology.[57]

The so-called "romance" of Brown's "heroic" refusal of a large sum of money for his painting—much like the reputation he desires to protect and that which allowed Jesse Trefusis to borrow vast sums of money to expand his business—resides outside the objectivity of the object and the concept of vital anthropological need. Moreover, such constructs as romance, prestige, status, and so on, in the end, may be more important to defining value than Trefusis ever realizes.

This is, perhaps, the final paradox or antinomy of *An Unsocial Socialist*—that neither Shaw nor his protagonist is quite fully aware of just how contemporary theories of value in the novel actually are. Trefusis concludes his letter, the novel's "Appendix," by mocking the fledgling novelist's representation of "the state of affairs between us by a discourse on 'surplus value'" essentially "cribbed from an imperfect report of one of my public lectures" (*US*, 259). Plagiarized or not, conceptions of surplus value and the profit it designates drive the practices of the ruthless capitalism Trefusis' father represents. Yet, at the same time, the discourse of value in the novel goes well beyond the parameters of Marxian surplus value and the imperative for greater profitability inherent to capitalism; at times, this discourse even goes well beyond the fundamental premises of marginalism and the consumption it privileges. The most intriguing paradox of *An Unsocial Socialist*, then, may be that Shaw's socialist seems incapable of recognizing just how radical his socialism is.

Notes

1. Stanley Weintraub, "Introduction" to *An Unfinished Novel by Bernard Shaw*, 12.
2. Dietrich, *Bernard Shaw's Novels*, 148, 149.
3. Susan Cannon Harris, *Irish Drama and the Other Revolutions*, 20.
4. See Chapter Two of Harris's *Irish Drama and the Other Revolutions*, 57–95.
5. Here, I am referring to Declan Kiberd's chapter "George Bernard Shaw and *Arms and the Man*" in *Irish Classics* (Cambridge: Harvard University Press, 2000), 341; and Silver, *Bernard Shaw: The Darker Side*, 71.
6. It should be added that the remaining fragments of *An Unfinished Novel*, composed in May and June of 1887 with additions in early 1888, contain some of these elements as well. The flirtatious Mrs. Maddick, for example, blushes several times during her conversations with Dr. Kincaid. In the closing, intimate conversation between the pair, she "reddened, ashamed of herself" (85) and "became very red, but an irrepressible gleam of fun shot through her embarrassment [sic]" (87). To take another example, her husband Dr. Maddick, not unlike several better-known Shavian characters, attempts to perform a role for which he is ill-suited, in this case that of a

"young, handsome, and dashing man." His failure in this role—unlike, say, the more successful social performance of Sholto Douglas's mother, the wealthy dowager in *The Irrational Knot*—is largely due to the unfortunate fact that he lacked "money enough to be more than a passable imitation" (52). Perhaps most important, Kincaid, like Trefusis, decries the effects of poverty on workers, particularly health issues originating in exhaustion, malnutrition, and alcoholism (68).

7. Weintraub briefly describes the circumstances of this addition in his "Introduction" to *An Unfinished Novel*, explaining that Swan Sonnenschein had actually suggested the addition of a preface and Shaw countered with this letter (18–19).
8. Oscar Wilde, "The Soul of Man under Socialism," in *The Soul of Man under Socialism and Selected Critical Prose*, ed. Linda Dowling (London: Penguin Books, 2001), 132.
9. Weintraub, 12.
10. Kiberd, *Irish Classics*, 347.
11. I specify "slightly more than five weeks" to account for two pieces of mildly conflicting evidence on this point. In his letter to Henrietta, Trefusis notes that for "five weeks" he has "walked and talked and dallied with the loveliest woman in the world" (11), while Henrietta's mother observes that her daughter has been married for "nearly six weeks" (10).
12. See Ahmed, *The Cultural Politics of Emotion*, 82–89.
13. Dietrich, *Bernard Shaw's Novels*, 146. As Dietrich observes, earlier characters in Shaw's novels including Robert Smith, Owen Jack, and Lydia Carew embark upon similar projects.
14. The first quotation in this sentence is from Silver, 71; the second is from Dan H. Laurence, *Collected Letters 1874–1897*, 62.
15. Silver, 67, 69.
16. See Silver, 66–68.
17. In the early pages of *Bernard Shaw and Totalitarianism: Longing for Utopia* (New York: Palgrave Macmillan, 2013), Matthew Yde references George Orwell's remark about a largely overlooked "sadistic element" in Shaw's work and alludes to a "sadistic streak" in Silver's readings of Shaw (10). Yde argues for a more complex and multidimensional Shaw than he finds in Silver's readings.
18. In "*Jitta's Atonement*: The Birth of Psychoanalysis and 'The Fetters of the Feminine Psyche,'" Peter Gahan references this line from Shaw's *On the Principles of Christianity* (1916). Gahan also quotes these lines from Shaw relevant to Jansenius's dilemma: "We must become mad in pursuit of sex: we become equally mad in the persecution of that pursuit. Unless we gratify our desire the race is lost: unless we restrain it we destroy ourselves" (qtd. in Gahan, 157). In such formulations, while not replicating in all its

nuances the death-instinct of *Beyond the Pleasure Principle* (1920; English translation, 1922) and elsewhere in Freud, Shaw nonetheless approaches theorizations of the opposition of life and death in much post-Freudian thought.
19. Later, while revealing his and Henrietta's identities to Miss Wilson, Trefusis repeats this formulation of their marriage and intimacy, reproducing the tension between desire and negative affect. He tells Miss Wilson that their marital "bliss" was "perfect," but that the same elements of their association that "attracted" him "so strongly" at first "repelled him so horribly afterwards." Consequently, he feels reluctant to resume connubial relations "just yet" (102).
20. Silver emphasizes that Shaw was "especially concerned" over his own "indifference to others," and it distresses him because "it may have been as responsible as his poverty for the breakdown of the romance with Alice" and her accusation that he was like a machine (72).
21. Silver, 55, 74.
22. For a brief discussion of the Jewess on the nineteenth-century stage, see my *"Something Dreadful and Grand": American Literature and the Irish-Jewish Unconscious*, 88–99. Shaw was certainly familiar with *Ivanhoe*, as both letters and his allusions to Scott in theatre reviews confirm. He also lampooned mercilessly Daly's various productions of Shakespeare and adaptations of European comedy. *Leah, the Forsaken* was also an infrequent attraction in Sarah Bernhardt's repertory as well. It would have been difficult, in other words, for anyone so culturally literate as Shaw to remain ignorant of the figure of the exotic Jewess in nineteenth-century culture.
23. See Harley Erdman, *Staging the Jew: The Performance of an American Ethnicity, 1860–1920* (New Brunswick: Rutgers University Press, 1997, 40).
24. See, for example, "MR DALY FOSSILIZES," a review of his 1895 adaptation *The Railroad of Love*, in *Our Theatres in the Nineties* 1: 163–68, which asks the unflattering questions, "What is to be done with Mr Daly? How shall we open his mind to the fact that he stands on the brink of the twentieth century..." (163)? Here, Shaw alleges that Daly perpetrates not merely "old-fashionedness," but the "most dangerous sort of old-fashionedness" (165). His review of Daly's adaptation *The Countess Gucki* in July, 1896, is similarly dismissive (*OT* 2: 188–94).
25. *Leah, the Forsaken* was produced at New York's Metropolitan Playhouse on February 10, 2017, and ran until March 12, its first revival in New York since 1966.
26. Augustin Daly, *Leah, the Forsaken* (London/New York: Samuel French/Samuel French & Son, 1863), 21. All further quotations from this play will be followed by page number in the text.

27. I discuss this speech and response to it in *"Something Dreadful and Grand,"* 93–96. When, for example, Sarah Bernhardt featured Leah in her repertory for her appearance in Chicago in 1892, the *Chicago Daily Tribune* on March 1 hailed her delivery of the "famous curse" as not only having "moved" but "fairly lifted the audience to its feet." In this register, as the *Tribune's* reviewer phrased it, Leah embodies with "dignity" a "much-wronged, deeply-loving woman."
28. Zygmunt Bauman, "Allosemitism: Premodern, Modern, Postmodern," in *Modernity, Culture and "the Jew,"* eds. Bryan Cheyette and Laura Marcus (Cambridge: Polity Press, 1998), 143.
29. Elaine Showalter, *The Female Malady: Women, Madness and English Culture, 1830–1980* (London: Virago, 1985), 129.
30. Showalter also describes the ways in which women in Charcot's photography at times mimicked the gestural repertory of the stage and thus "performed" hysteria, confirming again the link between cultural and scientific discourses (145–64).
31. Like *An Unsocial Socialist,* this later play also alludes specifically to hysteria. In an awkward cross-examination by her lover's widow, Jitta laughs *"hysterically"* and moments later warns her interlocutor, "Dont make me laugh any more: I am afraid I shall go into hysterics" (*CPP* 6: 441). For a discussion of Shaw's knowledge/criticism of Freud and Freudian elements in the play, including hysterical symptoms, see Gahan's *"Jitta's Atonement,"* 138–47, and *Shaw Shadows,* 102–11.
32. Kiberd, *Irish Classics,* 341, 359, 344.
33. Kiberd, *Irish Classics,* 351.
34. Sally Peters, *Bernard Shaw: The Ascent of the Superman* (New Haven: Yale University Press, 1996), 39. Peters' discussion of the dates of Hetty's birth and death features other factors as well, such as leap year, the "pagan significance of the winter solstice" in December, and an article in the London *Times* on the longest day of the year. See Peters, 38–40.
35. Dietrich, *Bernard Shaw's Novels,* 158, 155.
36. Silver, 71.
37. Silver, 68.
38. My thanks to Richard Dietrich for pointing out to me Stevenson's reading of Shaw's novels in serial form. For a widespread discussion of doubling in drama, fiction, and film, see Katherine H. Burkman, *The Drama of the Double: Permeable Boundaries* (New York: Palgrave Macmillan, 2016).
39. The narrator's specific allusion to Jansenius's "love" of money might be regarded, much like the description of his daughter's exotic beauty, as the product of Shaw's accession to negative stereotyping of Jews in late-Victorian culture. Also, as Shavians are well aware, this issue arose again with Shaw's 1938 play *Geneva.*

40. Georg Simmel, "Authority and Prestige," in *The Sociology of Georg Simmel*, 183.
41. Simmel, 184.
42. Peters, 12.
43. Discussing Oscar Wilde's "The Portrait of Mr. W.H.," Patrick R. Mullen observes that both Wilde and Marx recognize the "social mode of equivalence" in the concept of value. This is as much to say that value's relationship to labor is only one means of understanding it. See *The Poor Bugger's Tool: Irish Modernism, Queer Labor, and Postcolonial History* (New York: Oxford University Press, 2012), 22–27.
44. See the first paragraph of the expanded 1889 version of *The Portrait of Mr W.H.* in *The Soul of Man Under Socialism and Selected Critical Prose*, which includes the sentiment, "all Art being to a certain degree a mode of acting" (33). Here Wilde's narrator is referring to the artist, not the subject or medium of the art, as an actor who attempts to "realize" his or her "own personality on some imaginative plane" outside the "tramelling accidents and limitations of real life" (33). But throughout particularly the latter half of *An Unsocial Socialist*, portraits, headstones, photograph albums—even country estates and funeral processions—act as substitutes for the feelings, memories, or hypotheses of their subjects or owners.
45. See Antonio Negri, "Value and Affect," *boundary 2* 26.2 (1999): 77–88. Negri's opening sentence argues that for two centuries political economists have failed to decouple "value from labor. Even the marginalist currents and neoclassical schools, whose vocation is dedicated to this decoupling, are forced to take this relationship into account..." (77).
46. Michael Hardt, "Affective Labor," *boundary 2*, 26.2 (1999): 91. Hardt's essay is in many ways a response to Negri's "Value and Affect," which he translated.
47. The fact that the portrait of Trefusis's father depicts him wearing his "masonic insignia" may also be significant, as Trefusis immediately isolates it as the nexus of an objection he lodged against him. In this way, much like the *punctum* Roland Barthes theorizes in *Camera Lucida: Reflections on Photography*, trans. Richard Howard (New York: Hill & Wang, 1980), this insignia, this "sting," "cut," or detail in the photographic image both "bruises" him and effects a rupture in the dispassionate survey or *studium* of the picture (26–27).
48. Ruth Livesey, "Morris, Carpenter, Wilde, and the Political Aesthetics of Labor," *Victorian Literature and Culture* 32.2 (2004): 606.
49. Roach, *Cities of the Dead*, 36, 33.
50. Wicksteed, *The Common Sense of Political Economy*, 37.
51. This sentence greatly simplifies Wicksteed's discussion of a consumer's satisfaction as it relates to the supply of "total" goods, including those com-

plementary or alternative to the commodity in question. In a later chapter, "On the Nature of Curves of Total Satisfaction," he speculates on the "purely abstract" notion of subjective value attached to each increment of a commodity (474). He concludes that "the importance to us of increased supplies of any one commodity depends not only on the degree to which we are supplied with that commodity, but also on the degree to which we are supplied with all other alternatives or complementary commodities" (482).
52. Wicksteed, 45.
53. Smith, qtd. in Jevons, *The Theory of Political Economy*, 85–86.
54. Jevons, 86–87.
55. Jean Baudrillard, *For a Critique of the Political Economy of the Sign*, trans. Charles Levin (St. Louis: Telos Press, 1981), 63.
56. Baudrillard, 80, 84.
57. Baudrillard, 70.

CHAPTER 7

Postscript: Embodied Shaws

In *Irish Drama and the Other Revolutions*, Susan Cannon Harris portrays a Bernard Shaw who both complements my portrait and is useful to consider in juxtaposition to it. Extending Sally Peters' observation in *Bernard Shaw: The Ascent of the Superman* that "most of the radical thinkers on sexuality" in late Victorian London were "socialists and feminists, thereby linking political liberation for women with that of homosexuals," Harris considers the role this "revolutionary *eros*" plays in conceptions of socialism undergoing revision and refinement at the *fin de siècle*.[1] At the same time, she acknowledges that Shaw attempted to "purge his dramatic universe"—and, I might add, his novelistic universe as well—of this "transgressive eros."[2] This deliberate purging seems most directly, if complexly, applicable to Trefusis's "escape" from Hetty Jansenius's "carnival of love" in *An Unsocial Socialist* and his later deployment of her portrait as a therapy to suppress his "natural amativeness." As Arnold Silver concludes, Shaw's socialist is "ludicrously confused in his pronouncements on love and in his behavior toward women"[3]; and, as a consequence, it is arguable that *eros*, revolutionary or otherwise, is incompatible with the socialism Trefusis endeavors to cultivate. Still, as Harris wisely emphasizes in assessing the importance of embodiment in theorizing socialism, Shaw *did* have a body, a "vulnerable" one at that, "just like ours."[4] So, if "desiring bodies" like Hetty's don't predominate in Shaw's canon, other bodies do, complete with the feelings and emotions I have tried to brush into my interpretive canvas.

Of course, Trefusis's is hardly the only politico-sexual revolution—or counterrevolution, in his case—in Shaw's five novels, which are populated by other characters and bodies; and some are indeed desiring bodies. In the context of the emancipatory sexuality of late-Victorian New Women, for instance, Marian Lind and Susanna Conolly's unhappy fates in *The Irrational Knot* can be attributed not only to society's castigation of those who disdain traditional marriage and a capitalism that exploits working women such as Susanna, but also to their revolutionary desire. That is to say, Susannna's child born out of wedlock and Marian's flight from her marriage are equally the products of revolution, in the latter case Marian's surprisingly frank recognition of and accession to her desire. As she confesses to her cousin Nelly before leaving for New York with Sholto Douglas, Marian had ill-advisedly made a "disinterested marriage with a man whom I felt I could respect as my superior," and, in so doing, ignored her "instincts," what she describes as an "overpowering impulse—a craving" that "defies logic" (*Knot*, 265). To be sure, as Harris notes, Shaw harbored considerable ambivalence about some aspects of this revolutionary eros, citing as an example the 1889 Cleveland Street scandal involving London's gay subculture, class privilege, and the press. The incident exposed the operations of a male brothel frequented by, among others, young aristocrats, and motivated Shaw's letter on November 26 appealing to "champions of individual rights" to join him in protesting the excessive punishment ("twenty years penal servitude") that could be levied against two adult men who had "freely consented" to an entirely "private act" (*CL1*: 231), a punishment he denounces as a "relic of Inquisition law" (*CL1*: 232).[5] Yet, while Harris identifies allusions to sexual and political revolutions in a preface he wrote in 1912 for a special edition of *John Bull's Other Island*, Shaw also revealed his view of homosexuality as the result of "being born with one's natural instincts turned against nature by a freak of nature." His use of terms like "abhorrent" to describe this desire confirms how "strongly the rhetoric of inversion and perversion generated by the sexual revolution … conditioned Shaw's ambivalence about Ireland's alterity."[6] This variety of desiring body is difficult to find in Shaw.

The relationship, then, between sexual revolution and politico-economic theory—or, expressed more precisely, between desire and socialism—in Shaw's case is complicated. But clearly the Shaw I depict in the preceding pages does not advocate strenuously for an "embodied, desire-driven, pleasure seeking socialism which challenges the contempt for sexuality that still recurs in some strains of Marxism," however much sympathy characters like Marian and Susanna create.[7] On the contrary, as I mentioned in chapter four in relation to Owen Jack's unsettling epiphany in *Love Among the Artists* that he possesses a "heart and affections like other men" and that, moreover, he both *hankers* for a wife and *grovels* after money, desire is explicitly linked to capitalism and acquisitiveness in the novel, not to socialist antagonism to class privilege and the unearned wealth of a feckless and indolent aristocracy. If Jack is regarded as an avatar of Shaw, a figure who later in the novel flatly refuses Madge Brailsford's overtures of affection, then, like Trefusis, this Shavian double chooses the lonely hermitage over the cravings a term like "hanker" connotes. The only difference between these two protagonists is the specific discipline of the hermitage to which each retires; Jack's is a solitary world of art and music, while Trefusis's is one of politico-economic theory. Both characters have expelled from these domains the pleasure-seeking, "desire-driven," and embodied subject that Harris theorizes as central to a "queer socialism," a subject that does not ignore the body or suppress its longings, but rather endorses it as central to a revolutionary theory and social practice.

However, such an eviction does not mean that embodiment is not equally central to Shaw's representation of late-Victorian culture, its increasingly virulent strain of capitalism, and—at times—the social results of its predominance. There exists, for both Shaw and the characters he creates, another kind of embodiment, one highly sensitive to sensation and emotion. Recalling Brian Massumi's aphorism from *Parables of the Virtual: Movement, Affect, Sensation* quoted earlier, in Shaw's fiction "the skin is faster than the word," as intensity is "embodied in purely autonomous reactions" made manifest on the skin.[8] Many of these intense and automatic reactions have little to do with capital, commodity acquisition and exchange, or labor—think here of Shaw's blush when his inadvertently rolled sleeves are called to his attention, Nelly's sudden tears at hearing Conolly's beautiful singing of a haunting ballad in *The Irrational Knot*, or Smith's disgust with his menial employment in the early chapters of *Immaturity*. Other embodied reactions, however, intense ones at that, are directly connected to material and materialism: Smith's pained weekly settling of accounts with his landlady and Jack's unease while walking in Hyde Park with Mary. Even emergences of desire in Shaw's fiction are frequently inflected by capital, Smith's merciless self-accounting in the throes of his infatuation with the exotic dancer he returns to see at the Alhambra Theatre, for example. And, of course, there is the instantaneous exhilaration and feelings of greatness that

Gerald Bridges obtains from suddenly becoming rich—or luxuriating in the rhetorical flourishes of Shakespeare or Thomas Otway in "The Theatre of the Future." This other embodied Shaw and Shavian character, one who feels and experiences the most human of affects with intensity as he or she negotiates the increasingly monetized economy and fast-moving metropolis that Sigmund Freud and Georg Simmel theorize, has been the real subject of this study.

NOTES

1. Peters, 168; Harris, 24.
2. Harris, 19.
3. Silver, 61.
4. Harris, 28.
5. For a useful summary of the Cleveland Street incident, see Ritschel, *Bernard Shaw, W.T. Stead, and the New Journalism*, 54–55.
6. Harris, 57–58.
7. Harris, 23.
8. Massumi, 25.

WORKS CITED

Ahmed, Sara. *The Cultural Politics of Emotion*. New York: Routledge, 2004.
Ahmed, Sara. "Happy Objects." In *The Affect Theory Reader*, edited by Melissa Gregg and Gregory Seigworth, 29–51. Durham: Duke University Press, 2010.
Albert, Sidney P. "Reflections on Shaw and Psychoanalysis." *Modern Drama* 14.2 (1971): 169–94.
Altieri, Charles. *The Particulars of Rapture: An Aesthetics of the Affects*. Ithaca: Cornell University Press, 2003.
Badiou, Alain. "Being, Existence, Thought: Prose and Concept." In *On Beckett*, edited by Nina Power and Alberto Toscano, 79–112. Manchester: Clinamen Press, 2003.
Barthes, Roland. *Camera Lucida: Reflections on Photography*. Translated by Richard Howard. New York: Hill & Wang, 1980.
Bentley, Eric. *Bernard Shaw, 1856–1950*. New York: New Directions, 1957.
Bleicher, Joseph. "Leben." *Theory, Culture and Society* 5 (2006): 343–45.
Bloch, Ernst. *The Principle of Hope*, vol. 1. Translated by Neville Plaice, Stephen Plaice and Paul Knight. Cambridge, MA: MIT Press, 1995.
Brophy, Brigid. *Black Ship to Hell*. New York: Harcourt, Brace & World, 1962.
Burkman, Katherine H. *The Drama of the Double: Permeable Boundaries*. New York: Palgrave Macmillan, 2016.
Carlson, Marvin. *The Haunted Stage: The Theatre as Memory-Machine*. Ann Arbor: University of Michigan Press, 2001.
Cleary, Joe. "Toward a Materialist-Formalist History of Twentieth-Century Irish Literature." *boundary 2* 31.1 (2004): 207–41.
Clover, Joshua. "Value/Theory/Crisis." *PMLA* 127 (January 2012): 107–14.

Daly, Augustin. *Leah, the Forsaken*. London/New York: Samuel French/Samuel French & Son, 1863.
Darwin, Charles. *The Expression of the Emotions in Man and Animals*. 1872. 200th Anniversary Edition. Oxford: Oxford University Press, 2009.
Davis, Jim, and Victor Emeljanow. *Reflecting the Audience: London Theatregoing, 1840–1880*. Iowa City: University of Iowa Press, 2001.
Dent, Alan, ed. *Bernard Shaw and Mrs. Patrick Campbell: Their Correspondence*. London: Victor Gollancz, 1952.
Derrida, Jacques. *Writing and Difference*. Translated by Alan Bass. Chicago: University of Chicago Press, 1978.
Dietrich, Richard Farr. *Bernard Shaw's Novels: Portraits of the Artist as Man and Superman*. Gainesville: University Press of Florida, 1996.
Dietrich, Richard Farr. "Shavian Psychology." *SHAW* 4 (1984): 149–71.
Dietrich, Richard Farr. "Shaw and Yeats: Two Irishmen Divided by a Common Language." *SHAW* 15 (1995): 65–83.
Dukore, Bernard. *Money & Politics in Ibsen, Shaw, and Brecht*. Columbia/London: University of Missouri Press, 1980
Eagleton, Terry. "Commentary." *New Literary History* 35 (2004): 151–59.
Eagleton, Terry. *Sweet Violence: The Idea of the Tragic*. London: Blackwell, 2003.
Ekman, Paul. "Cross-Cultural Studies of Facial Expression." In *Darwin and Facial Expression: A Century of Research in Review*, edited by P. Ekman, 169–222.
Ekman, Paul, ed. *Darwin and Facial Expression: A Century of Research in Review*. Cambridge, MA/Los Altos, CA: Malor Books, 2006.
Erdman, Harley. *Staging the Jew: The Performance of an American Ethnicity, 1860–1920*. New Brunswick: Rutgers University Press, 1997.
Ervine, St. John. *Bernard Shaw: His Life, Work and Friends*. New York: William Morrow & Company, 1956.
Ferguson, Niall. *The Ascent of Money*. New York: Penguin, 2008.
Foucault, Michel. "Nietzsche, Freud, Marx." In *Aesthetics, Method, and Epistemology*, edited by James D. Faubion, 269–78. New York: The New Press, 1998.
Freud, Sigmund. "An Autobiographical Study." Volume 20 of Freud, *Standard Edition*.
Freud, Sigmund. "Case Histories: Fräulein Anna O. (Breuer)." Volume 2 of Freud, *Standard Edition*.
Freud, Sigmund. *Civilization and Its Discontents*. Volume 21 of Freud, *Standard Edition*.
Freud, Sigmund. "Further Remarks on the Neuro-Psychoses of Defense." Volume 3 of Freud, *Standard Edition*.
Freud, Sigmund. *The Future of an Illusion*. Volume 21 of Freud, *Standard Edition*.
Freud, Sigmund. *The Interpretation of Dreams*. Volume 4 of Freud, *Standard Edition*.

Freud, Sigmund. *Introductory Lectures on Psychoanalysis.* Volumes 15–16 of Freud, *Standard Edition.*
Freud, Sigmund. "The Libido Theory and Narcissism." Volume 16 of Freud, *Standard Edition.*
Freud, Sigmund. *On Dreams.* Volume 5 of Freud, *Standard Edition.*
Freud, Sigmund. "On Narcissism: An Introduction." Volume 14 of Freud, *Standard Edition.*
Freud, Sigmund. *The Standard Edition of the Complete Psychological Works of Sigmund Freud,* edited by James Strachey, 24 vols. London: The Hogarth Press and the Institute of Psycho-analysis, 1953.
Freud, Sigmund. "The Uncanny." Volume 17 of Freud, *Standard Edition.*
Frisby, David. "Introduction to the Translation." In Georg Simmel, *The Philosophy of Money* (1900). Translated and edited by David Frisby, 1–49. London: Routledge, 1978.
Gahan, Peter. *Bernard Shaw and Beatrice Webb on Poverty and Equality in the Modern World, 1905–1914.* London: Palgrave Macmillan, 2017.
Gahan, Peter. "Bernard Shaw: Dégringolade and Derision in Dublin City." *SHAW* 32 (2012): 39–58.
Gahan, Peter. "Introduction" to Shaw's "Six Fabian Lectures on Redistribution of Income." *SHAW* 36 (2016): 10–15.
Gahan, Peter. "*Jitta's Atonement*: The Birth of Psychoanalysis and 'The Fetters of the Feminine Psyche'." *SHAW* 24 (2004): 128–65.
Gahan, Peter. *Shaw Shadows: Rereading the Texts of Bernard Shaw.* Gainesville: University Press of Florida, 2004.
Gay, Peter. *Freud: A Life for Our Time.* New York: W.W. Norton, 1988.
Goodstein, Elizabeth S. *Georg Simmel and the Disciplinary Imaginary.* Stanford: Stanford University Press, 2017.
Goux, Jean-Joseph. *Symbolic Economies: After Marx and Freud.* Translated by Jennifer Curtiss Gage. Ithaca: Cornell University Press, 1990.
Gray, Richard T. "Accounting for Pleasure: Sigmund Freud, Carl Menger, and the Economically Minded Human Being." *PMLA* 127 (January 2012): 122–30.
Grene, Nicholas. "The Maturity of *Immaturity*: Shaw's First Novel." *Irish University Review* 20 (Autumn 1990): 225–38.
Hardt, Michael. "Affective Labor." *boundary 2* 26.2 (1999): 89–100.
Harrington, Austin, and Thomas M. Kemple. "Introduction: Georg Simmel's 'Sociological Metaphysics': Money, Sociality, and Precarious Life." *Theory, Culture & Society* 29.7–8 (2012): 7–25.
Harris, Frank. *Bernard Shaw: An Unauthorised Biography Based on Firsthand Information.* London: Victor Gollancz, 1931.
Harris, Susan Cannon. *Irish Drama and the Other Revolutions: Playwrights, Sexual Politics and the International Left, 1892–1964.* Edinburgh: Edinburgh University Press, 2017.

Holroyd, Michael. *Bernard Shaw, Volume 1: 1856–1898. The Search for Love.* New York: Random House, 1988.

Holroyd, Michael. *Bernard Shaw, Volume 2: 1898–1918. The Pursuit of Power.* New York: Random House, 1989.

Horney, Karen. *Our Inner Conflicts: A Constructive Theory of Neurosis.* New York: W.W. Norton & Company, 1945.

Jevons, William Stanley. *Money and the Mechanism of Exchange.* New York: D. Appleton and Company, 1900.

Jevons, William Stanley. *The Theory of Political Economy.* Revised and enlarged edition. London: Macmillan and Company, 1879.

Kiberd, Declan. *Irish Classics.* Cambridge, MA: Harvard University Press, 2001.

Kiberd, Declan. *The Irish Writer and the World.* Cambridge: Cambridge University Press, 2005.

Kornbluh, Anna. *Realizing Capital: Financial and Psychic Economies in Victorian Form.* New York: Fordham University Press, 2014.

Krutch, Joseph Wood. *The Modern Temper.* New York: Harvest Books, 1929.

Lacan, Jacques. *The Four Fundamental Concepts of Psycho-Analysis.* Translated by Richard Sheridan. New York/London: W.W. Norton, 1977.

Laplanche, Jean. *Life and Death in Psychoanalysis.* Translated by Jeffrey Mehlman. Baltimore: Johns Hopkins University Press, 1970.

Le Gallienne, Eva. *The Mystic in the Theatre: Eleonora Duse.* Carbondale: Southern Illinois University Press, 1965.

Livesey, Ruth. "Morris, Carpenter, Wilde, and the Political Aesthetics of Labor." *Victorian Literature and Culture* 32.2 (2004): 601–16.

Martín, Gustavo A. Rodriguez. "Bernard Shaw Adjusted for Inflation: Evolution of Wealth." *SHAW* 36 (2016): 82–116.

Massumi, Brian. *Parables for the Virtual: Movement, Affect, Sensation.* Durham: Duke University Press, 2002.

Mullen, Patrick R. *The Poor Bugger's Tool: Irish Modernism, Queer Labor, and Postcolonial History.* New York: Oxford University Press, 2012.

Mulvey, Laura. "Visual Pleasure and the Narrative Cinema." *Screen* 16 (Autumn 1975): 6–18.

Negri, Antonio. "Value and Affect." *boundary 2* 26.2 (1999): 77–88.

Ngai, Sianne. *Ugly Feelings.* Cambridge, MA: Harvard University Press, 2005.

Nietzsche, Friedrich. *On the Genealogy of Morals and Ecce Homo*, edited by Walter Kaufmann. New York: Vintage, 1989.

Noccioli, Guido. *Duse on Tour: Guido Noccioli's Diaries, 1906–07.* Translated by Giovanni Pontiero. Amherst: University of Massachusetts Press, 1982.

Nordau, Max Simon. *Degeneration.* English Translation. London: William Heinemann, 1898.

Pearson, Hesketh. *Bernard Shaw: His Life and Personality.* London: St. James's Library, 1942.

Peters, Sally. *Bernard Shaw: The Ascent of the Superman*. New Haven: Yale University Press, 1996.
Reynolds, Jean. "The Talking Cure." *SHAW* 26 (2006): 27–36.
Rice, Elmer. *The Living Theatre*. New York: Harper & Brothers, 1959.
Rice, Elmer. *Minority Report: An Autobiography*. New York: Simon and Schuster, 1963.
Ricoeur, Paul. *Memory, History, Forgetting*. Translated by Kathleen Blamey and David Pellauer. Chicago: University of Chicago Press, 2004.
Ritschel, Nelson O'Ceallaigh. *Bernard Shaw, W.T. Stead, and the New Journalism: Whitechapel, Parnell, Titanic, and the Great War*. London: Palgrave Macmillan, 2017.
Ritschel, Nelson O'Ceallaigh. "Shaw, Murder, and the Modern Metropolis." *SHAW* 32 (2012): 102–116.
Roach, Joseph. *Cities of the Dead: Circum-Atlantic Performance*. New York: Columbia University Press, 1996.
Roach, Joseph. "Performance: The Blunders of Orpheus." *PMLA* 125 (October 2010): 1078–86.
Roche, Anthony. *The Irish Dramatic Revival 1899–1939*. London: Bloomsbury/Methuen Drama, 2015.
Rushdie, Salman. *Shame*. 1983. New York: Random House, 2008.
Salomon, Albert. "Georg Simmel Reconsidered." Edited by Gary D. Jaworski. *International Journal of Politics, Culture and Society* 8.3 (1995): 361–378. Originally published in 1963.
Schermer, Henry, and David Jary. *Form and Dialectic in Georg Simmel's Sociology: A New Interpretation*. Houndmills, Basingstoke: Palgrave Macmillan, 2013.
Schmitt, Cannon. "Interpret or Describe?" *Representations* 135 (Summer 2016): 102–18.
Sedgwick, Eve Kosofsky. *Touching Feeling: Affect, Pedagogy, Performativity*. Durham: Duke University Press, 2003.
Shaw, Bernard. *Cashel Byron's Profession*. 1882. *The Works of Bernard Shaw*, vol. 4. London: Constable & Company, 1930.
Shaw, Bernard. *The Common Sense of Municipal Trading*. Westminster: Archibald Constable & Company, 1904.
Shaw, Bernard. *Complete Plays with Prefaces*, 6 vols. New York: Dodd, Mead & Company, 1963.
Shaw, Bernard. *Immaturity. The Works of Bernard Shaw*, vol. 1. London: Constable & Company, 1930.
Shaw, Bernard. *The Intelligent Woman's Guide to Socialism, Capitalism, Sovietism and Fascism*. New York: Random House, 1928.
Shaw, Bernard. *The Irrational Knot*. 1880. *The Works of Bernard Shaw*, vol. 2. London: Constable & Company, 1930.

Shaw, Bernard. *Love Among the Artists*. 1881. *The Works of Bernard Shaw*, vol. 3. London: Constable and Company, 1932.
Shaw, Bernard. *Major Critical Essays*. London: Constable and Company, 1932.
Shaw, Bernard. "The New Theology." In *The Critical Shaw: On Religion*, edited by Michel Pharand, 27–40. New York: RosettaBooks, 2016.
Shaw, Bernard. "A Note on Aggressive Nationalism." *The New Statesman* 12 July 1913. Rpt. in *The Matter with Ireland*, edited by David H. Greene and Dan H. Laurence, 81–84. London: Rupert Hart-Davis, 1962.
Shaw, Bernard. *Our Theatres in the Nineties*, 3 vols. London: Constable and Company, 1948.
Shaw, Bernard. *Short Stories, Scraps & Shavings. The Collected Works of Bernard Shaw*, vol. 6. New York: Wm. H. Wise & Company, 1932.
Shaw, Bernard. *Sixteen Self Sketches*. London: Constable and Company, 1949.
Shaw, Bernard. *An Unsocial Socialist*. 1883. *The Works of Bernard Shaw*, vol. 5. London: Constable and Company, 1932.
Showalter, Elaine. *The Female Malady: Women, Madness, and English Culture, 1830–1980*. London: Virago Press, 1987.
Silver, Arnold. *Bernard Shaw: The Darker Side*. Stanford: Stanford University Press, 1982.
Simmel, Georg. "The Aesthetic Significance of the Face." Translated by Lore Ferguson. In *Georg Simmel, 1858–1918*. Edited by Kurt H. Wolff, 276–81.
Simmel, Georg. "Authority and Prestige." In *The Sociology of Georg Simmel*. Translated, Edited, and with an Introduction by Kurt H. Wolff, 183–85.
Simmel, Georg. "The Dramatic Actor and Reality" (1912). Translated by K. Peter Etzkorn. In *Georg Simmel: The Conflict in Modern Culture and Other Essays*. New York: Teachers College Press, 1968. 91–97.
Simmel, Georg. "La Duse" (1901). Translated by Thomas M. Kemple. *Theory, Culture & Society* 29.(7/8) (2012): 276–77.
Simmel, Georg. "The Metropolis and Mental Life" (1903), translated by Edward A. Shils. In *The Sociology of Georg Simmel*. Translated, Edited, and with an Introduction by Kurt H. Wolff, 409–24.
Simmel, Georg. *The Philosophy of Money*. Translated and edited by David Frisby. London: Routledge, 1978.
Simmel, Georg. "Selections from Simmel's Writings for the Journal *Jugend*." Translated by Thomas M. Kemple. *Theory, Culture & Society* 29.(7/8) 2012: 263–78.
Stewart, Kathleen. *Ordinary Affects*. Durham: Duke University Press, 2007.
Valente, Joseph. *The Myth of Manliness in Irish National Culture, 1880–1922*. Urbana: University of Illinois Press, 2011.
Vološinov, V.N. *Freudianism: A Marxist Critique*. 1927. Translated by I.R. Titunik. New York: Academic Press, 1976.

Walker, Francis Amasa. *Money*. 1877. New York: Henry Holt and Company, 1891.
Watt, Stephen. *Joyce, O'Casey, and the Irish Popular Theater*. Syracuse: Syracuse University Press, 1991.
Watt, Stephen. *"Something Dreadful and Grand": American Literature and the Irish-Jewish Unconscious*. New York: Oxford University Press, 2015.
Weintraub, Stanley, ed. *An Unfinished Novel by Bernard Shaw*. London/New York: Constable/Dodd-Mead, 1958.
Wicksteed, Philip H. *The Common Sense of Political Economy*. London: Macmillan, 1910.
Wilde, Oscar. *The Soul of Man under Socialism and Selected Critical Prose*, edited by Linda Dowling. London: Penguin Books, 2001.
Wolff, Kurt H., ed. *Georg Simmel, 1858–1918: A Collection of Essays with Translations and a Bibliography*. Columbus: The Ohio State University Press, 1959.
Wolff, Kurt H., ed. *The Sociology of Georg Simmel*. New York: The Free Press, 1950.
Yde, Matthew. *Bernard Shaw and Totalitarianism: Longing for Utopia*. New York: Palgrave Macmillan, 2013.
Žižek, Slavoj. *The Parallax View*. Cambridge, MA: MIT Press, 2006.

Index[1]

A

Achurch, Janet, 77
Affirmation, 18
   money and affirmation, 20–23, 27–29, 100–102, 111–112
   theatre and affirmation, 27–29, 144
   Tragedy and affirmation, 28
Ahmed, Sara, 12, 13, 38n33, 38n36, 38n37, 92, 94, 97–98, 130n12, 131n20, 148–149, 156, 172n11, 174n28, 184, 211n12
Albert, Sidney P., ix–x
Altieri, Charles, 12–14, 38n34, 38n38, 46, 159
Anxiety (varieties of), 48, 54–55
   See also Negative affects
Arac, Jonathan, 35n3
Archer, William, 77
Artaud, Antonin, 27–28

B

Badiou, Alain, 18–19, 39n50, 40n62, 40n63, 41n70, 144
Balfe, Michael, 105
Barker, Harley Granville, 78
Barthes, Roland, 214n47
Bateman, Kate, 188
Baudrillard, Jean, 129n3, 208–209, 215n55, 215n56, 215n57
Bauman, Zygmunt, 190, 213n28
Beckett, Samuel, 18–19, 27
Beeton, H.R., 65
Bentley, Eric, 132n23
Bernhardt, Sarah, 150–152, 213n27
Binet, Alfred, 83n9
Bleicher, Joseph, 86n40
Bloch, Ernst, 95, 130n14
Blush
   and contemporary affect theory, 148–149

---

[1] Note: Page numbers followed by 'n' refer to notes.

Blush (*cont.*)
  in Darwin's writing, 11, 150, 159, 173n21
  in Eleonora Duse's portrayal of Magda, 152 (*see also* Shaw, George Bernard, lectures, criticism, and other writing, "Duse and Bernhardt")
  and pallor, 166–167, 172n13
  in Rushdie, 168–170
  in Shaw's life and fiction, 10–11, 13–14, 136–137, 149–150, 154–156, 159–164, 166–167, 174n24, 174n25, 174n26, 196–197, 219
Breuer, Josef, 54, 72, 86n49, 191
Brophy, Brigid, ix, x
Burkman, Katherine H., 213n38
Burne-Jones, Sir Edward, 153

C

Campbell, Mrs. Patrick (Stella), 78, 88n63, 95–96, 124, 149, 153
Carlson, Marvin, 61, 84n21
Carpenter, Edward, 201
Carr, J. Comyns, 152–153
Chapman, George, 21–23
Charcot, Jean-Martin, xi, 83n9, 191
Cleary, Joe, 41n73, 65
Clench, Stanley, 5
Clover, Joshua, 40n57, 84n17
Craven, Hawes, 153

D

Daly, Augustin, 212n24
  Leah, the Forsaken, 187–190, 212n25, 212n26, 213n27
Darwin, Charles, ix, 10
  The Expression of the Emotions in Man and Animals, xi, 11, 38n28, 38n29, 148, 150, 156, 159–160, 172n9, 173n14, 173n15, 173n21, 174n27, 174n31
Davis, Jim, 40n58
Delbœuf, Joseph, 56
Derrida, Jacques, 27–28, 40n64, 40n65
Diamond, Cora, 11, 38n29
Dibden, Charles, 93–94
Dickens, Charles, 145
Dietrich, Richard Farr, 9, 10, 16, 37n20, 37n22, 38n23, 38n24, 99, 104–105, 131n19, 132n31, 132n32, 132n34, 157, 174n30, 177, 184, 210n2, 211n13, 213n35
Disgust, *see* Negative affects
Donne, John, 5
Dostoevsky, Fyodor, 194
Dukore, Bernard F., 31, 41n71
Dumas, Alexandre, 150
Duse, Eleonora, viii
  in *La Dame aux Camélias*, 150
  in *Magda*, 150–151
  Shaw's praise of, 151–152
  Simmel's praise of, 71, 151

E

Eagleton, Terry, 28, 41n67, 41n68, 41n69
Ekman, Paul, 173n16, 174n23
Eliot, George, 145
Ellis, Havelock, 47
Emeljanow, Victor, 40n58
Erdman, Harley, 212n23
Ervine, St. John, 3, 131n23, 132n24
Exchange value, *see* Value

F

Farr, Florence, 77
Ferguson, Niall, 107, 132n36, 149
Fitzball, Edward, 105

INDEX 231

Foucault, Michel, 3, 35n6
Freud, Sigmund, ix, 3, 19, 81n1, 92, 153–154
 dream work, 46–48, 60, 80
 free association, 45
 money and debt in dreams, 43–47
 overdetermination, 46, 81, 82n4
 works; "The Archaic Features and Infantilism of Dreams" (Lecture XIII), 62; "An Autobiographical Study," 54, 60, 72, 88n66; "Anxiety" (Lecture 25), 83n13, 83n14; *Beyond the Pleasure Principle*, 148; "Case Histories: Fräulein Anna O.," 191–192; *Civilization and Its Discontents*, 39n43, 123, 146–148, 157, 172n4, 172n5, 172n12; *The Future of an Illusion*, 147; *The Interpretation of Dreams*, 2, 43–44, 47–48, 56–58, 63, 72, 82n4, 82n5, 84n18, 84n19, 158; *Introductory Lectures on Psychoanalysis*, 54–55; "The Libido Theory and Narcissism," 74, 185; "The Manifest Content of Dreams and the Latent Dream-Thoughts" (Lecture VII), 60–61, 82n3; "Mourning and Melancholia," 62; *On Dreams*, 43–46, 58–61; "On Narcissism: An Introduction," 185; *The Problem of Anxiety*, 54; "Remembering, Repeating, and Working-Through," 62; *Studies on Hysteria*, 54, 191–192; "The Uncanny," x, 53–54; "Wish Fulfillment" (Lecture XIV), 61
Frisby, David, 35n1, 70, 86n41, 86n43

G
Gahan, Peter, vii, viii, 9, 36n10, 37n21, 39n44, 40n61, 130n9, 131n22, 167, 175n34, 175n35, 211n18, 213n31
Gay, Peter, x, 35n1, 82n7, 86n49, 87n52, 88n66
George, Henry, 66
Goodstein, Elizabeth S., x, 70–73, 81, 86n42, 86n47, 86n50, 86n51, 87n54, 87n55, 88n60, 88n65
Goux, Jean-Joseph, 39n51, 63, 83n11, 83n12, 84n24
Gray, Richard T., 16–17, 22, 39n41, 39n42, 39n45, 39n46, 39n54, 55, 66, 84n15, 84n16, 85n28, 85n29
Grene, Nicholas, 99, 132n30

H
Hardt, Michael, 200, 214n46
Harrington, Austin, 88n57
Harris, Frank, 2–3, 35n4, 35n5, 36n8, 36n9, 79, 80
Harris, Susan Cannon, 90, 129n2, 131n19, 178, 207, 210n3, 210n4, 217, 218, 220n2, 220n4, 220n6, 220n7
Hearst, William Randolph, 4
Henderson, Archibald, 99
Holroyd, Michael, viii, 4, 36n9, 65, 77, 85n26, 85n32, 88n61, 88n62
Horney, Karen, x, 37n19
Hysteria, 190–192

I
Ibsen, Henrik, ix, 64, 73, 78, 153
Irving, Henry, 25–26, 40n60, 152

J

Jary, David, 86n46, 86n50
Jevons, William Stanley, viii, 16, 70, 75, 85n39, 206–207
  Money and the Mechanism of Exchange, 88n59, 130n9
  The Theory of Political Economy, 66–67, 85n30, 85n31, 131n18, 215n53, 215n54
Jewess, The Tragic, *see* Daly, Augustin, *Leah, the Forsaken*; *La Juive*; Scott, Sir Walter, *Ivanhoe*
Joyce, James, 4, 188
Jung, Carl, 185

K

Kant, Immanuel, 33
Kemple, Thomas B., 88n57
Kiberd, Declan, 4, 5, 36n13, 179, 182, 192–193, 197, 210n5, 211n10, 213n32, 213n33
Kornbluh, Anna, 5, 17, 37n15, 39n43, 39n47, 39n48, 39n49, 39n56, 133n42, 145–146, 171n1, 171n2, 171n3, 172n6, 172n7
Krafft-Ebbing, Richard von, 83n9
Krutch, Joseph Wood, 28, 41n66

L

Lacan, Jacques, 67, 74, 85n36, 88n58, 90
La Dame aux Camélias, 150, 152
La Juive, 187
Laplanche, Jean, 85n36
Laurence, Dan H., 186
Le Gallienne, Eva, 151–152, 173n20
Lenin, V.I., 178
Livesey, Ruth, 214n48
Lockett, Alice, 184, 186–187, 190, 200–201
Lukács, Georg, 44, 82n2

M

Marginal economics, 16–17, 66–68, 75
Marginal value, *see* Value
Martín, Gustavo A. Rodríguez, 5, 8, 36n14, 37n18
Marx, Karl, viii, 3, 23, 49, 65
Massumi, Brian, 13, 38n35, 132n29, 219, 220n8
Material psychology, 1–6, 8, 14–18, 48, 149
  in *Love Among the Artists*, 139–142
  or "psychic economy," 17–18, 145–146
Menger, Carl, 16, 17, 55, 66, 70
Mill, John Stuart, 157
Moe, Ledelle, xi
Molière, 178
Money, adventitious (or earned income), 30–34
  and artistry, 138–141
  as capital, 129n1
  as currency or sign of commensurability in exchange, 52–53, 130n5, 130n9
  profectitious (inherited or given income), 30–34
Morris, William, 201
Mosenthal, S.H., 187
Mullen, Patrick R., 214n43
Mulvey, Laura, 175n33

N

Negative affects, 6
  anxiety, 55–56, 149, 179, 196–197
  disgust (and repulsion), 91–92, 94–95, 115–116, 184
  shame, 12, 34, 97–98, 115–116, 148–149, 156–157, 162–164, 168–171, 179, 196–197
Negri, Antonio, 214n45
Nethercot, Arthur, ix

Ngai, Sianne, 92, 94–95, 130n13, 130n14
Nietzsche, Friedrich, 73, 104
  On the Genealogy of Morals, 3, 36n7
Noccioli, Guido, 151, 173n17, 173n19
Nordau, Max Simon, 72–73, 87n52
  Degeneration, 4, 18, 49, 83n9, 87n56

O
O'Casey, Sean, 98
Odets, Clifford, 98
O'Neill, Eugene, 28
Otway, Thomas, 21–23, 220

P
Pearson, Hesketh, 66, 72, 82n7, 85n27, 86n48
Performance
  role playing in dreams, 56–59, 61–62
  social, 1, 3, 11–12, 46, 201–203
  See also Roach, Joseph
Peters, Sally, 197, 213n34, 214n42, 217, 220n1
Pinero, Sir Arthur Wing, 27
Poe, Edgar Allan, 194

R
Reynolds, Jean, 98–99, 132n27
Rice, Elmer, 4, 36n12
Ricouer, Paul, 62–63, 84n22, 84n23
Ritschel, Nelson O' Ceallaigh, vii, viii, 37n19, 87n56, 220n5
Roach, Joseph, 35n2, 35n3, 38n30, 38n31, 38n32, 214n49
  surrogation, 11, 61–62, 201–202
Robins, Elizabeth, 153

Roche, Anthony, 6, 37n16
Rushdie, Salman,
  Shame, 168–170, 175n36, 175n37, 175n38

S
Salomon, Albert, 86n45, 87n53
Schermer, Henry, 86n46, 86n50
Schmitt, Cannon, 44, 81n2
Scott, Sir Walter, 212n22
  Ivanhoe, 187
Sedgwick, Eve Kosofsky, 92, 94, 130n6, 130n7, 130n11, 148, 150, 172n8, 172n10, 174n29, 174n32
Shakespeare, William, 21, 27, 29, 55, 136, 178
Shame, *see* Negative affects
Shaw, Charlotte (Townsend), 77
Shaw, George Bernard
  childhood and adolescence in Ireland, 2, 33–34, 79–81, 92–93
  feelings of shame or disgust, 3, 91–94, 197
  lectures, criticism, and other writing; *The Common Sense of Municipal Trading*, 7, 25, 37n17, 40n59; "Duse and Bernhardt," 150–152; "The Idolatry of Money and How to End It," 6; *The Intelligent Woman's Guide to Socialism, Capitalism, Sovietism, and Fascism*, 68–69, 91–93, 96–97, 107, 129n1, 131n16; "Mr Daly Fossilizes," 212n24; "The New Theology," 9–12, 38n25, 38n26, 38n27, 47; "A Note on Aggressive Nationalism," 87n52; *Our Theatres in the Nineties*, 7,

Shaw, George Bernard (*cont.*)
150–152; "The Sanity of Art: An Exposure of the Current Nonsense about Artists Being Degenerate," 18, 49; "Six Fabian Lectures on Redistribution of Income," 36n10; *Sixteen Self Sketches*, 2, 18, 34, 65–66, 77, 79–80, 83n9, 93, 128; "Why We Idolize Millionaires," 7

novels; *Cashel Byron's Profession*, 137, 145–171, 180; *Immaturity*, 1, 3, 14, 36n8, 87n52, 90, 95, 96, 99; 103–117, 128, 129, 131n23, 135–136, 144, 186; *The Irrational Knot*, 6, 85n39, 90, 91, 93–95, 99, 101–102, 112, 116–127, 129, 136, 137, 155–156, 160, 218–219; *Love Among the Artists*, 9, 111, 135–144, 154–155, 165, 179, 186, 219; *An Unsocial Socialist*, 15, 66, 90, 102, 137, 171, 177–210, 217, 219

plays; *Androcles and the Lion*, 78; *Arms and the Man*, 182, 192–193; *Buoyant Billions*, 20, 77, 97, 102, 103, 111, 127, 131n16; *The Devil's Disciple*, 77, 151; *Fanny's First Play*, 78; *Geneva*, 213n39; *Jitta's Atonement*, 37n21, 191–192, 211n18; *John Bull's Other Island*, 178, 218; *Major Barbara*, 20, 89–90, 93, 98, 102, 116; *Man and Superman*, 128, 169; *The Millionairess*, 20, 77, 97, 100–103, 109, 111, 112, 128; *Misalliance*, 20, 63–65, 73–75, 78, 80, 83n10;

Mrs. Warren's Profession, 30–32, 34, 41n72, 82n6; *On the Rocks*, 48–53, 63, 65, 94; *Pygmalion*, 99, 180; *The Shewing-up of Blanco Posnet*, 4; *Why She Would Not*, 20, 97, 127–128, 181

short fiction; *An Unfinished Novel*, 210n6; "Don Giovanni Explains," 24, 76–77; "The Miraculous Revenge," 21, 24, 39n53; "The Theatre of the Future," 1, 18–29, 48, 109, 136, 144, 201, 220

views of Freud and psychoanalysis, 9, 18, 83n9, 97

views of psychoanalysis offered by his characters, 49–51

Shaw, George Carr, 36n9, 197
Shaw, Lucy, 5
Showalter, Elaine, 190–191, 213n29, 213n30
Silver, Arnold, 9, 98, 132n25, 132n26, 179, 184, 186, 211n15, 211n16, 212n20, 212n21, 213n36, 213n37, 217, 220n3
Simmel, Georg, ix, 19, 23, 52, 35n1, 69–78, 87n52, 90, 92, 196

works; "Authority and Prestige," 196, 214n40, 214n41; "The Dramatic Actor and Reality," 173n18; "La Duse," 71, 151–152, 173n18; "The Metropolis and Mental Life," xi, 108–109, 130n5, 130n8, 132n37, 133n38, 133n39, 133n41, 143, 144n1; *The Philosophy of Money*, x, 2, 39n55, 69–71, 73–76, 79, 97, 129n4, 130n9; *Sociology*, 71

Sims, G.R., 5
Smith, Adam, 206, 207

Sonnenschein, Swan, 177, 211n7
Spencer, Herbert, 11, 38n29
Stevenson, Robert Louis, 194
Stewart, Kathleen, 132n28
Strümpell, Ludwig, 55, 63
Stricker, Salomon, 56
Sudermann, Hermann
  Magda, 150–152

T

Tennyson, Alfred Lord, 153
Terry, Ellen, 77–78, 153
Thirlwall, Connop, 141
Tomkins, Silvan, 91–92, 148, 156–157, 172n16
Trebitsch, Siegfried, 7–8
Trollope, Anthony, 145
Tucker, Abraham, 141
Tucker, Benjamin, 4

U

Use value, *see* Value

V

Valente, Joseph, 153, 160, 174n22
Value, 63
  in *An Unsocial Socialist*, 198–200, 202–205
  exchange value, 206–210
  as product of workers' labor, 65, 198–200
  use value, 52–53, 55, 208–209
  value and people (dowry, prostitution, wergild), 52, 75–76, 120–122
  value, feeling, and subjectivity, 23, 52, 55–56, 74–77, 104
Vološinov, V. N., 15–16, 38n39, 39n40

W

Wagner, Richard, 73
Walker, General Francis Amasa, 85n39, 96–97, 130n9
Walras, Léon, 67
Watt, Stephen, 40n60, 131n21, 132n35, 212n22
Webb, Beatrice, ix
Webb, Sidney, ix
Webster, John, 21–23
Weintraub, Stanley, 210n1, 211n7, 211n9
Wergild, *see* Value
White, Arnold, 5, 7, 15
Wicksteed, Philip, viii, 65, 68, 70, 75, 198
  The Common Sense of Political Economy, 67, 85n32, 85n33, 85n34, 85n35, 85n37, 85n38, 204–206, 214n50, 214n51, 215n52
Wilde, Oscar, 4, 6, 192, 201
  The Portrait of Mr W.H., 199, 214n44
  "The Soul of Man under Socialism," 181, 211n8
Wolfe, Cary, 11, 38n29
Wolff, Kurt H., 86n44

Y

Yde, Matthew, 185, 211n17
Yeats, W.B., 9

Z

Žižek, Slavoj, 40n57

The manufacturer's authorised representative in the EU is Springer Nature Customer Service Centre GmbH, Europaplatz 3, 69115 Heidelberg, Germany. If you have any concerns regarding our products, please contact ProductSafety@springernature.com

Printed and bound by CPI Group (UK) Ltd, Croydon, CR0 4YY
23/03/2026
02076662-0006